Risk–Benefit Analysis
in Drug Research

Risk–Benefit Analysis in Drug Research

Edited by

J. F. Cavalla

Wyeth Laboratories, Taplow, Maidenhead,
Berkshire, England

Proceedings of an International Symposium
held at the University of Kent at Canterbury, England,
27 March 1980

MTPPRESS LIMITED

International Medical Publishers

LANCASTER · BOSTON · THE HAGUE

Published by
MTP Press Limited
Falcon House
Lancaster, England

Copyright © 1981 MTP Press Limited
Softcover reprint of the hardcover 1st edition 1981

First published 1981

ISBN 978-94-015-7134-0   ISBN 978-94-015-7132-6 (eBook)
DOI 10.1007/978-94-015-7132-6

Mather Bros (Printers) Limited, Preston

Contents

List of Contributors

Sir Douglas Black
Royal College of Physicians,
11 St Andrew's Place,
Regent's Park,
London NW1 4LE, England

Professor A. M. Breckenridge
Department of Pharmacology and
   Therapeutics,
University of Liverpool,
Liverpool L69 3BX, England

Dr R. W. Brimblecombe
Vice-President, Research and Development,
Smith, Kline and French Laboratories,
Welwyn Garden City,
Herts., England

Dr J. F. Cavalla
Research Director,
Wyeth Laboratories,
Taplow, Maidenhead,
Berks. SL6 0PH, England

Dr C. N. Christensen
Vice-President,
Lilly Research Laboratories,
Indianapolis,
Indiana, USA

Dr A. D. Dayan
Wellcome Research Laboratories,
Beckenham,
Kent BR3 3BS, England

Professor C. T. Dollery
Royal Postgraduate Medical School,
Hammersmith Hospital,
Ducane Road,
Hammersmith,
London W120HS, England

Dr J. F. Dunne
Senior Medical Officer, Pharmaceuticals,
World Health Organization,
1211 Geneva 27, Switzerland

Rt Hon. David Ennals, MP
Former Secretary of State for Social Services,
The House of Commons,
London SW1A 0AA, England

Professor D. G. Grahame-Smith
Rhodes Professor of Clinical Pharmacology,
University Department of Clinical
   Pharmacology,
University of Oxford,
Radcliffe Infirmary,
Oxford OX2 6HE, England

Dr W. H. W. Inman
Director, Drug Surveillance Research Unit,
University of Southampton,
Southampton SO2 3FL, England

Dr P. A. J. Janssen
Janssen Pharmaceutica,
B-2340 Beerse, Belgium

Dr S. Lock
Editor, *British Medical Journal*,
Tavistock Square,
London WC1H 9JR, England

Dr J. Maddox
Editor, *Nature*,
4 Little Essex Street,
London WC2R 3LF, England

Dr B. B. Newbould
Research Director,
ICI Ltd: Pharmaceuticals Division,
Alderley Park, Macclesfield,
Cheshire SK10 4TG, England

LIST OF CONTRIBUTORS

Sir Edward E. Pochin
National Radiological Protection Board,
Harwell, Didcot,
Oxon., OX11 0RQ, England

Mr J. D. Spink
Regulatory Controller,
The Wellcome Foundation Ltd,
187 Euston Road,
London NW1 2BP, England

Preface

The appreciation of risk like the awareness of beauty lies very much in the eyes of the beholder. It involves a value judgement and can never be absolute. Yet paradoxically, modern society is demanding ever greater degrees of safety in the medicines it takes, to the extent that nothing short of the total absence of risk will be tolerated.

Since 1960, and mainly as a result of the thalidomide tragedy, governmental regulation of testing and use of new medicines has grown apace throughout the world. It has derived impetus not only from the understandable wish of the public to seek protection, but also from the anxiety of bureaucrats and politicians not to be seen to have made mistakes. Both these concerns have been inflamed by the recognition of the media that all drugs make news and horror drugs make the best news of all.

Prior to this time the physician and his cures enjoyed a relatively supportive public. It was true that quacks existed and were recognized as such but, in the main, people wanted to take medicines and expected them to do them good. Side-effects were little recognized and when observed were often attributed to the disease rather than the cure. Only as education grew and communication improved did it begin to be appreciated that medicines might cause disease as well as prevent it. With the concomitant growth of the pharmaceutical industry in the second half of this century and the consequent introduction of many potent new medicines, the concern for safety became overriding; to the extent that many traditional remedies were dropped for fear of their side-effects.

While in most cases the concern for safety is a direct humanitarian response embodying the desire of all to prevent suffering, on occasions it is tainted by venal motives. No one can be seen publicly to support hazard, though cigarettes are still advertised and highwire acrobats applauded. When medicines are being considered, however, an emotional response seems to be elicited and rational discussion obscured. Moreover, special pleading either for commercial gain in the form of financial compensation for damage done or political advantage in seeking public control of an essentially entrepreneurial industry can often be detected. All these factors tend to militate against rational discussion of an essentially pragmatic problem. Evermore the quest for absolute safety and abolition of all risk in medicines prevents the assessment of the comparative risk–benefit equation.

This book records an attempt by several parties to determine how this paradox can be resolved: how best to equate the risk involved in taking a new medicine with the potential benefit it can bestow. It is timely such an effort was made. The international pharmaceutical industry is responsible for most, if not all, the new medicines now being offered to man. It supports an extensive and growing research effort throughout the world to undertake this task yet, perversely, as the expenditure has increased so the discoveries have lessened. With the growth in cost and the decline in invention, smaller companies have moved out of ethical research. In the United Kingdom alone, a dozen research units have closed in the last 15 years as a result either of mergers or business failure. In the view of many in the industry the time has now come when further demands for safety coupled with ever greater regulatory control might well jeopardize the future of the enterprise. In effect it will become so difficult and so onerous a task to introduce a new medicine that no one will be prepared to take it on. Already it is costing in excess of $20 million and taking over 12 years to bring a new drug to the marketplace. Only substantial reversal of the trend can bring effective change.

It was in this climate that the Society for Drug Research decided to arrange a meeting to discuss the whole question of risk–benefit analysis in drug research. Invited speakers included politicians, members of government regulatory bodies, representatives of the media, physicians, clinical pharmacologists, toxicologists and research directors. At no time was there an adversarial approach to what was said. All accepted the need to discuss a serious problem with the aim of achieving a consensus for resolution.

Clearly surcease in regulatory control is necessary if drug research as we know it is to survive. For this, responsible leadership is required to educate the public to accept the fact that medicines like surgery must always possess some small element of risk if their benefit is to be made manifest.

J. F. CAVALLA

1
Risk–benefit in medicine

SIR EDWARD E. POCHIN

Perhaps the first thing to say about risk–benefit analysis is that everybody does it every day; and the second is that it usually cannot really be done, at least in any quantitative way. We are, in fact, surely making some kind of risk–benefit evaluation every time we choose between alternatives: we are weighing the advantages against the disadvantages. Our assessment may be heavily influenced by habits, by traditions, by a few misconceptions and by yesterday's headlines, but some sort of judgement will be made. To do this job properly however, and to strike a true balance between risk and benefit, we need two sorts of information that we usually have not got. We need a factual and, essentially, a numerical estimate of all components of the risk, as well as of the benefit, if we are to dignify the process by the name of risk–benefit analysis. Much more important and much more difficult, however, we need to have some idea of how much weight should be put on the different components of the risk and of the benefit; and we need to assess numerically the relative importance of these various components. We may say to ourselves that the risk is a small one, and not much of a worry, or we may call it a small risk but an unpleasant one that we do not like to take, or we may recognize that the benefit is trivial, but we want it. Our personal weighting factors are often more important than the bare arithmetic of profit and loss.

To tackle the problem of risk–benefit analysis it is essential to be numerical about the size of the risk, as well as to be concerned with the weighting that should be put, for example, on the safety of the drug or its value in treatment, and the weighting that other people will put on these factors. Because inevitably any tidy-minded risk–benefit equation will come out in apples and pears—in factors that are not easily expressed in commensurable terms.

This is particularly true in medicine and in public health problems, where one will be dealing with deaths, with non-fatal diseases, and with non-fatal disabilities to which relative weighting factors must be attached; and one must

1

be aware also of the anxieties and stresses about the possibility of those deaths, diseases and disabilities.

Obviously this is a very large and awkward problem, even when we take the easy way out, of looking only at numbers of deaths on both sides of the equation, and ignoring, or putting less weight on, the non-fatal components. Even then it is not easy. For example, what about advising someone to have an operation that carries a 2% risk of immediate death at the time of the operation but that offers a 10% chance of avoiding death from fatal malignant disease two years later? Or, is it worse to cause one death by vaccinating a healthy child, or to allow one death to occur through having failed to prevent the disease by doing so? We are comparing one death with one death, but they are not equal deaths, and the comparison is made no easier by the risks of vaccination being so low. There were about three deaths per year between 1967 and 1976 from the effects of vaccination (England and Wales[1], categories E933 and 934), during a period in which an average of 4 million vaccinations were carried out each year (against the seven diseases listed in 'Social Trends'[2]), indicating a risk of fatality in the region of one in a million such vaccinations.

How can we visualize what 10^{-6} means as a risk? We can obtain some perspective by a comparison with other circumstances giving rise to the same risk, for example, that cigarettes appear to carry a risk of causing death of a little over 10^{-6} per cigarette smoked[3], any such death involving an average of about 5 years' loss of life expectancy. Numerically, therefore, vaccinations may have had a risk equal to that from one cigarette in terms of deaths attributable to each; or to a packet of cigarettes if the risk were expressed as the average years of life expectancy lost per vaccination.

However difficult it may be to appreciate the importance of different types of risk, this appreciation can only be helped by assessing numerically the magnitude of the risks or the frequency of the benefits, so that decisions can be influenced, at least in part, by a factual knowledge of their likely consequences. Certainly we cannot add apples and pears, but we may know that we would rather have two pears than five apples.

It is useful therefore, that this habit of risk watching seems to have proliferated so much in the past few years[4, 5]. It does not answer questions, but it poses the questions in a more exact form and can help one to guide one's decisions in the light of the facts. It is a curiously obsessive habit. It is almost like collecting stamps or engine numbers, and in a way it is about as juvenile. But at least numbers are produced, and actions can be rated according to the likelihood of certain specified consequences, particularly of harmful biological effects. This, I believe, has a certain value, as long as no-one believes that it will get him all the way to answering the question.

Even when this is done, one is obviously only looking at the findings in a particular problem under particular circumstances, as averaged over a certain period of time, and one can only say that if circumstances do not change, then it is to be expected that the risk will not change, and the risk estimate, of so many effects per million exposed to a particular challenge, can be used in forecasting. One point that has to be clearly remembered, however, is that in events having a low risk, for example of death, the number of deaths will be very small unless very large populations are considered. One has to be very much aware therefore of the confidence limits of the risk estimates that emerge. For example, if we see[6] that in 23 000 liver biopsies there were four deaths, that figure of four has 90% confidence limits from 1.4 to 9.2 on ordinary Poisson statistics, and so one must be fairly wary about the accuracy of any rate derived.

Also, obviously, one has to be wary about the way in which the estimate lumps together a variety of different levels of hazard. I have quoted the liver biopsy data as an example. This hazard of liver biopsy will vary in people of different ages. It certainly varies in groups with different severity of liver disease. It will be considerably affected by the likelihood of bleeding, so will vary with the blood coagulability and the degree of portal hypertension and doubtless with many other factors. The cake may be split into as many sections as one wishes, with finer and finer subdivisions, until finally it is all crumbs and there is nothing profitable to use. Any good statistician can claim that every average is nonsense because it could have been split a little bit more finely, or a lot more finely. But, if one assays for a particular population and can hope for reasonable homogeneity within the population, one can get a figure that applies as an average to a similar population; and this can help.

There is one obvious example in which this sort of analysis can help, and has helped, in the work that has been done on X-ray screening for cancer of the breast, in a number of countries. Obviously the survival rate of patients with cancer of the breast can be increased, or we hope it can be increased, by the earlier diagnosis that is obtained by X-ray screening of the healthy population. On the other hand, the irradiation of the breast may itself induce a certain number of cancers, and the task is to find that number. There is thus a risk–benefit problem in the screening of healthy populations for cancer of the breast and we need to know which wins. Does the screening programme induce more cancers than it saves, or save more than it induces? More specifically, we want to know above what age to screen, and below what age we shall be worse off by screening because of the irradiation. This is a situation in which the induction rate of breast cancer from radiation at a given dose is quite reasonably reliable[7]. There is good evidence on the rate of induction at low dose. That is simply because data have been obtained on studies by fluoroscopy in the course of pneumothorax treatment, and each individual exposure was at reasonably low dose. One can get, therefore, a good figure for the induction at the appropriate dose of X-rays, or only somewhat higher, and there are reasonably good data on the age variation of this induction rate. Obviously the rate of induction will vary with the type of examination, because the mean X-ray dose to breast will vary. The mortality of the breast tumours that may be induced by radiation must be known, as must the time interval between irradiation and detection of the cancer or death from it. These latencies for radiation-induced malignancies are long, probably of the order of 20, 25 or more years median interval between irradiation and even the detection of an induced malignancy. Thus when one is reviewing the age at which to perform such examinations, one is concerned with this figure of latency; and one will of course need to know also the natural incidence and mortality at different ages without a screening programme.

Studies of this sort have been done in a number of countries, and the most reliable and extensive suggest that above the age of 50 in women we are winning; more cancers will be detected than will be induced. Obviously examinations at greater ages will carry less penalty because of the long latency, if induced cancers are not expressed during the remaining lifetime. Obviously also more will be detected by such examination at these ages because the incidence is rising rapidly with age. Above this critical age of about 50, therefore, it seems likely that more will be detected and prevented than are induced[8], and below the age of 50 it may be the reverse.

There is particularly good work from Japan on screening for stomach cancer[9]. This malignancy is responsible for the greater part of all cancer mortality in Japan. It is also an important cancer to try to detect by mass survey of healthy people, because it is one which is very liable to be fatal, unless detected before symptoms have started to develop. Also, X-ray examination is really the only practicable method of screening on a mass scale, whereas for the breast there are alternatives.

The quantitative basis that has been used in Japan is very much helped in its precision by the fact that, because of the commonness of stomach cancer there, screening was started in 1960, and as many as 4 million people were screened in this way during 1978. Iinuma and his colleagues, therefore, had good evidence as to the frequency with which otherwise undetected stomach cancers were found by the technique of screening that they used. They had good evidence on the frequency with which the cancers so detected were cured, or how frequently they caused death despite their being so detected and they had the data on the variation of all those figures with age and sex. They obtained information on the radiation dose, from the examinations that were made, to all the body organs within the radiation beam; and there are now good data on the induction rate of malignancies for most of the main body organs by radiation[10, 11]. It was, therefore, possible to estimate with some confidence in this survey the number of cancers that might be detected and the number induced, and make a comparison with the natural incidence rate and the mortality without screening.

Since he was concerned with age variation, Iinuma compared the two situations, with screening or without, in terms of the years of life expectancy lost. Table 1.1 shows for males the years of life lost with screening because of cancers induced, and these drop rapidly with age at examination. Taking account also of the mortality from cancers that caused death in spite of the screening programme, an estimate is obtained of the total loss of life in years per thousand person-years of screening. Without screening and with only a small average radiation dose to the population, by X-rays given to patients who came up because of symptoms, cancer induction forms a trivial component of the risk but the later diagnosis of the naturally occurring cancers gave substantial estimates of life loss.

Table 1.1   Radiological screening for gastric cancer in Japan, showing years of life lost per 1000 men from induced and gastric cancer

	From Cancers	*Age*		
		25–30	*30–35*	*35–40*
With screening				
Greater average radiation	induced	1.20	0.92	0.67
Earlier diagnosis	gastric	0.44	0.87	1.38
	total	1.64	1.79	2.05
Without screening				
Less average radiation	induced	0.01	0.01	0.01
Later diagnosis	gastric	1.12	2.23	3.52
	total	1.13	2.24	3.53
Net benefit from screening; years (per 1000)		−0.51	+0.45	+1.48

(Iinuma, *et al.*)

Thus, screening of the populations between age 35 and 40 shows a gain of 1.5 years per thousand, at ages 30 to 35 the gain is 0.5 years, but screening at age 25 to 30 results in a loss of life expectancy. The total risks and benefits balance at an age of about 30, both for males and for females, above which there is a gain by preventing more cancers than are induced, and below which there is a loss by inducing more than are prevented in the younger age groups. Quite obviously there are a lot of uncertainties in this analysis, but, given the assumptions that were made, and the care with which it was done and the large number of factors taken into account, it does indicate that for the Japanese population, screening is likely to be profitable in saving life above the age of 30. These studies of screening programmes are important particularly because the programmes may involve large numbers of people and therefore appreciable numbers of cancers might be induced by radiation; and other risks might be involved in other types of screening procedure.

There are similar problems, in some ways more difficult, in looking at the use of various procedures in medical or clinical research, procedures such as studies by X-rays and radio-pharmaceuticals. There is no reason to apologize for giving examples in which radiation risk analysis is involved. Radiation hazards have been very much better studied and documented than very many environmental chemical hazards, and many pharmacological hazards. There has been a great deal of work on the epidemiology of radiation induction of malignancies and of genetic effects and estimates are now reasonably reliable[10].

Table 1.2   The radiation exposure levels of patients undergoing various diagnostic tests using X-rays and radionuclides

Equivalent whole-body dose (mrem)	Number of types of diagnostic tests using:	
	X-rays	Radionuclides
0.01	—	1
0.1	—	3
1	1	21
10	18	33
100	14	25
1000	—	5
10 000	—	—
Geometrical mean dose	74 mrem	37 mrem
Risk	8×10^{-6}	4×10^{-6}

In medical research, for example using radiopharmaceuticals, no problems need to arise if the test is being done for clinical purposes in any case, and it is merely its results that are being studied. The position is usually similar even if somewhat larger activities are used, or rather larger samples of blood are removed for the purposes of research. But, if healthy or other volunteers are being examined, who cannot be expected to benefit from the tests, then it is important to look at the risk–benefit balance and ensure that the risk to the individual is trivial, and that the size of the benefit certainly outweighs the risk.

But how small is the risk likely to be? Table 1.2 shows, for the range of conventional X-rays, the amount of radiation exposure involved. For a group of 30 or so typical diagnostic procedures the geometric mean dose is of about 70 mrem. (This value is the 'effective' whole body dose, either from radiation of the whole body uniformly, or as the whole body dose equivalent in number of harmful effects to doses delivered to individual body organs.) Conventional radionuclide investigations give a rather lower figure. The risks of inducing any fatal effect implied by these geometric mean values are of about 8×10^{-6} for X-rays, and 4×10^{-6} from radionuclide examinations. For perspective on the mean doses, the whole body receives about 100 mrem per year from natural sources and has always done so. As perspective on the size of the risk (although not necessarily on its acceptability) the smoking of six, or three cigarettes corresponds in risk of fatal effect to the 8 or 4×10^{-6} mean risks of typical examinations by X-rays or radiopharmaceuticals.

How far is this simply a theoretical calculation? Three studies have been made on large numbers of patients after particular radiological procedures in which there has been a detectable cancer incidence above expectation (Table 1.3). Following multiple fluoroscopies, when the patient was facing the tube so that the breast received a somewhat higher dose than usual, the breast cancer induction rate corresponded to a mortality of about 10^{-4} per examination[12]. The use of diagnostic X-rays involving the pelvis of a mother during pregnancy was followed by a small excess of cancers in the fetus, as expressed during the first 10 years of life, in this case with a mortality[13] of about 2×10^{-4}. Studies of treatment for ringworm involving a few rads to the thyroid in about 11 000 children showed a detectable excess of thyroid cancer. The mortality of radiation-induced cancers of the gland is low so that again there is likely to have been a fatality risk of about 10^{-4} per treatment[14].

Table 1.3   Radiological procedures involving a detectable cancer incidence above expectation

Procedure	Type	Cancer incidence	Mortality
Fluoroscopy (facing tube)	Breast	2.10^{-4}	1.10^{-4}
In utero, pelvic X-ray	All types	2.10^{-4}	2.10^{-4}
Thyroid dose, 7 rad	Thyroid	9.10^{-4}	1.10^{-4}
Thorotrast (25 ml)	Leukaemia		120.10^{-4}
	Liver		500.10^{-4}

We are seeing X-rays and radiopharmaceuticals therefore with typical estimated risks of a few deaths per million, and evidence of certain such procedures with observed risks which are factors of 1.5 or 2.0 orders of magnitude higher than this. (The use of Thorotrast, the thorium oxide contrast medium, involved very much higher risks, in the order of 6×10^{-2} per examination.)

In view of this range of hazards that can be estimated for radiopharmaceuticals or X-rays, the World Health Organisation (WHO), some 3 years ago, produced a report[15] on the use of investigations involving radiation in research on man, as well as in other circumstances. They divided the diagnostic tests that could be used with radiation into three categories (Table 1.4).

The boundaries between WHO's categories correspond to 50 mrem, 500 mrem and 5 rem whole body doses. The average risk of causing a fatal malignancy in a man of 40 can be estimated to be in the region of 4×10^{-6} at the boundary between categories I and II, this estimate varying in proportion to dose in the higher categories[16].

How can one illustrate the size of these risks? The average loss of life expectancy would be small, varying from less than half an hour from the effects of category I, to 1 or 2 days in category III, if it was justifiable to average the duration of life loss from an induced cancer amongst all recipients of the test. Or, on a more reasonable comparison, the radiation risk of fatality at the boundary between categories I and II would equal the average likelihood that a man aged 35 would die from natural causes on any one day, or, at the top of category III, that a man of 60 would die from such causes during any week of the investigation.

If these are the risks, what about the benefits? Quite obviously the results of a piece of research cannot be predicted before it starts. Very often the result cannot be predicted even when the research has been completed, because it will take time to work out, together with its implications and the help that it may give. But, we can say something about the orders of magnitude in these categories. In my experience, a large planned study of human metabolism or disease would involve perhaps 25 volunteers. Looking at the upper limit of category II, a category which covers most radionuclide investigations, for each investigation involving 25 people there will be a risk of about one death

Table 1.4 Categories of research project involving irradiation of human beings

	WHO Category		
	I	II	III
Effective dose equivalent (mrem)	50	500	5000
Risk of fatal malignancy exposure at age 40 ($\times 10^{-6}$)	4	40	400
Average loss of life expectancy exposure at age 40	30 min	5 h	2 d

per 800 separate investigations. Adding in major genetic defects, the risk becomes one per 400 investigations[11, 16]. The benefit cannot be predicted, but if 400 investigations of substantial size did not, in time and world-wide, save one life, then you may feel that the research department needed its Head examining. On this sort of argument, we can expect that sound clinical or metabolic research with conventional radiopharmaceuticals is likely to be highly cost-effective, expressing 'cost' in terms of lives saved or lost, and that the benefit looks likely to be substantially greater than the risk numerically.

This, of course, is not everything. The ethics involved in inviting someone, or allowing someone, to offer to act as a volunteer come into the question. The risks, even if small, are sustained by the volunteer but the benefits are reaped by others. I believe, however, that people who willingly volunteer for such investigations would wish to accept a numerically small risk in contributing to potentially valuable and well-conducted medical research.

In the practice of medicine itself, obviously, an urgency for diagnosis or for therapy might if necessary justify considerably greater risks. In his paper[17] in 1974 on death after taking medicaments, Girdwood stresses the uncertainties and imperfections in the survey, but on 30 drugs that he reviewed, the median number of deaths was four per million prescriptions. We are thus in the same region of risk as for radiological procedures: one X-ray equals two drug prescriptions equals two radioisotope tests. Girdwood's risks ranged up and down by one or two factors of ten, and his highest was 150 deaths per million prescriptions. The risk from radiopharmaceutical tests also range up and down by one or two orders of magnitude (Table 2) with risks of a few hundred per million at the highest levels. For most usual X-ray procedures the range of radiation risk appears to be somewhat narrower, although in certain cases some element of hazard may result from the use of contrast media and from the modes of administering them.

I have already mentioned the estimated hazard of liver biopsy. In two large studies reported in the mid-1960s[6, 18], 16 deaths occurred as a result of about 100 000 biopsies, giving a risk of 160 per million (with 90% confidence limits of

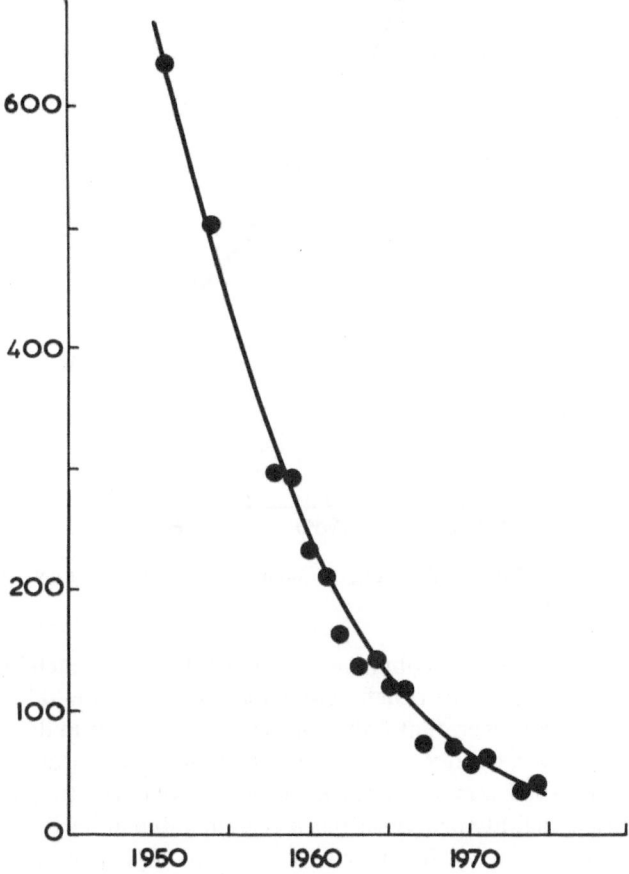

Figure 1.1 Number of deaths attributed to anaesthetics, per million operations in England and Wales, 1951/1973 (reference 20)

100 and 240 per million). Low as this risk may be, it is already 20 to 40 times the mean values for X-ray or radionuclide tests, and 100 times that of vaccinations.

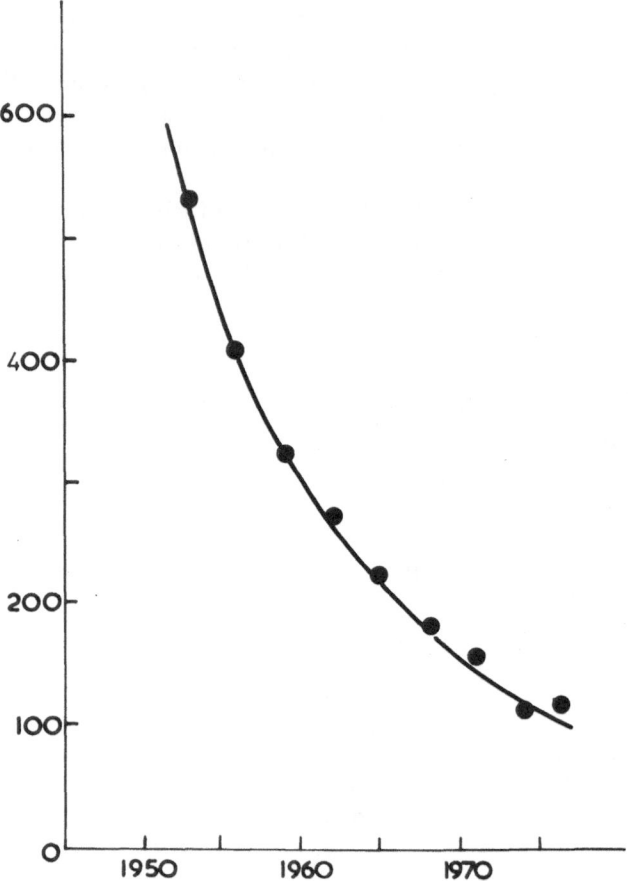

Figure 1.2 Number of maternal deaths, per million maternities in England and Wales, 1952/1977 (reference 22)

While it is thus possible to obtain estimates of the risk of such biopsies, it is very difficult to evaluate the benefit with which this risk should be compared. We can imagine, however, that if the correct diagnosis was in doubt, the gain could well be much greater than a 10^{-4} risk of death, provided that the diagnosis established was one that helped positively in treatment or in prognosis (because a definite prognosis has a certain value in itself, even where it does not guide treatment). It is worth noting that 10 years earlier, a series of 20 000 liver biopsies[19] reported in 1953 carried the ten times larger risk of 1.7×10^{-3}.

Similar rapid reductions of risk from a given form of treatment are very conspicuous in the safety of anaesthetics given at the time of operation (Figure 1.1). Here there is a rapidly falling risk from about 600 deaths per million operations in 1950 down to a value in the region of 40 per million in 1970[20]. These are supposedly deaths from the anaesthetic rather than from the disease or from the surgeon, but it is obviously a difficult demarkation to make with precision. The anaesthetic risk in dental practice or during electro-convulsant therapy is said to be much lower, and probably about 10×10^{-6}, while that during caesarian section has been reported[21] to be substantially higher (in 1970–72) at about 300×10^{-6}.

There has thus been a drop during two decades, of the deaths from anaesthetic by rather more than one order of magnitude. Here again it is easy to state the risk and hard to state the benefit. This is inevitable, because procedure can be standardized, but not the patient. For our purposes at this symposium, however, it may be felt, rightly or wrongly, that what are accepted as conventional techniques in medicine are justified on present risk–benefit criteria. We are looking therefore, at the range of risks in medicine which seem to be regarded as justified in the circumstances in which they are used.

Another risk which is falling fairly rapidly, is the number of maternal deaths per million maternities (Figure 1.2). This risk has dropped from 500, to below 100, per million in the last three decades[22]. This would suggest that maternity is a highly cost-effective procedure, in the sense that about 10 000 lives are achieved at the expense of one lost, putting the equation in terms of basic cost–benefit numerology.

On the other hand, the risk to the mother in legal abortions fell by a factor of ten or more between 1968 and 1972 (Figure 1.3)[23] and has remained about constant at between 40 and 50 per million since then. If one considered only the maternal benefit, and assessed this purely in terms of length of life lost or gained, a total of say 50 years of life lost in one out of 20 000 legal abortions would be in risk–benefit balance if there was average gain of one day's life expectancy in the remainder. The obvious inadequacy of this comparison, however, emphasizes very clearly the importance of the weighting to be applied to different aspects of maternal benefit and to the consideration of the fetus. The true balance of risk–benefit will depend very critically on the relative weighting between the life of the mother and the death of the aborted child.

In much medical therapy, weighting comes in very strongly. How should the difference be weighted between better health achieved by use of a drug, and rare but severe toxic effects from that drug? How is the equation to be balanced between the cure of a chronic disease and the occasional fatal effect of therapy? How is 10 years of improved health in 99 people to be compared with a 50-year loss of life in the hundredth?

In severe renal disease, the operative risks of a transplant may well outweigh the problems and hazards of renal dialysis, but it is becoming clear that, in addition to the operative risks, there may be added some risks of cancer resulting from the immunosuppressive therapy. Kinman, Sheill, Peto and Doll[24] have estimated an excess frequency of malignancy, commonly from malignant lymphoma and skin tumours, occurring during the first 4 years or so after immunosuppressive treatments (using courses of azathioprine, cyclophosphamide and chlorambucil). These treatments, designed to prevent rejection of the transplant, carried a 1.3% risk of tumour induction and a 0.4% risk of mortality from the induced tumours during the period of observation, a mortality risk about 100 times the present average fatality rate from the anaesthetic in surgical operations.

In the treatment of severe and progressing disease, high risks may need to be

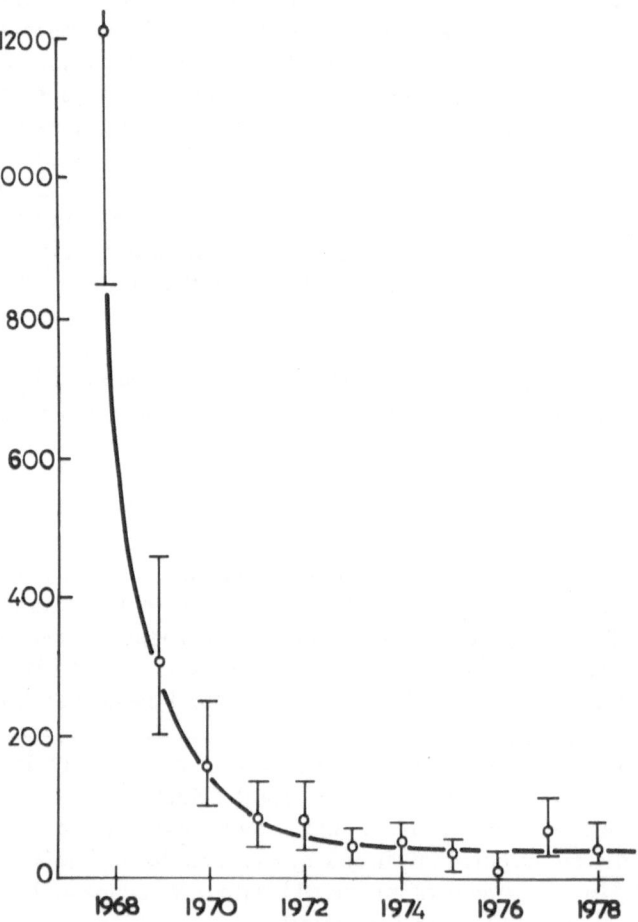

Figure 1.3 Number of maternal deaths per million legal abortions (with 90% confidence limits), England and Wales, 1968/1978 (reference 23)

taken. Valagussa and his colleagues in Milan have reviewed[25] the risk of cancer induction as a result of treating patients with Hodgkin's disease by radiotherapy, or various drugs, or both. They found a 7.3% excess incidence of solid cancers, and a 2.4% incidence of leukaemia, developing at an average interval of 5 years after the start of these treatments. Their figures are calculated on a life-table basis of surviving patients, so it can be presumed that their 10% malignancy risk is associated with 90% of survivors without malignancy at a comparable period.

To formulate a risk–benefit equation in this situation, of course, we need to know the average years of survival of patients with Hodgkin's disease before these forms of therapy were available, to compare with the survival of the 10% who developed malignancies and the 90% who did not. It is apparent, however, that the greatly prolonged survival of the majority of treated patients now constitutes a nett gain in the benefits of present treatments over their risks.

We encountered a somewhat similar situation in treating patients with active and metastasized thyroid cancer with radioiodine. In about half of these patients, there was considerable destruction of tumour tissue and metastases, owing to the selective concentration of radioiodine in the primary and all secondary deposits, whether they had been detected clinically or not, and often a complete abolition of all remaining cancer tissue, even to the highly sensitive scanning tests which can detect residual deposits of only 10 or 20 mg of functioning tumour tissue. But, in four patients out of over 300 now treated, leukaemias developed which must be attributed to the radiation delivered in the course of the therapy[26]. A 1% risk of inducing a second and fatal malignancy may seem clearly acceptable as the risk of treating an existing, metastasized and actively spreading cancer, as most of these treated cancers were. But this evidence shows that the benefits are not obtained without risk and that for a cancer which often only develops slowly, intensive radioiodine therapy may at some stages of the disease involve on average a greater risk than benefit.

I shall not discuss cost–benefit analysis in any detail because that was not my brief. However, it is to be noted that it has been suggested[27] that a programme for the detection, and, if abortion is accepted, the prevention, of Down's syndrome may cost about £2000 per case prevented. The successful treatment of cancer of the testis by radiotherapy has been estimated[28] to cost about £250 worth of machine time and staff time, and the treatment of Hodgkin's disease similarly costs between £300 and £400. Detecting hypothyroidism in children at birth, of which the frequency is of the order of 300 per million[29], can be very easily coupled with tests for phenylketonuria.

So how safe does a drug have to be? It is important to start by saying that nothing is fully safe. This is very obvious in occupational statistics. One can look at a list of conventional occupations, and determine the number of deaths per year per million employed[30]. The risks of accidental death run from a few per million per year to 100 or more per million per year in manufacturing industries. In other conventional occupations they range up from a few hundreds to a few thousands of deaths per million per year attributable to occupational causes. And occupational exposure to carcinogenic or other chemicals has been responsible for mortality rates even in excess of 10 000 per million exposed per year[30].

There is thus a very wide range of occupational risks, and there is clearly an equally wide or wider range in medical procedures. We have seen a variation from simple diagnostic methods of nuclear medicine or radiology which may carry a risk of a few deaths per million tests, to the very effective modern therapy of Hodgkin's disease which may cause a few deaths per hundred treatments, a range of four orders of magnitude in risk. Against this background, the maximum acceptable risk from a drug should clearly be related to the urgency of need for that drug and the severity of the disease in which it is needed, as well as the amount of value that it has in that disease. Many other considerations come into this question, such as the availability of alternatives of equal consistency of performance, keeping qualities or purity, and perhaps of greater safety. Whatever the answer to your question, there will be no one answer – the justifiable risk must be justifiable by its benefit, and by a benefit which cannot be obtained by even safer means. But if the clinical need is urgent, then a clinical risk ought to be acceptable.

This is not an easy problem, even formally; and indeed the medical profession still quotes periodically a very defensive adage, '*primum non nocere*'.

Certainly harm should not be done unnecessarily, and certainly the risk of harm should not exceed the likelihood of benefit, but that is what risk–benefit analysis is all about. But it will surely often be a responsible action to allow some risk of harm in order to achieve on balance a substantially greater prospect of benefit.

So perhaps we should not be asking how safe does a drug have to be, but how unsafe it might quite properly be for use in circumstances in which its benefits clearly exceed its risks, and where no safer alternative therapy for a serious disease is available. These must surely be the necessary criteria for the safety of drugs provided that the right weight is given to the nature of the symptoms or effects prevented, and to the quality as well as the length of life that is gained. The objective arithmetic of risk–benefit analysis may be simple. The balancing of the perceived risk–benefit equation is more difficult and more important. But a knowledge of the size of the risks and the amount of the benefits should surely be an essential component in reaching a proper judgement on how safe any drug needs to be.

References

1. *Mortality Statistics (1977) England and Wales* (1979). Office of Population Censuses and Surveys. Series DH1 No. 5 (London: HMSO)
2. *Social Trends 9. 1979 Edition* (1978). (UK) Government Statistical Service. Thompson, E. J. (ed) (London: HMSO)
3. Doll, R. and Peto, R. (1976). Mortality in relation to smoking: 20 years' observations on male British doctors. *Br. Med. J.*, **2**, 1525
4. Wilson, R. (1979). The daily risks of life. *Technol. Rev.*, February
5. Pochin, E. E. (1978). Estimates of industrial and other risks. *J. R. Coll. Phys.*, **12**, 210
6. Thaler, H. (1964). Uber vorteil und Risiko der Leberbiopsie Methode nach Menghini. *Wien. Klin. Wochenschr.*, **29**, 533
7. Boice, J. D. Jr., Land, C. E., Shore, R. E., Norman, J. E. and Tokunaga, M. (1979). Risk of breast cancer following low dose radiation exposure. *Radiology*, **131**, 589
8. Breslow, L., Thomas, L. B. and Upton, A. C. (1977). Final reports of the National Institute *ad hoc* Working Groups on mammography in screening for breast cancer. *J. Natl. Cancer Inst.*, **59**, 467
9. Iinuma, T. A., Tateno, Y. and Umegaki, Y. (1979). Benefit vs. risk analysis of stomach cancer mass screening. In Okada, S. (ed.) *Radiation Research – Proceedings of the 6th International Congress of Radiation Research*, (Tokyo)
10. *United Nations Scientific Committee on the Effects of Atomic Radiation, Report to the General Assembly 1977* (Sales No. E77.IX.I) (New York: UN)
11. *Recommendations of the International Commission on Radiological Protection* (1977). ICRP Publication 26, Annals of the ICRP **1** (3), 1 (Oxford: Pergamon Press)
12. Boice, J. D. Jr. and Monson, R. R. (1977). Breast cancer in women after repeated fluoroscopic examinations of the chest. *J. Natl. Cancer Inst.*, **59**, 823
13. Stewart, A. M. and Kneale, G. W. (1970). Radiation dose effects in relation to obstetric X-rays and childhood cancers. *Lancet*, **2**, 1185
14. Modan, B., Baidatz, D., Mart, H., *et al.* (1974). Radiation induced head and neck tumours. *Lancet*, **1**, 277
15. *Use of ionizing radiation and radionuclides on human beings for medical research, training and non-medical purposes* (1977). World Health Organization, Technical Reports, Series 611 (Geneva: WHO)
16. *Problems involved in developing an index of harm* (1977). ICRP Publication 27, Annals of the ICRP **1**, (4), 1 (Oxford: Pergamon Press)
17. Girdwood, R. H. (1974). Death after taking medicaments. *Br. Med. J.*, **1**, 501
18. Lindner, H. (1967). Grenzen und Gefahren der perkutanen Leberbiopsie mit der Menghini-Nadel: Erfahrungen bei 80,000 Leberbiopsien. *Dtsch. Med. Wochensch.*, **92**, 1751
19. Zamchek, N. and Klausenstock, O. (1953). Liver Biopsy (concluded) II The risk of needle biopsy. *N. Engl. J. Med.*, **249**, 1062
20. Office of Health Economics. Report No. 55 on Anaesthesia, February 1976
21. Editorial, 'Anaesthetic deaths' (1979). *Br. Med. J.*, **1**, 703
22. *Mortality Statistics of Childhood and Maternity*. Office of Population Censuses and Surveys. DH3 No. 4 (1977) and Birth Statistics FMI No 3 (London: HMSO) (1979)
23. Lewis, T. L. T. (1980). Legal abortion in England and Wales 1968–78. *Br. Med. J.*, **1**, 295
24. Kinlen, L. J., Sheil, A. G. R., Peto, R. and Doll, R. (1979). Collaborative United Kingdom–Australasian study of cancer in patients treated with immuno-suppressive drugs. *Brit. Med. J.*, **2**, 1461
25. Valagussa, P., Santoro, A., Kenda, R., *et al.* (1980). Second malignancies in Hodgkin's disease: a complication of certain forms of treatment. *Br. Med. J.*, **1**, 216
26. Pochin, E. E. (1969). Long term hazards of radioiodine treatment of thyroid carcinoma. UICC Monograph Series Vol. 12, Thyroid Cancer (Berlin: Springer-Verlag)

27. Hagard, S. and Carter, F. A. (1976). Preventing the birth of infants with Down's Syndrome: a cost–benefit analysis. *Br. Med. J.*, **1**, 753
28. McEvedy, M. (1980). (Letter) *Br. Med. J.*, **1**, 648
29. Hulse, J. A., Grant, D. B., Clayton, B. E., *et al.* (1980). Population screening for congenital hypothyroidism. *Br. Med. J.*, **1**, 675
30. Pochin, E. E. (1974). Occupational and other fatality rates. *Community Health*, **6**, 2

2
The effect on industry

B. B. NEWBOULD

INTRODUCTION

During the last 20 years both the pharmaceutical industry and the regulatory authorities established by governments to safeguard the interests of the public have striven to minimize the risks to patients initially exposed to and subsequently treated with new drugs.

The object of this presentation is two-fold. First, to cover those parts of a typical drug development programme most affected by initiatives designed to minimize risk. Second, to present certain data to quantify the effects of some of these initiatives on the pharmaceutical industry.

Table 2.1 outlines the nature of the timescale a bioscientist has to contend with in the search for new drugs. It is noteworthy that a colleague who

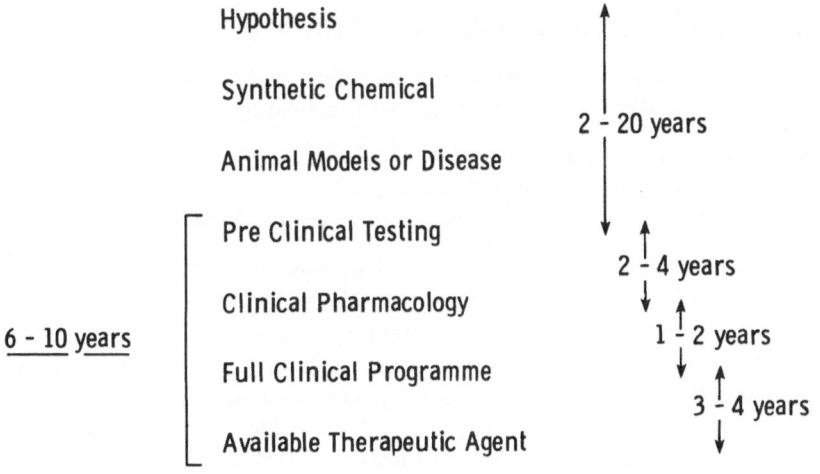

Table 2.1 The time scale of drug development

embarked on what turned out to be a most successful career as a 'drug-hunter' in the late thirties, made a major contribution to medical science in three different areas. Today a young bioscientist with post-doctoral experience entering industry in his late twenties would be extremely fortunate to nurture one compound through from novel concept to an established place in medical therapy during the course of an industrial career.

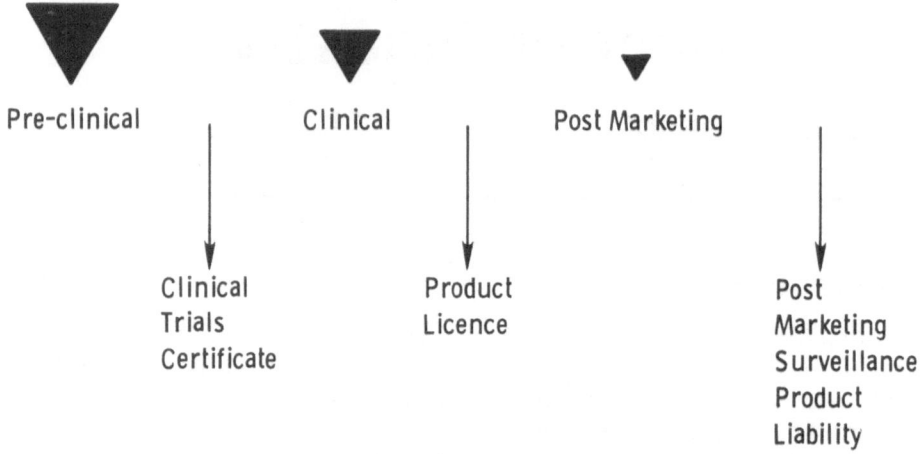

Table 2.2   Risk–benefit – the effects on industry

This discussion will consider three phases of drug development, namely safety evaluation in the laboratory, clinical evaluation and post-marketing activities (including product liability).

SAFETY EVALUATION IN THE LABORATORY

The effects of increasing requirements for safety evaluation in the laboratory can be conveniently broken down under three headings:

(a) increases in the number of tests;
(b) increases in the magnitude of tests;
(c) increases in the administrative systems related to the tests.

Because the most striking increases in demands for more data have taken place during the last 10 years, this paper analyses data from 1972 and 1978. It will not deal in depth with the different demands of different regulatory bodies. Suffice to say, a company wishing to develop a new chemical entity internationally has to generate a total package of data which exceeds the requirements of any one regulatory body considered in isolation. Some examples of increases in the number of tests and increases in the magnitude of such tests are depicted in Table 2.3. The most important changes to note are:

(1) Three-month tests in rodents and non-rodents are now almost redundant. Whereas in 1972 most authorities accepted tests over three months in two species (rodent and non-rodent) as a basis for decision making for a product licence, by 1978 a minimum of six months had become the norm. Shorter periods of study are acceptable prior to clinical trials of short duration. But, because an increasing number of new drug entities are destined for use in chronic disease states and precious toxicological resources could be wasted by conducting repeat studies, there is now an increasing tendency to embark on six-month tests on declaring a compound a new-drug candidate.

Table 2.3 Number of animals used in safety tests 1972 and 1978

Tests	1972	1978
Acute toxicity		
Rodents	40	40
Prolonged toxicity	3 months	6 months
Rodents	90	240
Non-rodents	40	50
Carcinogenic tests		
Rodents	250	500
Reproductive tests		
Teratology		
Rabbits	40	48
Rats	140	140
Fertility		
Rats	Not required	180–400 initial and offspring for three generations

(2) The number of animals used in many tests have increased – in the case of carcinogenicity tests by 100%.

(3) Fertility tests have been introduced by many authorities as a requirement prior to sale and by the Committee for Safety of Medicines ,CSM) as a requirement prior to clinical trial. The results of carcinogenicity tests are not normally required prior to application for a product licence but there are examples of carcinogenicity test results being required before clinical trial with certain classes of compounds.

Having dealt in outline with some of the general changes between 1972 and 1978, one study, a non-rodent test, will be examined to show the increase in effort required to initiate and complete the study between 1972 and 1978. Most of the increases in resource requirements are associated directly or indirectly with a doubling of the test period from 90 to 180 days and a 25% increase in the number of animals used. However, the costs of complying with the Food and Drug Authority's (FDA) requirements for good laboratory practice are not insignificant, accounting for some 12% of the effort. It is noteworthy that were it not for the considerable efforts and expense devoted during this period to increase efficiency by improved instrumentation and the introduction of computerized systems for data handling, this 180-day study would have required 565 man days for completion in contrast to the 480 days detailed in Table 2.4.

Table 2.4 Analysis of typical non-rodent study: 1972 and 1978 (designed to satisfy CSM/FDA)

	1972 (90-day) study Man days	1978 (180-day) study Man days
Preparation of protocol	3	7
Trial	190	335
Reporting	80	105
Study director role	2	12
Quality assurance group	—	21
	275	480 (565)

NB: Use of improved working methods has resulted in saving of 85 man days in 1978

Cost of GLP compliance = 61 man days – (12%)

Data obtained from another laboratory concerned with satisfying the safety evaluation requirements of another regulatory body (the Environmental Protection Agency) where the basic safety evaluation tests are very similar to those required by drug authorities, confirm and extend the trends above (see Table 2.5).

Table 2.5 Analysis of effort required to satisfy EPA: 1972 and 1979

Study	Effort in man days	
	1972	1979
Ninety-day rat feeding	150	680
Ninety-day dog feeding	178	465
Two-year rat feeding	520	1600
Rat reproduction	326	1107
Mouse carcinogenic	295 (for 80 weeks)	1350 ($\simeq$ 2 years)
Rabbit teratology	120	172
Rat teratology	84	185
	1673	5559

As a lead into a brief commentary on the clinical trial phase of drug development, it is salutary to examine the time scale for tests and report preparation and processing by different authorities for a single dose study in patients (Table 2.6). At the time of writing, clinical trials could commence in

Germany about six months after the decision to proceed to trial. In the UK it would take at least three times longer.

Table 2.6 Time scale (weeks) for tests/report preparations and processing by authorities for single-dose study in patients

Time	Germany	Holland	Sweden	UK	USA
Do tests and prepare documents	24–36	24–36	24–36	52–130	24–36
Processing time	0	2–4	2	23–32	4
Total	24–36	26–40	26–38	75–162	28–40

CLINICAL TRIAL STAGE

In contrast to the large increases in data requirements for pre-clinical safety studies between 1972 and 1978–80 there has been little change in data requirements at the clinical trial stage. However, the scene is rapidly changing in association with the introduction by the FDA of its proposed regulations on good clinical practice.

It is difficult if not impossible to estimate the effect that these regulations will have on risk benefit ratios. However, there is no doubt that they will have a profound effect on the workload of the teams involved in the design, conduct and evaluation of the results of clinical trials and will significantly increase the effort required to compile the data in a form suitable for submission.

POST-MARKETING ACTIVITIES

Post-marketing activities will, without doubt, pose a bigger challenge to the intellect than any of the topics covered so far. It is perhaps for this reason that, until recently, action by both industry and regulatory bodies has been tentative and appropriately sensitive to the issues involved.

Dealing first with post-marketing surveillance, it can quickly be appreciated by reference to Table 2.7 that large numbers of patients have to be included in a study to detect with reasonable confidence a unique side-effect. For example, about 5000 patients would be required to have a 99% chance of detecting a unique adverse reaction with an incidence of 1:1000. The problems are horrendous in terms of number of patients required, if the adverse effect is superimposed on a normal background incidence (Table 2.8).

The four basic techniques for post marketing surveillance studies are:

1. Voluntary reporting of adverse effects;
2. Trend analysis of morbidity and mortality incidence data;

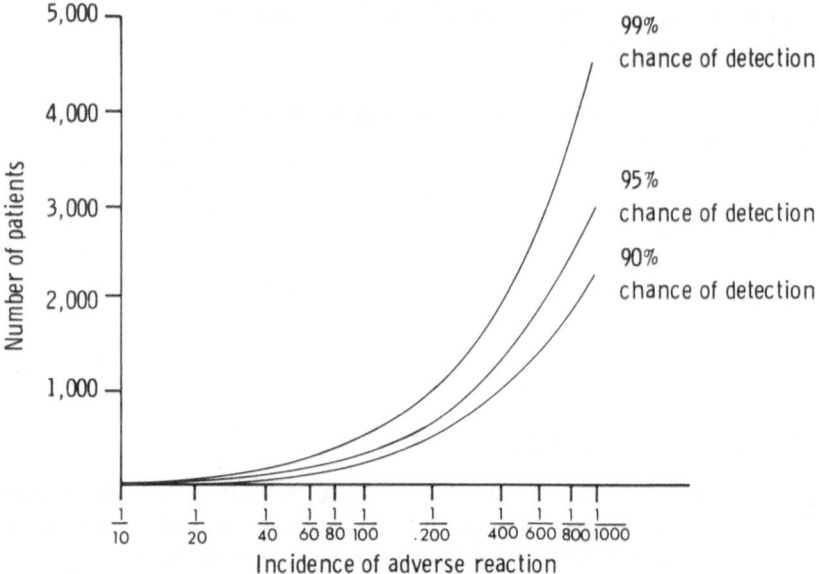

Table 2.7 The number of patients required to test for a unique adverse reaction with no background incidence

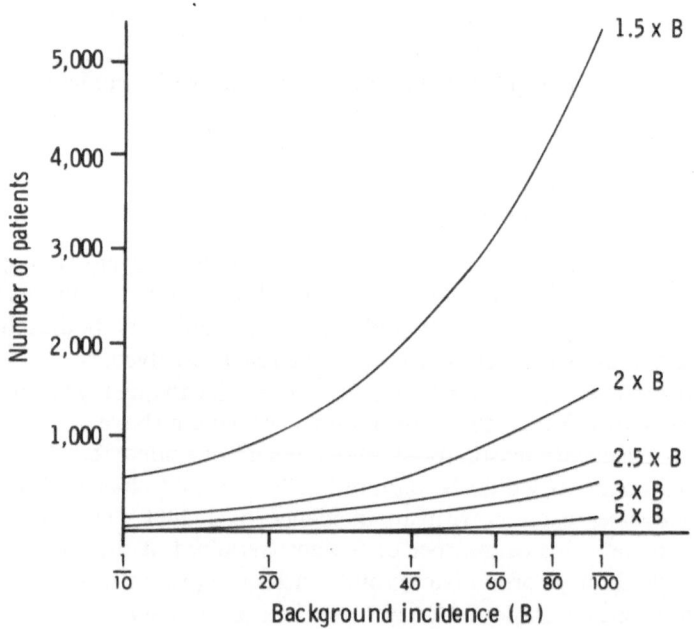

Table 2.8 The number of patients required to test for a unique adverse reaction with background incidence

3. Follow-up surveillance of patients exposed to a specific drug;
4. Retrospective study of drug use by patients suffering from a specific condition and of a similar group without specific condition (case control study).

However, do not be deluded into thinking that the issue is as simple as it first appears since in a recent study conducted by IMS under contract from a US government/industry consortium, some 22 variations on these four basic techniques were developed. Clearly, more extensive research will be required before the 'mists begin to clear' and appropriate methodology can be defined for different classes of compounds.

PRODUCT LIABILITY

Although it has been stated repeatedly by commentators from industry and academia that there is no such entity as a non-toxic drug, with growing knowledge and publicity of product liability the prospects for the 1980s are that there will be an increasing number of 'product liability claims' justified or not, related to medicines. Industry and government must work closely together to formulate sensible and honourable policies to appropriately compensate those that inadvertently suffer from unforeseen side-effects despite the huge and increasing efforts expended to minimize risk.

CONCLUSION

In heading towards a summary and conclusion to this presentation, it is necessary to pause and attempt to answer the questions:

'What does all that has been alluded to so far do to reduce the risk/benefit ratio?
and
'What impact do these initiatives have on the drug-hunters?'

Unfortunately, the first question cannot be answered. Although in all probability each and every action initiated has some good in it there is no way that one could attempt to quantify the overall improvement to the risk–benefit ratio.

The answer to the second question is readily quantified within ICI. During the period 1970 to 1980, the proportion of technical expenditure devoted to innovative research has fallen from greater than 50% in 1970 to less than 37% in 1980. Although during this period the ICI group has increased its total investment in innovative research, expenditure on development has increased 50% more rapidly.

In summary, this presentation has identified a sequence of events which individually and collectively bear a strong resemblance to the different phases of bacterial growth! (Table 2.9). The lag and log phases are clearly identifiable for the total activities. Whether or not a stationary or preferably a decline phase is reached will be dependent on a continued sensible interaction between industry and representatives of government acting on behalf of the community, i.e. the regulatory authorities. The growth characteristics of the mutants such as post-marketing surveillance and product liability have yet to be determined.

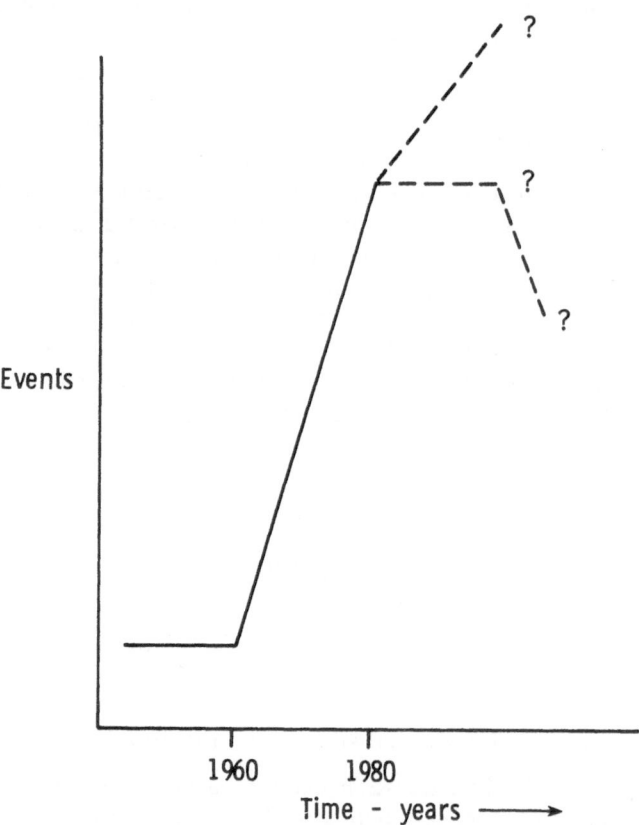

Table 2.9   Increasing amount of information and development work required by the regulatory authorities

Before concluding, it is worth offering a quote from Professor Kerr, who stands outside the interface between industry and the regulatory authorities on the issue of risk–benefit ratio:

'Information overkill has already begun. It is best seen in the advertisements in the *American Journal of Medicine* where drug manufacturers discharge their legal responsibilities by printing at the limits of visibility, lists of side-effects, including the rare, the vanishingly rare and the probably non-existent.'

In conclusion, this discussion has attempted to quantify the effects on industry of sincere attempts to reduce the risk–benefit ratio during the last 10 years. The effects on industry are striking and quantifiable. The effects on the lowering of the risk–benefit ratio are impossible to quantify. However, re-duction of this ratio is highly desirable to all parties. To this end, continued individual and collective contributions are required from all those involved in:

(1) Pre-clinical toxicity requirements,
(2) Clinical trial requirements,
(3) Post-marketing surveillance,
(4) Product liability,
(5) Harmonization of regulatory requirements and mutual recognition of approvals between regulatory authorities.

The latter is highly desirable but must provide for 'give and take' between regulatory authorities and industry so that the ultimate total information package required is not greater than the sum of its parts.

3
The effect on the public

J. MADDOX

The pharmaceutical industry has had a hard time in the past few years, since
the thalidomide affair in the early 1960s. I want to look into some of the ways
in which the industry's relationship with the general public might be improved. And it's perhaps as well to start by recognizing that the pharmaceutical industry is not alone. People in general worry about the side-effects of
drugs, but people at large also worry about a great many other consequences
of the operations of other industries – pollution of water from paper mills,
motor car exhausts, chemicals in the environment and so on. I think the
industry will be better able to face the difficult years ahead if it can somehow
recognize that it hasn't been singled out, by public opinion, for a unique place
in some public pillory.

The closest analogy, I think, is between the pharmaceutical industry and the
nuclear power industry. In the 1950s, the nuclear power industry was widely
regarded as a potential saviour of the industrialized West. Everywhere, but in
Britain especially, people were alarmed at the difficulty of digging enough coal,
the traditional source of bulk energy. In Britain, people were vividly aware, in
the 1950s, of how in 1947 the country ground almost to a stop because of the
physical shortage of coal. Inevitably, the promise of independence from the
old-fashioned way of keeping warm and productive caught the public
imagination, and right up to the early 1960s nuclear power was regarded as a
latter-day miracle.

Now, of course, the public mood is quite different. Historically, what
happened is that at the end of the 1950s, governments began to appreciate that
if nuclear power promised a more or less inexhaustible supply of energy, for
the time being at least, petroleum from the Middle East was apparently also
plentiful and, more to the point, cheaper. At the same time, public opinion had
become alarmed – rightly in my opinion – at the accumulation of radioactive

fallout from nuclear weapons tests. Nuclear engineers are now acutely aware of how this change of mood has affected their work. From being the darlings of British industry, they have become the group whose professional skills are most often suspect. Each new proposal for building a reactor is opposed by increasingly well-organized pressure groups. It is, of course, ironical that this should have happened at a time when it is clear that the promise of cheap oil from the Middle East has quite disappeared – for reasons which, in my opinion, should have been recognized a long time ago.

Some of my best friends work in the nuclear industry – and some of them also work in the pharmaceutical industry. My impression is that the nuclear engineers have a greater sense of having been wronged by this change of public attitudes than any other group I know. Why is it, they ask, that the public is so consistently suspicious of our technology, so suspicious of our personal motives and so willing to cut its own throat by denying itself the full use of a way of escaping from some of the problems of energy supply that haunt us just now? These are serious questions, which governments in the West as well as the nuclear engineers are going to have to face more courageously in the future than they have in the past.

When you think of it, the pharmaceutical industry has gone through a very similar transition. In the years immediately after the Second World War, it enjoyed the highest public esteem. Especially because of the introduction of antibiotics, the general public regarded the pharmaceutical industry as an indispensable source of public health. New types of drugs were welcomed with enthusiasm, and there was great public applause for what seemed to be the inexorable battle against infectious disease and the struggle for the more effective treatment of other conditions. For each idealistic chemist who may then have believed that by the development of new drugs it would be possible to make sure that people died only of accidents and old age, there were a thousand people outside the laboratories who considered that that was their legitimate expectation.

Much of that optimistic dream has, of course, already come true. Infectious disease has indeed been beaten back to the point at which such casualties as there are can be blamed not on the pharmaceutical industry and its products but on the inevitable difficulty of making sure that the people who need drugs actually receive them – the reasons are administrative rather than technical. And the anti-hypertensive drugs, the diuretics and the beta-blockers have helped to prolong the lives, and to enhance the quality of life, of a great many people who would in previous times have been chronically handicapped. So why is the pharmaceutical industry in the dog-house?

In my opinion, the trouble about thalidomide was only the presenting symptom of what has gone wrong, but it's easy to underestimate the import-ance of those events. The pictures of children born deformed that filled the newspapers for years on end were bound to create a vivid impression in the public mind that drugs can have unexpected side-effects. The fact that physicians and the pharmaceutical industry had been saying this all along counted, at the time, for very little. The general public made the discovery for itself, in the most dramatic way, and the lesson will not now be lost. But you'll also remember that the thalidomide affair coincided more or less in time with the beginning of that excited period during which people at large became self-conscious about the environment.

Historically, the origins of the environmental movement of the 1960s lie, in my opinion, in people's recognition that a sufficiently prosperous society could enjoy the benefits of industrial development without suffering the accompanying disbenefits. You could hope to build steel plants and paper mills without putting at risk the clean air and clean water that people commonly regarded as their birthright. At bottom, in other words, the environmental movement was born of a recognition that you could have your cake and also eat it provided that you were prepared to pay the price. Inevitably, of course, the environmental movement had wild excesses – there were some who argued that there need be no price to pay, or that it would be possible to enjoy the benefits of an advanced society without the industrial development which is the foundation of our prosperity. But these were excesses. The hard and rational core of the environmental movement – which still survives, but which has been modified by the financial stringencies of the past few years – inevitably reinforced public anxiety about the side-effects of drugs.

The result is that the pharmaceutical industry has become the focus for a great deal of public concern. It differs, however, from the nuclear power industry in at least one important respect. Broadly speaking, the nuclear engineers have found in the past decade that governments will not permit the exercise of their skill. The pharmaceutical industry, on the other hand, finds that its products are even more widely used than ever – and in spite of the regulatory systems which have evolved in the past 20 years, new drugs are still brought on to the market – but that the public expects that unwanted and unexpected side-effects should be eliminated.

There is, of course, an element of irrationality in all this. Whatever steps are taken to identify in advance the side-effects of new drugs, nobody can afterwards put his hand on his heart and proclaim that side-effects will not appear. Indeed, there is a good deal of force in the argument that it is only possible to ensure that a drug used in the treatment of human beings can be tested adequately by using it in the treatment of human beings. And, of course, it's also possible to argue that many drugs with beneficial therapeutic properties but also with unwelcome side-effects should nevertheless find a place in medical practice because their benefits, their value to patients and to society at large, are likely far to exceed such damage as they may do to a small number of those treated.

I think it's fair to acknowledge that these propositions are not widely accepted by the general public. It's also fair to say – as many in the industry do

– that this public expectation is unreasonable, irrational. If the public wants the benefits of a new drug, and if informed opinion says that guarantees against side-effects are not feasible, surely the public attitude is irresponsible.

In my opinion, however true that assertion may be, it does no good to try to change public opinion simply by saying that the public impression of what the pharmaceutical industry is about is simply and mischievously wrong. The nuclear industry – this is one reason why the analogy is valuable – has found that to its cost. And in any case, where the public fear of the side-effects of new drugs is concerned, there is a case for saying that the public are, if not right, justified.

That argument goes like this. A new drug, or a new technology of any other kind, offers social benefits of some kind but also risks. It's easy enough for the public at large to grasp what the benefits are likely to be. If somebody crippled by rheumatoid arthritis hears that there's a wonder drug on the way that had been shown in clinical trials to deal effectively with people in his condition, he'll not find it hard to imagine how his life could be changed. He'll go along to his doctor immediately, and he'll be asking for a prescription to put him right. In the nature of things, however, the wonder-drug may have unwanted side-effects, and they'll be strange side-effects – to the person who looks for a cure for his rheumatoid arthritis, it'll seem bizarre that he should be at risk of having something happen to his heart, or his liver, or his eyes. It doesn't matter that the risk may be numerically very small. It's an unfamiliar risk. It's one that appears to have no connection with the condition that's been cured. It's one that's bound to be regarded as a kind of extra threat to life and health. It's a risk that's bound to be resented. The nuclear industry has the same difficulty. The risks of radioactivity are entirely unfamiliar to ordinary people.

In my opinion, the pharmaceutical industry cannot expect that this ambivalence in public attitudes towards new drugs will go away either by the passage of time or as a result of the insistence that all new drugs carry the risk of unwanted side-effects. Public opinion is not like that. What is needed is a much more sensitive way of educating public opinion than any of the conventional ways of doing the job.

Fortunately, there are ways in which the pharmaceutical industry could set out to do that job. Paradoxically, the first need is that the industry should more willingly go along with the notion that it is not solely responsible for the safety of new drugs. Everywhere in the past decade or so, governments have found it necessary to set up regulatory bodies which license the introduction of new materials, and to that extent take away from the industry the final judgement of when the benefits of a new therapeutic material can be held to outweigh whatever risks may be entailed. This, given the depth of public feeling on the subject, is inevitable. So the industry is not fully responsible. It should, in my opinion, welcome these developments and make it plain to everybody concerned, but especially to potential users of new drugs, that complaints should be addressed, so to speak, not to itself but to the regulatory bodies – the Committee on the Safety of Medicines, for example.

But, you will say, what good will that do? On the one hand, the regulatory bodies are no better able to take responsibility for the safety of new drugs than are the manufacturers. Indeed, it's explicitly laid down that the approval of a regulatory body does not absolve the manufacturer of a new drug from liability for such side-effects as there may be. The regulatory bodies are also at odds with the industry in one crucial aspect – there is a common belief within industry, and some evidence to support it, that the activities of the regulatory bodies have reduced the pace of innovation. It is also clear that the ways in which they set about their task leave much to be desired – why else should there be just now such widespread interest in quite different ways of assessing the side-effects of new drugs, post-marketing surveillance and all that? And in any case, is there not the prospect that manufacturers of drugs will be explicitly saddled with responsibility, financial responsibility in particular, for the side-effects of new drugs by the legislation now being framed to specify the strict liability of all manufacturers for whatever ills emerge from the use of their new products? The manufacturers, you will say, are locked in to ultimate responsibility.

I do not think the problem is as stark as that. But, equally, I do not seriously pretend that the pharmaceutical industry will be able in the foreseeable future to shelter behind the regulatory bodies. For really, when you think of it, the responsibility for the use rather than the licensing of new drugs rests not with committees but with physicians. Only they, in my opinion, are able to shoulder responsibility for the decisions that are made each day about the prescription of particular drugs for particular patients. And, when you think of it, only they are able to carry out the educational task that has to be tackled if the public attitude towards pharmaceutical innovation is ever to be 'rational', as the saying goes.

It therefore seems to me that physicians, but general practitioners in particular, must now be asked to regard the prescription of a new drug as a rather solemn business. They cannot expect to discharge their duty to their patients or to medicine as a whole by giving their patients a slip of paper and sending them to the chemist's with it. They must, instead, explain what kind of chemical the new drug contains, what kinds of benefits they expect to follow from its use, what kinds of side-effects have already been identified and then, they have to say, 'and of course it's a new drug, so that there may be other side-effects that haven't been noticed yet'.

It may seem that I'm asking a lot of physicians, but I do not believe that they can discharge their duty if they do less. You may also say that my proposal is unrealistic – patients would not understand what they were being told by these enlightened physicians and, anyway, many physicians are unlikely to be able to shoulder these tasks. Frankly, I do not think these objections carry any weight at all. The courses of action that I propose have not seriously been tried. Physicians, by and large, are intelligent people. We all tend to underestimate the extent to which ordinary people can take into their heads quite complicated notions about the way in which a potential benefit must be balanced against a potential risk. Obviously, it will not be easy to reconcile the ways in which drugs are at present promoted to physicians with the need that the industry's representatives should spend as much time talking about the side-effects as about the benefits of a drug, but in the long run the benefits to the industry of such a practice would in my opinion, be immense.

None of this will of course get the regulatory bodies off the industry's back – they've come to stay. And none of this will deal with the legal issues that now confront the industry – strict liability, no-fault insurance and so on. How should these questions be tackled?

As an observer of the scene, I find that I'm repeatedly being told that the present practice of the regulatory bodies impedes the introduction of new drugs. I'm prepared to believe much of what I'm told. I'm also willing to accept that the public, as a result, is denied the benefits of many innovations, sometimes because they are unreasonably delayed and sometimes because they never find their way on to the market. In the long run, the community is the loser.

The issue of strict liability is likely to have more serious consequences, still hard to predict. If companies are required to shoulder more or less indefinite responsibility for whatever side-effects new drugs may have, many of them may decide to turn to quite different fields of activity, food manufacturing perhaps. Others may change their corporate structures so as to minimize the financial risk, with the result that the cost of marketing and distributing drugs will be increased, the public will pay more and the community will again be the loser.

People are constantly saying that these are terrible prospects, and that something should be done. I agree. But what? If the truth is what the industry says – that existing and promised legislation threatens to deny the community the benefits of new drugs – that is a political issue of great public interest. It should be tackled in the way that other political issues are tackled, by public debate, parliamentary debate and ultimately by government decision and action. I do not believe that sophisticated societies like that we live in would be unable to face up to such problems. But they will not do so unless they are asked to do so. And so, in my opinion, the industry had better stop wringing its hands and telling people like me how unfairly it's being treated. Rather, it should set out to make sure that the political issue with which it grapples is widely recognized for what it is, and widely discussed where political issues should be discussed – in the House of Commons and places like that.

Discussion of Chapters 2 and 3

CHAIRMAN: Dr J. COOMBES

Chairman: We have heard from those two extremely broad surveys of the problem of a whole number of new issues and directions that we might pursue. One point in relation to Mr Maddox's talk. What is very difficult to quantify is the benefit that has been lost because of the figures that Dr Newbould presented, that is the number of people who have been transferred from working on new drugs to developing drugs. What are the new drugs that have never been made available as a consequence? How that is to be quantified, I just do not know.

We have seen the very profound effect that regulations are having on the pharmaceutical industry, particularly in relation to its research, and we have had from Mr Maddox a somewhat astonishing account of how complicated issues of risk and benefit are, how it is not real risk but perceived risk that counts and how difficult it is to translate people's awareness of risk into action. I cannot think that anyone works out whether it would be worth the £5 train fare to go by train because the risk of driving into London by car would be much greater. No one indulges in such calculations. Those who smoke, can similarly put aside all risk calculations and enjoy the habit.

It is an elaboration of the problem that we have heard this morning. There is the direct effect, and there are the intangible decisions that are made by the public.

Dr J. Davoll (Director, Conservation Society): I am no longer affiliated to the pharmaceutical industry so I can speak as someone who has had experience in it but is perhaps less inhibited.

I should like to agree with quite a lot of what Mr Maddox said but there are one or two points that I felt could be amplified. For example, the nuclear engineers who once asserted that nuclear power was safe were moved from that stance by public pressure from outside by anti-nuclear groups. While I would agree that very often those groups were just as exaggerated in their denunciation of the dangers as were the nuclear engineers in their assertions of safety, it remains true that the nuclear people did appear to be moving under public pressure. That leaves a legacy of distrust in the public mind so that when the engineers say, 'Now we admit that there is this risk', the public may feel that they are not admitting what the risk really is.

Turning to the pharmaceutical industry, there have been cases, all well known, where evidence has been suppressed or played down so as to facilitate the marketing of drugs. It is known, too, that companies will market drugs in countries to the limit of the permissiveness of such countries' regulations. This, I am sure, is well known to all of us. The drug industry is seen by the public, and I think rightly, as not being in a neutral position on these things.

I would underline Mr Maddox's point. The utmost openness is needed if things are not to stall completely. I accept that there is a danger of regulations becoming so onerous that this may happen. Having left the industry some 10 years ago, I was particularly impressed by the relative heights of the piles of documents.

I have a subsidiary point about drugs already on the market, for example, Valium. Industries always advertise so as to sell something to deal with a problem. There is very little advocacy of perhaps changing lifestyles or of making other modifications in society that would reduce the need for drugs, and I think that there is over-prescription of drugs which are for minor transient anxieties that are really part of the human condition. Here again one does feel that the pharmaceutical industry needs some countervailing, so as to put the other point of view, and it would be wise for the industry to accept that this is the case. I agree with Dr Newbould that the more openness we have on this the more everybody will benefit, although in the short run some of the things will seem harder to do. The rewards will come later.

Dr J. M. Mungavin (ABPI): I speak in a personal capacity as a doctor with some experience of doctor/patient relationships.

To come to the heart of the last speaker's proposals, I must make it clear that as a doctor I think it would be quite impossible to have patients sharing the prescribing decisions. The doctor in Britain has shed much of his magic in the last 20 years from his position as the Edwardian father figure, but I do not think that he is so stupid as to shed the last shreds of this and to bring the patient into prescribing decisions. Nor indeed do I think that the patient wants it. At one stage in my medical career I was a registrar anaesthetist, commissioned by an enthusiastic surgeon to explain the procedures of gastrectomy and partial gastrectomy to his patients. I can still remember the glazed look that used to come across the faces of quite senior executives when I got on to stage 3 reduction of their gastric ulcer.

Nor do I believe that we shall be able to have a special position for our industry (this is more in the regulatory field) in product liability. A very important decision was taken in the Commission, or the Council of Ministers, when the proposal of Viscompte D'Avignon that the pharmaceutical industry in the Common Market be made a special case as regards product liability was rejected. I believe that the government has now accepted that they will have to legislate eventually for a no-fault liability without exception in regard to pharmaceuticals.

With respect to Mr Maddox, I am afraid that the suggestion is a non-runner.

Dr D. M. Burley (Ciba-Geigy): I completely agree with Mr Maddox that public opinion must be recognized and respected, but it is important to realize that as a commodity it is highly subject to manipulation. It can be mobilized to adopt a warlike attitude to another country. It can be influenced to throw out a political party, or to pillory some unfortunate individual for a private misdemeanour. On the subject of medicine, health and drugs, its views can be directed by politicians, pressure groups or individual reporters through the various communication media. Many of us would now say that a totally disproportionate amount of time and energy is being devoted to disasters of various kinds and this applies to all walks of life not just to medicine and far too little space is accorded in the medical area to the benefits of scientific research and endeavour. The real question is how can a more favourable attitude be achieved. I should be interested in Mr Maddox's view, and possibly that of Dr Lock (tomorrow).

Mr J. Maddox: To deal with the two last points at this stage.

First, I am not nearly as depressed as some people are at the supposed manipulability of British public opinion. On the whole, people's attitudes are not the same as the composition of the average newspaper's news stories. Indeed, I think it is quite impressive that in spite of the way that the newspapers may bring forth all kinds of scare-stories about nuclear power, or drugs, or this, that and the other, the man in the street is actually a lot more level-headed. Nevertheless, I agree it is more than unfortunate that so many exaggerated tales of disaster are told. The difficulty is that so long as the speculation about what the benefits may be is inhibited either by lack of information or sheer intellectual uncertainty, it is very hard indeed for the newspapers to deal with things fairly. But on that point I am not nearly as depressed as the questioner (Dr Burley) appeared to be.

On the question of whether doctors ought to share more fully with their patients responsibility for the choice of medicines, I know that a great many doctors' honest experience is that this is very difficult to do. I believe that until doctors try harder, and if they fail then try harder still, it will be exceedingly difficult to get a fully informed and enlightened public opinion. I know it is difficult, but therefore there is all the more reason for paying a lot of attention to how best to do it.

Dr J. G. Collier (St George's Hospital Medical School): John Maddox's suggestion of sharing responsibility is important and realistic. To share responsibility requires information, and my worry is that the information content of the prescriber is inadequate for such a proposal. If we consider important drugs, we now know the risks of many of those drugs, and that those risks are increased by poor prescribing. I should like to think that 'the public' includes the GP, who is a part of the public in this respect.

Take, for instance, propranolol, which is known to have many beneficial effects as well as clearly unwanted effects, and these we know. Those effects, when unwanted, have been produced by ignorant prescribing in many instances. It is the drug's fault to an extent, but the major burden should be taken by the GP. I would suggest that the worry of sharing is that not enough information reaches the level of the patient. I suspect that all the information is available, and has been made available in many instances by the industry, which is doing a tremendous amount. The greatest weakness in the chain is now the prescriber.

Dr C. J. Mugglestone (Schering Chemicals): My company, in common with a number of other manufacturers, markets oral contraceptives. The 11% drop in sales of these products over the past year or so is probably a direct effect of the fear of the public in response to one or two pieces of information about over-thirties, smoking, etc., in combination with the Pill.

In my view nothing is free from risk. Every one of the participants would agree that a pharmacologically active compound, a good pharmacologically active compound, has effects and side-effects. Perhaps the sooner we get that across to the public, the better. How we do it I do not know. I do not know that I agree with Mr Maddox's suggestions. Time with the GP is one of the great problems and trying to explain to the patient would be very difficult. One way might be to take a lead from the cigarette manufacturers. I bought a packet of their tranquillizers last night which said, 'Cigarettes can seriously damage your health'. Perhaps we should say on our pills, 'These pills may have side-effects'.

Mr F. Steward (University of Aston): Dr Newbould talked of the difficulty of quantifying the benefits of regulatory change. One approach to this problem is to look at the rate of withdrawal of new drugs that have been marketed in Britain and have later proved to be unsatisfactory. If the rate of withdrawal of unsatisfactory drugs introduced before regulatory control as opposed to after is compared, then it is a much higher proportion in the period before regulations were introduced than subsequently. That would seem to give some indication of a positive quantifiable benefit of regulatory control.

My second point concerns Mr Maddox's talk on public involve ment. He seemed to concentrate on the involvement of the public in the decision to prescribe. A lot of public concerns are about the process of regulation itself and the degree to which the public is involved in that process. The Genetic Manipulation Advisory Group (GMAG) is an interesting body in acknowledging a repre- sentative role for the public and for trades unions in the expert advisory process on decisions concerning risk. Does Mr Maddox think that a good approach to adopt, and if so, is it applicable to the Committee on Safety of Medicines, for example?

Dr B. Newbould: It was interesting to hear the comment on rates of withdrawal. That is one area where some attention could be focused to quantify the nature of the problem and the improvement in the risk–benefit that has accrued through the increased activities of regulatory bodies. One would have to look at it in depth before one could agree that it was a good method, and perhaps the only method of evaluating that will give an impartial assessment.

One of the problems is that we do take a lot of compounds out of development as a result of adverse findings in laboratory animals. There are occasions, and I know of one, where such a compound has been picked up again, in another country for example, and developed for sale, sold, and found not to have the adverse effects that were predicted from the animal results. I did not go into this particular aspect because it is not easily quantified in that we do not have the data, but all in all, we have to continue to scrutinize carefully what we are producing and try to form a judgement as to whether or not it is realistic.

The other point that I could have brought in, and would have liked to have done but for that it would have made my theme too complicated, is the tremendous pressures from other quarters on what we are doing. From, for example, those concerned with animal welfare. When we try to balance out all these considerations then we see that those involved with central decision-making have a tremendous and growing problem, because the pressures are arising from every conceivable source.

However, I shall certainly look at that data on the rate of withdrawal and see whether it is able to give us some evidence that these activities during the last 10 years have increased the value of risk–benefit analysis.

Mr Maddox: An interesting question about GMAG (the Genetic Manipulation Advisory Group). I should explain that because of the obvious conflict of interest between again becoming a journalist and being a member of such a committee, I had to resign a few months ago. It seemed to be a very interesting innovation. There were four lay members of a committee of about 20, and there were also four people, mostly scientists, who had been appointed by trades unions. To begin with, the scientist members of the committee found us a great nuisance because they did not understand what we were talking about, but as the weeks or months went by they discovered that it was educative for them as well as for us that they should have to explain what they were doing in simpler language than was convenient.

There were, nevertheless, a number of difficulties about the GMAG experiment which seem almost unavoidable if a government committee is dealing with information that is necessarily confidential on either commercial or other grounds. First, the lay members cannot talk freely, and therefore cannot go about talking in such a way that the public at large will sense that in fact everything is going fine and that is as important in drugs as in genetic manipulation, indeed more so because more money hangs on it.

The other sort of difficulty is that committees like that, and this is a very personal view, are likely always to be over-cautious. It is very hard to expect that the Committee on the Safety of Medicines should set its sights a little lower given the public pressures provided by the newspapers, the civil service, and so on. For that sort of reason, the ideal in the long run is to find a way of making the Committee on the Safety of Medicines a less crucial part of the process of bringing drugs on to the market. That would be my goal, but I would not for a minute suggest that it could be done unless the public was in a very different frame of mind to what it is at present.

Mr J. Spink (Wellcome Foundation): Mr Maddox's point about the question of shared responsibility is one of the most interesting and controversial points to have been made this morning. I would first question whether there can be a true sharing of responsibility when we are talking about the prescribing of drugs. It is really a question of the informed consent. It is often said that the only person who can give an informed consent is another doctor, because one really needs to understand all about medicine, or at least everything surrounding the medication that is proposed, before being able to say that the patient is sharing the responsibility with the doctor.

I should then like to question, and I would be very interested to hear whether Mr Maddox has taken this point into account, whether it is desirable that there should be this sharing, because where there is a sharing of responsibility there is also a sharing of liability, and this can be to the disadvantage of the patient in reducing the compensation that would be payable to him in the event of injury.

Under the proposals of the Common Market Directive, the notification of a hazard will be a defence for the manufacturer and one of the very few defences to be left with him. This touches on the question of what kind of liability we are talking about. Mr Maddox referred to no-fault liability. With great respect, we are not talking about no-fault liability. The only country to have no-fault liability is New Zealand. We are talking about strict liability. No-fault liability is a compensation scheme where never-mind-who has caused the accident, the patient is paid, and that is perfectly all right. But we are not talking about that. We are talking about strict liability in which there will be a defence for the manufacturer whereby if the hazard is notified by the manufacturer and his warning is then passed on to the patient, the patient's position could very well be prejudiced in regard to the matter of compensation. I wonder if, therefore, in the light of that, it would still be considered desirable that the responsibility for the treatment should be shared.

Mr Maddox: The short answer is yes. It is understandable, I think, that medical people should be impressed with the difficulties of this, but they are by no means as serious as they would seem at first sight. At present a great many doctors do implicitly involve patients in responsibility for prescribing when they tell the pharmacist to put on the bottle of pills, 'Take no more than once a day', or 'Take one pill once a day'. This would implicitly suggest that if the patient takes two, or ten a day he may get into trouble.

Doctors could make a start by explaining to patients why they say 'one tablet after every meal', and in the case of dangerous drugs such as barbiturates it would obviously make sense for the doctor to say, 'Not more than two a day', or, 'when going to sleep', and to add the information 'If you do, you may go into a coma and be in trouble'. I know that to some that might seem like an invitation to suicide, but in practice I am sure that unless doctors do get into that frame of mind when dealing with their patients, not merely about drugs but all kinds of other matters, that it will be very hard to get a sensible relationship between patients and doctors.

One could imagine, even in the case of entirely novel drugs where the side-effects had not yet been identified, how doctors might go about it. They might well say, 'Mrs Jones, here is a new drug. The manufacturers have been able to demonstrate that it has the following benefits, and I therefore believe it will help you and your condition, but we must acknowledge that it is a drug whose use is so short that we cannot yet be sure that it may not have side-effects.' It seems only humane, and equitable, that a doctor should share his own anxieties with his patient in that way. If the result now and again is that the patient says that he or she would prefer not to take the risk, that too is a risk, but in the interests of a more enlightened public opinion it is a risk well worth taking.

I agree about no-fault, what I have just said deals with that point too.

Mr J. Spink (Wellcome Foundation): With respect, Mr Maddox has not quite answered the second part of my question. If the patient is warned of the hazard, it will affect that patient's right to compensation. We are not talking about no-fault. We are talking about strict liability, when the notification of a hazard will become a defence. If there was a straight compensation scheme, the question of whether or not the patient was warned would not be at issue, but in strict liability that question is at issue, and the patient, who may be so injured that he needs assistance for the rest of his life, would be barred from any assistance by having been warned of the hazard.

Mr Maddox: The fact that the introduction of new drugs may sometimes lead to the need for companies to pay compensation to patients is not a very important consideration in my, perhaps naive, point of view. I was much more concerned with the extent to which by sharing responsibility for drugs, and indeed other aspects of medical treatment with patients, doctors would help encourage the much better appreciation by patients of how tricky modern medicine is.

On the question of compensation, if the doctor has in a sense acquired the informed consent of his patients in this way, then it would be right and proper that the patient should to some extent not do as well out of any compensation awards there might be. But I cannot for the life of me think that the compensation issue is the central one. It is the kind of relationship that matters.

Prof. A. Bennett (Kings College Medical School): We have spoken largely of drugs that have gone on to the market and are then prescribed to patients, but not much has been said about the other aspect of the question, that is getting drugs quickly into the patient when those drugs are thought to have desirable biological activity. I am not sure that the public is the body that is the best arbiter on this. It is much more the responsibility of the regulatory authorities and government to ease the burdens of getting drugs quickly into a man for a very short, limited period, and then the importance of prolonged studies can be stressed where they are worthwhile.

Dr J. H. Shelley (Boehringer Sohn): On the question of shared responsibility with regard to decision to treat, Dr Cartwright, were she here, could give much more information on this.

First, there are a lot of data, and a lot of studies have been done on the question of sharing decisions to treat. Drug treatment may be a very small part of the whole. We have been equating treatment with the prescription of drugs, and really this is not so by any means. Studies have shown that the patient's expectations, and those of the doctor, his or her previous experience of the disease, the patient's relationship to the GP, age, sex and social class have all been investigated and have been reported in the literature with regard to successful outcome of discussion on treatment choice, i.e. course of treatment, what type of treatment should be adopted in different situations, etc. There is already information on the question of shared responsibility, and Cartwright is one of the people who has done a lot of work on it.

Dr L. Z. Saunders (Smith, Kline and French Research): Mr Maddox said we have very few data on the benefit of new drugs since the war. We have even fewer data on the benefit of the proliferating tests that the regulatory agencies are asking to be done in animals. It is not possible to enlarge on this without possible pre-empting later speakers and I shall wait on them, but this is a good juncture to make the point in juxtaposition to Mr Maddox's contribution.

Prof. C. T. Dollery (Royal Postgraduate Medical School): A comment, first, about the context of this discussion. It is relevant to all questions of risk and benefit.

There is a tendency to assume that all drugs are given for death-dealing conditions, but the majority are not. Many drugs are quite properly given to relieve pain, which may be severe but which may be relatively minor and to relieve anxiety which may be severe or minor, or depression, or even to shorten a febrile illness which would itself have been self-correcting but which has a shorter duration because an antibiotic is given. In that sense drugs can be looked upon almost as a convenience, or as a consumer product, rather than as a life-saving one, and clearly the standards of safety that have to be applied to a drug that is given in that sense are different and more stringent than those that are required for a drug that would be given, say to treat tuberculosis or something of that kind.

The second assumption that seems to underlie the discussion is that all drugs are innovative and novel. Anybody who has sat on a drug regulatory body realizes that only a tiny minority of the drugs that come forward are of that kind. Special requirements are needed for the first drug, like cimetidine, or propranolol, but it is rather difficult to argue the same for the third, fourth, fifth, tenth or twelfth of the same kind. It is proper that more stringent standards should apply to drugs that show a very little innovation, and that therefore do carry with them unknown risks, but rather accurately quantifiable benefits, since they seem to be very similar to existing drugs. By the time that a drug is marketed, one usually knows whether it is substantially innovative or not, although at the clinical trial stage that is not always known.

The third point, and the last in setting the context, is that unfortunately for all of us, once an effective treatment in an area of medicine has been discovered, the requirements for the next advance in that area will be more difficult, because no one is asking to achieve the same level, but to achieve something that is better than that. That does set a higher standard of appraisal, both from the standpoint of efficacy or safety, because we really should not be accepting a new medicine unless its balance of efficacy and safety for the condition being treated is better than the best of the existing drugs. The more we achieve, the more difficult it is to do better in the future.

Although I sympathize with Dr Newbould, to a certain extent the lengthening of the development cycle and its complexity are inevitable. My criticisms would be on the selection of the areas of the development cycle where the emphasis is placed. Currently, an excessive emphasis is placed on preclinical testing, and perhaps not always sufficient on clinical testing.

My final point arises out of that, but not directly, and it is to comment on what Mr Maddox said. I enjoyed it immensely, but there is a tendency for liberal intellectuals like him, and I hope myself, to assume that the whole world is populated with people who are similar in their attitudes to us. One need only sit in outpatients for a relatively short time to realize that that is not quite true! However, I do think that it is inevitable, and proper, and right that we should give more information to our patients, not just about decisions about drugs but about everything that we do in medicine. I was extremely impressed the first time I went to the United States, nearly 20 years ago now, to find the argument that took place at the bedside if a patient's dose of a drug was due to be changed. The patient wanted to know why. It is still relatively rare for a British patient to ask such forceful questions as an average American patient will. We must do it because the patient is a human being; he will collaborate better with treatment; he will have a better understanding of all that is involved. But it is extremely difficult to convey a sufficient knowledge of biology that he genuinely participates in the decision as an informed person rather than, as it were, acceding to a decision, but feeling that he has been properly consulted. There is a difference in emphasis there. That might even apply to the Genetic Manipulation Advisory Panel, but it would certainly apply in outpatients.

4
The necessary role of government

D. ENNALS

Today the whole question of the intervention of government in the absolute freedom of private industry is in question. This is partly because we have a government which, in theory, is committed to a non-interventionist policy. Recently Professor Milton Friedman, whose theories are held in great respect by the present government, related the theory of non-intervention in the process of free market forces to the pharmaceutical industry. Answering the question, 'how far should we set up machinery to protect ourselves' he launched into an attack upon agencies of intervention which could have applied as much to the Committee on the Safety of Medicines (CSM) as to the US Food and Drug Administration. While accepting that in his view the situation for the pharmaceutical industry in Britain was better than in the United States, he argued the case for leaving the testing of drugs to the industry itself and above all to avoid what he called 'the judgement of the bureaucrats'. Whether the distinguished experts of the Committee on the Safety of Medicines would recognize this description of them is hard to say!

Interest is also immediately highlighted by the case against the manufacturers of Debendox, bought in Orlando, Florida, by the parents of four-year-old David Mekdeci who was born with a number of physical malformations. The fact that Richardson-Merrell, had had to pay out about £100 million in damages after Triparanol had been withdrawn in 1962, shortly before thalidomide was put on the market by the same firm, seemed to Dr Kenneth Hambley, writing in *Pulse* on 8 March to be irrelevant. His article was called 'The Sunday Scaremongers'. But these so-called scaremongers are

---

The publisher draws the attention of the reader to an alternative point of view expressed elsewhere in this volume (see pages 146 and 167)

not too wide of the mark. The jury unanimously concluded that Debendox was unsafe and had caused David's deformities and awarded $20 000 to cover the boy's medical expenses, though not the $12 million compensation the plaintiffs had sought. Extraordinarily the firm claimed that the verdict did not impugn the drug's safety. 'The court's verdict is not important in our assessment of the safety of the drug', they said. What an extraordinary attitude to take in the wake of a court ruling. The attitude of the Department of Health and Social Security is no less puzzling. A spokesman said, 'The mere fact of the verdict doesn't make that much difference. The Committee on Safety of Medicines will wish to study the evidence and give their views when they feel the time is right'. That appears to be intolerably complacent after the ruling of the court in Florida. The present Secretary of State, Patrick Jenkin, should suspend the use of Debendox in Britain until there has been a thorough review of all the evidence by the CSM and to do otherwise would be irresponsible.

Dr Cavalla has referred to 'the contrary pressures exerted on a legislator to effect safety on the one hand with protection of maximum liberty on the other'. It goes back at least 360 years. Legislation to protect the consumer against the grosser malpractices of traders goes back to early medieval times, and in the case of medicines, an Act of 1540 empowered the physicians of London to appoint four inspectors of 'Apothecary wares, Drugs and Stuffs'. From the early seventeenth century these inspecting doctors were joined in their inspections by representatives of the Society of Apothecaries. During the nineteenth century the Pharmaceutical Society of Great Britain was established and legislation was introduced to control the retail supply of poisons and to establish a register of pharmacists. In 1858, statutory provision was made for the publication of the *British Pharmacopoeia*. Between then and 1875 the Food and Drugs Act laid down penalties for the adulteration of drugs. In 1925 the first Therapeutic Substances Act introduced controls over 'biological' products, such as vaccines and sera, which could not be assayed by chemical analytical methods. This Act provided for the licensing of manufacturers and the control of strength and quality of the product. By virtue of the provisions of the Pharmacy and Poisons Act of 1933 and later Acts dealing with antibiotics and certain other products, lists of medicines which could be supplied only on prescription were prepared.

However, except in relation to the 'biological' substances and dangerous (e.g. narcotic) drugs no limitation was placed on the freedom of an individual manufacturer to put a new medical product on the market. Most of the established manufacturers did in fact carry out thorough tests and trials, but were not obliged by statute to do this. The need for further legislation was already being considered when, in November 1961, the revelation of the effects of thalidomide called public attention to the inadequacy of existing measures. In 1962 a joint sub-committee of the Standing Medical Advisory Committee recommended the establishment of an expert committee to review the evidence available for new drugs and offer advice on their toxicity. As a result of these recommendations a Committee on Safety of Drugs was established by the health ministers in 1963 under the chairmanship of Sir Derrick Dunlop and began work with effect from the 1 January, 1964.

The pharmaceutical industry voluntarily agreed to submit data on new products and to abide by the committee's advice. The Minister of Health announced that he would publicize cases where the committee's advice was disregarded, and the committee was given the full support of the pharmaceutical and medical professions. The joint sub-committee also recommended that there should be new legislation giving statutory backing to the committee's advice, and comprehensively overhauling all legislation relating to medicines. After a period of review and consultation, a White Paper, 'Forthcoming Legislation on the Safety, Quality and Description of Drugs and Medicines', was published in September 1967. The Medicines Act based on these proposals received the royal assent in October 1968, and is the basis of government intervention in 1980.

It is worth recalling briefly why governments in general (not just in the UK) should become so intimately involved, particularly when on other activities of potentially greater impact on public health (such as alcohol, smoking, fluoridation, the compulsory wearing of seat belts to prevent accidents) action has so often been avoided by successive governments. I hope you will allow me to return to those examples later. In the case of drugs there seem to me to be four factors which compel governments to act:

(1) The public's fear of exploitation by powerful multi-nationals interested only in profits,
(2) The emotional impact of news of deformed babies,
(3) Unrealistic public expectations of safety of drugs (leading to dismay when expectations are unfulfilled),
(4) Fear of the unknown (not knowing what long-term effects a new drug might have).

Reverting to a historical summary it is interesting to see that the *Lancet* in 1920 said, 'the time has now come to ensure the same protection against fraud and error in the case of complicated remedies that we already enjoy in the case of simpler ones'. The manufacturers were said to be strongly in favour of control 'because it protects both themselves and the public from the activities of those who are inefficient and dishonest'. These are strong words. There was, even then, not only a recognition that advancing technology carried with it both potential for great benefit and for drugs which would transform the treatment of so many physical and mental conditions but also the potential for harm, if only for a small minority of people. There was a growing recognition that there needed to be some sort of organization commanding resources and expertise greater than any individual company to protect not only the consumers but the pharmaceutical industry itself.

It is hardly possible to exaggerate the enormous effect of the thalidomide tragedy on public opinion. It gave massive weight to public awareness that drugs could have wholly unexpected side-effects and rightly created pressure for an independent check on the work of drug innovators. It was this pressure that led of course to the Medicines Act with its full panoply of controls. The government learnt its lesson. I wish the doctors and the public had learnt their lessons from this tragedy. Despite thalidomide, the taking of even non-essential drugs during pregnancy has not gone down in the past 10 years (and in America it has increased). A survey published in 1977 indicated that in Britain doctors prescribed drugs for 56% of women in the first three months of pregnancy, and an astounding 97% of women received some sort of medication during the nine months.

Perhaps we have gone pill mad in Britain. The public seem to believe that there is a pill for every ill and GPs too often go along with the theory. The quickest way to end a consultation is to write out a prescription. That is why I persuaded the British Medical Association to launch a joint campaign addressed to GPs to persuade them not to overprescribe and to look at the price tag before prescribing. It was backed up by posters and other material from the Health Education Council. I don't think it had much effect since doctors don't always appreciate advice from either the Secretary of State or the BMA!

But no one has any doubt about giving their advice to the Secretary of State! While I agree that public pressure for regulation of drugs may not be entirely rational or realistic, there is a consistent and continuing concern that government should look over the shoulder of drug manufacturers and protect the public from hazardous developments or shoddy or dishonest work. In this consumerist age it would be strange if this were not so. It is for government to decide, after the fullest possible consultation, whether further safety protection measures should be adopted, what the effects of such measures on industry, availability of goods and services, might be and how far the enthusiasm of the pressure group or of experts within government ought to be discounted. There is no formula, for each case is different. Usually, after ideas have been aired and discussed, a consensus emerges. Each social demand inevitably has a social cost.

What should the government's role consist of? The White Paper which preceded the Medicines Act mentioned that the 'pharmaceutical revolution', by introducing powerful and valuable new medicines, had given rise to new problems for which the then existing legislation was never designed. The Medicines Act subsequently provided for, inter alia, certification of new drugs before clinical trial and assessment of safety, quality and efficacy before grant of a product licence. The role of government in relation to drug research, development and marketing thus became much more extensive. In the nature of things it has, over the years, tended to grow rather than diminish because while there is seldom any concerted demand for the removal of controls aimed at safety, each sensation tends to renew the pressure on government departments and MPs to extend and intensify the controls.

So, what should be the objectives of this battery of controls and how should they be achieved? Some possibilities are:

(a) Setting data requirements determining what studies and tests are essential before drug is tried on patients; this means setting general standards to which industry must conform.
(b) Providing a body of experts to consider the data produced and reach a balanced judgement on whether the drug reaches an acceptable level of safety. quality and efficacy.

The setting of standards and the assessment of individual applications is an onerous task, especially since absolute safety cannot be guaranteed with new compounds. It requires a delicate judgement as to how rigorous pre-marketing testing should be, bearing in mind that one cannot prove a negative.

The Government is very fortunate to be advised by a body of eminent independent experts, the Committee on Safety of Medicines, under the chairmanship of Professor Scowen. On advice of that committee the Licensing Authority has issued notes for guidance on the kinds of studies which applicants will normally be expected to have conducted to test toxicity, effect on reproduction, etc. Such guidance inescapably has significant impact on research and development, though I understand that many companies would, for their own reasons, carry out these or similar studies in any case. The effect is therefore mainly one of codifying and of bringing the standards of all up to those of the best.

The government must decide as to whether a reasonable balance is struck between:

(a) Safeguarding the public from injudicious trial and marketing of new products.
(b) Risk of stifling innovation through over-rigorous controls.

The government has to form its view in the light of consultations and its perception of the public interest. There are, however, other, perhaps less obvious, elements in the government's role:

(c) International. With movement towards a free market of drugs within the EEC, gradual though it may be, government officials have to come to agreement with those of other member states. They must, for example, try to harmonize data requirements throughout the community so that data submitted in support of a licence application will be acceptable to all member states.
(d) The pricing of NHS drugs. It must recognize in pricing policy the importance of allowing adequate return from investment in research and development. This the last government sought to do in introducing the revised PPRS.

(e) Seeking to ensure that revision of legislation governing use of animals in laboratory experiments does not operate to discourage or impede development of new or improved drugs.

(f) How to encourage research into new drugs for relatively unremunerative uses, e.g. rare diseases. To some extent government has a direct role through use of government research facilities or through provision of research funds for specific purposes. The optimum size and extent of this role is not easy to judge and is likely to remain a matter for debate.

(g) Finally, a separate involvement through the control of laboratory conditions in interests of workers as well as consumers, such as Health and Safety Executive, advisory groups on dangerous pathogens and on genetic engineering, etc. Inevitably this is a role which tends to grow.

So we are talking about a multi-faceted role of government. Government activities have impact on drug research from several different angles. There are different government departments and bodies involved. Co-ordination is inevitably difficult. We are fortunate that in the UK consultation between industry and government is generally effective, more so, it seems, than in most other countries.

Over the years the government's involvement with industry has been characterized by a desire for fairness and impartiality and the Medicines Act contains various safeguards for industry. For example, application for a clinical trial certificate or product licence may not be turned down without reference to the CSM, and if the CSM is disposed to advise rejection, it must grant the right of making representations. The licensing authority may not take price into account in assessing an application. Naturally the government must concern itself with the health of the pharmaceutical industry as well as the health of patients, taking regard of the value to the nation of a vigorous, economically viable innovative industry.

The industry is of course an international one and the industry in the UK gains immeasurably from its multi-national character. During their last period of office, the last Labour Government did what it could to attract foreign companies to use the UK as a base for production. Britain has many advantages including the quality of its specialist and professional manpower but also the thoroughness and objectivity of UK clinical trials.

What of the future? The government's role cannot be static in the face both of advancing technology and the pressing consumerist demand for an increasingly leak-proof safety umbrella. There are always some weaknesses in any system. Here are two examples.

Products already on the market before 1 September automatically got a Product Licence. All of these pre-1971 products will in due course have been considered by the Committee on Review of Medicines under the chairmanship of Professor Wade but it seems likely that the committee will still take about 10 years to complete its mammoth task. When it came into existence in 1975 there were nearly 30 000 specialized drugs on the market and there are still 20 000 to be reviewed.

Secondly, doctors do not appear always to read or to act on the yellow Adverse Reaction Warning Leaflets. The DHSS has worked out a system of specially marked envelopes to draw attention to these warning leaflets and the situation may improve. But Jack Ashley has continued to campaign for legislation to make it mandatory on doctors to report adverse reactions. Easier said than done, but the present voluntary system leaves much to be desired. We must find ways of securing a more effective response from doctors and of ensuring that adverse reactions to drugs are properly brought to the attention of the CSM. It does seem strange that, according to recently published figures there were 65 000 adverse reactions noted by doctors, concerning 1700 drugs in the past 17 years yet only 14 yellow warnings were issued.

But at the same time as we consider how to make checks and controls more effective we ought to see whether there are ways of cutting down on bureaucracy. Regulatory agencies of all kinds ought periodically to stand back from their day-to-day activities and ask themselves whether all the controls are still necessary and relevant. We ought to view the costs of safety not only in financial terms but also in 'opportunity cost' terms. Thus, in terms of public health, might some diminution of effort here enable scarce resources, especially of skilled manpower, to be deployed elsewhere to better effect? It would be foolish and politically unthinkable to suggest that drug regulation be abandoned but experience may show that particular categories of product or particular activities within the long chain from the original research and development effort to eventual retail sale and supply present little hazard in practice. It is no doubt easier to indulge in such speculations in opposition than in government.

But if it is the saving of life which concerns us most then there are four measures on which a new government with a big majority in parliament should legislate. No, they have nothing to do with the control of drugs. They are:

To legislate to give health authorities the right to require fluoridation of water by the water authorities.

A legal requirement for all front seat occupants of motor cars to wear seat belts at all times.

A very substantial tightening up on legislation governing drinking and driving on lines suggested years ago in the Blennerhassett Report.

An end to all cigarette advertising except at the point of sale.

5
Problems facing a regulatory authority

D. G. GRAHAME-SMITH

If one asks the question, 'How safe does a drug have to be?', one needs to know its efficacy and indications for use. A cytotoxic drug used in the treatment of acute leukaemia is very dangerous but the risk is worth taking if there is a chance of remission. At the other end of the scale, and only speaking generally, many doctors would not now treat osteo- or rheumatoid arthritis with phenylbutazone in the long term because, although the drug is effective, the risk of adverse effects upon the bone marrow is unacceptable. This does not prevent the wise use of phenylbutazone in the short-term treatment of acute gout. Immediately, therefore, one sees that there are many factors to weigh up and decisions become very difficult. The controversy which ensues can be seen from the strong reaction that industry makes to the efforts of regulatory authorities, as epitomized by the following two views:

(1) 'Superior drugs will only be found by the inquisitive and candid researcher, living in a free world where ideals can still be realized and beautiful dreams can still come true. They will not be recognized by the complacent, unimaginative and lazy-minded bureaucrats, soaked in regulations, old prejudices and habits of mind. I strongly believe that creative thinking and action cannot but suffocate in a world of bureaucratic materialism, where force, power, conspiracy against work and selfishness are the main driving forces and charity is dead.' Janssen, P. (1979)

(2) 'It is high time that drug regulatory agencies contributed to more efficient research by relieving qualified research departments from the task of spending a major part of their intellectual and material

resources on studies which contribute neither to drug safety nor to the effective treatment of diseases for which no satisfactory therapy exists today.' Herr. E. B. (1977)

These criticisms need careful examination because so far only the free-enterprise western pharmaceutical industry has developed effective medicines. though this may be as much a product of the possession of trained personnel. tradition in chemical and biological research and available resources, as anything to do with the capitalist system and the lure of profits. Whatever the explanation, the pharmaceutical industry of the western world has been and will continue to be a potent source of new and effective medical therapies.

The problems facing a regulatory authority stem from the task of having the authority to make and impose regulations! It is rare that regulations are nice for anyone because they are intended either to make people do things that they do not wish to do or to prevent people doing things that they wish to do. As far as the regulation of the drug industry is concerned. both of these conditions apply. In these circumstances regulations are bound to be controversial and deserve careful consideration.

One might ask why have regulations at all. The answer to that is in order to provide an assurance in an open way that the quality. safety and efficacy of a drug comply with some pre-set standards. However. why can the market and

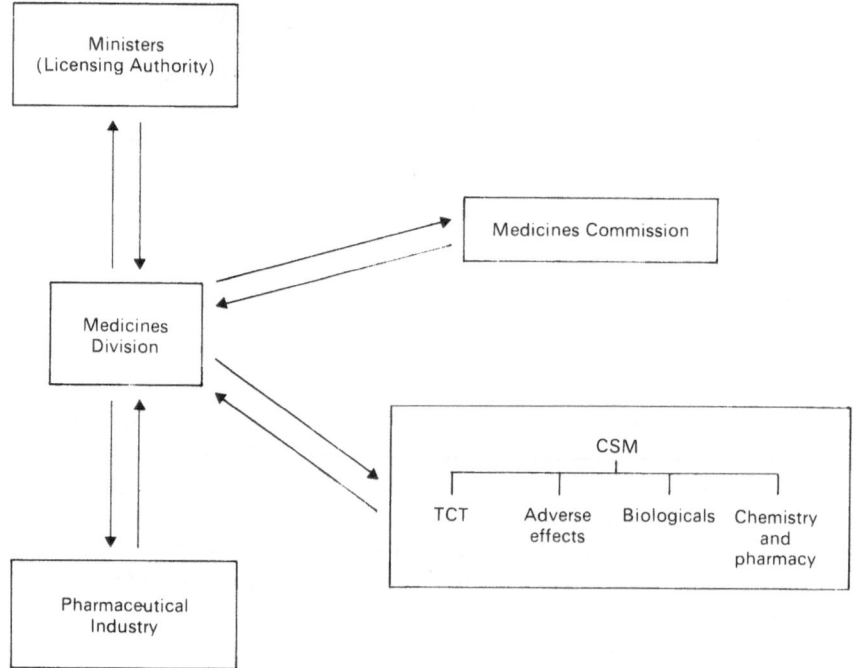

Figure 5.1   Organization of the regulatory systems

the law not take care of that? It could be claimed that market forces makes it unprofitable or, because of the developing litigation, downright foolhardy to market unsafe products. You might expect an unsafe drug to be quickly removed from the market, leading to the loss of a great deal of investment. It would follow then that the commercial and ethical interests of the pharmaceutical industry would ensure a reasonable degree of drug safety. This is undoubtedly so, but such an argument is probably too sophisticated for governments responsible for health care, the public and indeed for many doctors, and anyway would require a fairly sophisticated surveillance system. The same attitude could be taken toward efficacy but with much less confidence. It could be said that a drug which is not efficacious would not find a market and therefore would not be used, and that all the development and marketing costs would therefore be lost. If we lived in a world of objective and rational therapeutics no doubt this would be so. But our world falls below these standards and large quantities of drugs for which there is dubious evidence of efficacy are prescribed every day and produce a profit. Maybe if the medical profession were more critical about the drugs they used, this argument on efficacy would hold.

There is, in fact, an ambivalence on the part of the industry toward regulatory authorities because it is useful for industry to have some kind of agreed external standard to come up against. I think we all respond to that in whatever sphere of life we work. Any scientist benefits from having to produce work which comes up to the standards expected by his peers, standards which are perpetuated by scientific societies, by universities and by the publication of scientific journals. All these standards are external to the scientist and he keeps to them as best he can. So perhaps industry does get some protection and help from there being a regulatory authority, as long as, in principle, the regulatory authority is respected.

Having once decided that there should be regulations, how does one formulate and administer them? Without actually saying so, this is what the Medicines Act of 1968 did. The Act is a document of masterly vagueness which allows great latitude in how the interested parties sort themselves out in relationship to the licensing of medicines. The Act is interested in providing some standard of safety, quality and efficacy and it aims to do that by setting up the Medicines Commission to advise the licensing authority about matters to do with medicine. Figure 5.1 shows the organizations involved in the function of the resulting regulatory systems. It can be seen that the Medicines Commission acts through the Medicines Division, with what are called the Section 4 committees, that is the Committee on Safety of Medicines (CSM), with its various subcommittees and, of course, now the Committee on Review of Medicines. The Medicines Division advises the ministers according to the advice it receives, though it acts on a great number of matters in its own right. Really the Licensing Authority, the Medicines Division, the Medicines Commission and the CSM act in concert, but it is the CSM that tends to get the stick in terms of adverse reactions to regulatory policies. All the various bodies interact through the Medicines Division with the pharmaceutical industry, although more recently the CSM has spoken directly to the industry and, of course, the industry has a member on the Medicines Commission.

The tasks for which the Committee on Safety of Medicines was established are spelled out in the Act (Figure 5.2).

Medicines Act 1968

A committee may be established for:

1. Giving advice with respect to safety, quality or efficacy.

2. Promoting the collection and investigation of information relating to adverse reactions for the purpose of enabling such advice to be given.

Figure 5.2   Tasks for which the CSM was established

In a sense the criteria that the Committee adopt to give advice on these matters to the Licensing Authority are *ipso facto* the regulations under which the industry has to work. In fact, in most matters the licensing authority provides guidelines with the intention of allowing a fair degree of flexibility, but human beings and human institutions have a habit of being awkward and once industry starts to interact with a regulatory body, guidelines tend to get turned into regulations. Take, for instance, clinical trials in respect of drugs for long-term use, for example hypotensives, or drugs for rheumatoid arthritis. In these cases the CSM was often presented with the results of studies made over a few weeks in perhaps 20 or 30 patients as grounds for product licence applications and that kind of clinical use is quite insufficient for drugs that are likely to have very widespread use for a long time in an individual. Here, the decision as to the nature of the guideline was an arbitrary one. First the CSM said they would like to see the use of the drug in a reasonable number of people over a longer period of time and immediately, and quite understandably, industry came back and asked how many people and for how long. The Committee had to respond, picked a number out of the hat and said about 100 patients for 1 year. This immediately became a millstone around the Committee's neck because the industry said why 100 patients, why not 80; why 1 year, why not 9 months, and really there are no answers to these questions. Nonetheless, the guideline now remains about 100 patients for about 1 year because this seems a reasonable requirement under the circumstances. In this way a guideline can become an *ipso facto* regulation. The next problem faced by the regulatory authority was their guidelines themselves, and some of the difficulties met by the CSM in this respect are listed below in Figure 5.3. Most of these are concerned with safety and efficacy, the regulations for quality not being such a problem.

First of all, the science of toxicology is terribly imprecise in relation to drug development. Drug testing toxicology seems to have developed haphazardly and many of the guidelines that both the CSM and the industry keep to do not appear to have a very firm base. The requirements are all very sensible and have grown out of usage, but the mathematical rules that govern, for instance, the length of toxicity testing required for a certain length of clinical trial are unclear. The toxicological data produced is not imprecise but its interpretation often is and the imprecision of data on the risk–benefit balance for new drugs introduced onto the market is a serious matter that must be tackled by post-marketing surveillance. Of course, at the clinical trials stage with small numbers it is impossible to pick up anything except side-effects with high incidence.

1. Imprecision of toxicological science in relation to drug development.
2. Imprecision of data on risk–benefit balance for new drugs.
3. The problems of judging efficacy.
4. Tendency to arbitrariness when faced with *having* to make a decision without adequate data.
5. Regulations by precedent: (consistency!).
6. The changing base of scientific opinion – when is it stable?
7. How to balance pre-marketing testing and post-marketing surveillance (both for safety and efficacy).
8. How can you avoid regulating for the lowest common denominator?
9. The problem of the expert.

Figure 5.3 Problems for the regulatory authority

What is equally worrying is the appraisal of efficacy in large populations during ordinary clinical use. For instance, it is very difficult to get a real feel of the benefit of the common antidepressant agents in the depressed population at large. It took a long time to estimate the real benefit produced by, say, imipramine and amitriptyline and to define the strict indications for their use. Many trials, in fact, showed only minimal benefit. Now, because of ethical views that psychiatrists have, it is ethically unacceptable to test antidepressants against placebo and therefore one sees antidepressants being tested against imipramine or amitriptyline, knowing that probably one trial in five of those drugs against placebo would show a negative result. One has to accept evidence of the efficacy of a new antidepressant if it shows up equally as effective as imipramine or amitriptyline in one of those trials. This shows extreme gullibility, particularly as there is no good animal test system for showing definitively that a drug has antidepressant activity. One is on slightly surer ground with drugs used to treat hypertension.

Industry should realize that around the table at the Committee on Safety of Medicines are sitting a fairly hard-headed group of characters who have to adjudicate on scientific matters all the time. The standards they apply are the same, whether it be for safety and efficacy in a drug submission or a paper to be refereed for a journal. There cannot be two scientific standards. At no time is this more difficult than when considering a drug which is shown to have a biochemical effect, which is supposed to bring about clinical benefit. Oral hypoglycaemic agents in diabetes or the lipid-lowering agents in the majority of patients with coronary disease pose formidable problems in the assessment of clinical efficacy. What does one accept as evidence of their efficacy? In considering the results of the recent Anturan reinfarction trial, should reasonable men accept that Anturan protects against sudden death in the early months after a myocardial infarct? The results appear to be promising, but some people do not accept them as being more than chance occurrences, whilst others think the case is proven. There is often genuine disagreement about the assessment of efficacy during clinical trials, and even after marketing it usually takes quite a long time for a drug to find its proper place in clinical practice.

One continuing reason for concern is the tendency which regulatory authorities have towards arbitrariness when they have to make a decision without adequate data. This is the case with the rule about 100 patients for 1 year mentioned above which is clearly an arbitrary decision. Often there is insufficient hard data on many of the matters requiring decision and unfortunately the resources required to provide the data necessary for unequivocal decisions are not available in the circumstances of drug development, so the CSM will continue to make arbitrary regulations and occasionally get caught out by them. This is an unsatisfactory state of affairs, but it is the state of the art and all must learn to live with it, as best they can.

Another difficulty arises out of the need for the CSM to be consistent in its requirements of industry, which means that once a precedent has been set, even if it turns out eventually to be unnecessary or ill-advised, there is a tendency to follow it. For example, some years ago, the Committee was vexed by the spectre of analgesic nephropathy with respect to all the non-steroidal anti-inflammatory agents that were submitted. Until the genuine scientific basis of the problem was determined, the judgement of the Committee was swayed by fashionable clinical opinion, and they demanded quite rigorous tests of renal function on a large number of patients in order to err on the side of caution. Until the subject was totally reviewed and put into perspective, these tests were adhered to. In fact, it was a major scientific exercise to review the field and to reach the decision as to the significance of the renal effects and what to do about them.

Another problem is to judge when a particular scientific subject has reached a stable state, that is a point at which most reasonable men would say, 'It does look as if there really is something in this and we ought therefore to be dealing with the problem this way'. These are the circumstances in respect of mutagenicity testing at the moment, a subject on which the CSM and industry have had a lot of discussions. But there are other examples, the beagle bitch mammary gland tumours being a good one. The state of scientific opinion is something the CSM has to be aware of and the Committee must be ready to judge its significance in any particular respect.

Then, there is something that industry around the world frequently grumbles about and that is the length of time before they can conduct trials on human patients or get a product licence. Industry would often prefer to market more quickly and then do the postmarketing surveillance which would, of course, be essential for safety and efficacy. Whether this would be the best course is a matter of opinion. There are considerable problems with postmarketing surveillance. There are obvious advantages in conducting clinical trials on a very restricted basis at an early stage of drug development, but in this country I think the product licence is granted at about the right stage.

Sometimes people in industry think that the CSM is teaching its grand-mother to suck eggs and in some cases this may be true. But unfortunately not all pharmaceutical firms appear to have the diligence, talent and intelligence to do their drug testing for toxicity, safety and efficacy properly and so the whole of the pharmaceutical industry must adhere to regulations which are constructed for the lowest common denominator. This may be very irritating and unfortunate but is unavoidable.

There is a problem within the regulatory authority itself and this is the 'problem of the expert'. If a bunch of experts sits around a table for long enough, and they are all very friendly, get on well together and respect each other's opinions, then sooner or later they will feel sufficiently encouraged to speak up. Imagine the scene as a new non-steroidal inflammatory agent, another beta-blocker and yet another steroid cream comes onto the table, whilst with groans all round, the discussions get underway. Agreement seems almost reached when Professor Stromboli perks up to ask whether his colleagues have seen the paper and editorial in the *Archives of Totally Obscure Toxicology* on the induction of drug-metabolizing enzymes, causing premature involution of the organ of Zuckerkandl, which occurs in all tested ospreys if the drug is administered as a dose of $3\,kg/g$ intravenously every day for 9 months through the left central wing vein. Before anyone realizes quite what has happened, there exists a guideline for all drugs of this class saying that toxicity must be conducted by administration through the left central wing vein of the osprey in doses of $4\,kg/g$ daily for 9 months followed by full histopathology of the organ of Zuckerkandl. Regulatory committees have to be wide awake to avoid this sin.

The next main problem is how to set about administering the regulations. The main problem here is to avoid the supersolution, which is a solution to a problem that creates greater difficulties than the original problem (Herr, 1979). This is a well known sin on the part of bureaucracy generally and in 1978 a new Act in the USA has tried to reverse a definite trend to super-solutions in the regulation of medicines.

What the authority must attempt is to prevent the uncontrolled growth of bureaucracy, the demands for endless dotting of 'i's and crossing of t's' in toxicology and for ever more details in the data sheet.

It must find a way to avoid excessive but understandable caution on its own part. The problem is that any sensible individual is likely to err on the side of caution (an error unlikely to be challenged) rather than take on the enormous responsibility of passing a drug and risking the faint chance of a disaster.

How do you avoid trivial, pedantic interference with the process of drug introduction and prescribing? Examples are many and include writing data sheets that nobody takes any notice of, fiddling about with package inserts so that patients do not hurt themselves and the EEC practice of producing therapeutic guidelines to tell doctors and drug firms how cardiac glycosides should be developed and used. How do you encourage minimal bureaucracy or wise courage to take what might be an unknown risk? How do you encourage freedom for an industry and profession? These are all philosophical matters which must be worked out, but one practical consideration that must always be under review is how to ensure the adequacy of the regulatory machinery. If regulations there must be, then there must also be facilities available for their efficient administration. If these are not adequately provided, there will be impossible delays. If the Civil Service is so hard-pressed that it cannot properly man a Medicines Division when the industry through its licences is paying for adequate manning, then there has arisen a ridiculous state of affairs which should be taken up with the licensing authority.

One must now ask what are the effects of the regulations that are made and imposed, assuming that they can be measured. On the positive side, the public are supplied and treated with safe, good quality, effective drugs. The safeguards and resulting benefits provided by licensing regulations are usually reliable. The arguments centre upon the negative effects of the regulations. The regulatory authority is criticized for delaying drug development, causing very greatly increased costs, laying down demanding regulations which squander rare resources of manpower, time, money and animals and last, but not least, the regulations are accused of causing demoralization of industry and the stifling of its innovative spark. The Committee on Safety of Medicines decided last year to institute a working party to look at its requirements for clinical trials certification because it was here that industry grumbled about excessive regulations and long delays in the granting of clinical trial certificates. It has been an interesting exercise and there are strong hopes that ways can be found to allow clinical trials to go forward more quickly and in a more rational, developmental way. Undoubtedly, because of the tendency to arbitrariness, action on precedent and because of excessive caution, requirements have been demanded which are probably unreasonable.

Resources are limited and the industry, regulatory authorities and the public all have to be aware that if we squander our resources on unnecessary regulatory requirements there is going to be less available for innovative research and development, which would be a serious matter. I do not believe that industry is seriously demoralized, and after something of a doldrum for the last 10 years, we may now be on the verge of an era of new drug discovery and development based on developments in medical science over the last 10–15 years and an improved understanding of molecular pharmacology and pharmaceutical chemistry.

The next subject of concern for a regulatory authority is what the people think about the regulations. There are all sorts of interested parties who might have different ideas. There is the pharmaceutical industry which does not like regulations, there are regulatory authorities which exist for regulations, there is government which produces regulations to suit its own requirements and there are patients who could not care less about regulations but certainly want effective drugs for the treatment of their illness and who would like them to be safe but who, by and large, seem to understand and accept the idea of risk–benefit analysis and that when they take pills they take risks. There are exceptions, but it is extraordinary how patients who have, for example, gastrointestinal bleeds because of nonsteroidal anti-inflammatory agents and who are told so, shrug their shoulders and accept it philosophically. It is very rare that one sees a great resentment amongst patients who suffer adverse effects, though of course fetal abnormalities are another matter, as was the practolol syndrome. The discussions between industry and regulatory authorities hardly touch ordinary doctors, most of whom know little about the Committee on Safety of Medicines nor care very much what it does. There appears to be no record of what pharmacists think about regulations. Many health-care authorities in the NHS do care about what the Committee on Safety of Medicines says, particularly the teaching authorities, under whose aegis clinical trials are carried out and by whom ethical problems have to be considered. These authorities tend to take the CSM's word as law. Consumer organizations are usually hankering after more regulations and in one way or another minority groups pressurizing the government are responsible for many of the problems that the licensing authority faces. The media, of course, delight in nothing more than a medicines scandal and naturally the licensing authority, which bears the brunt of such scandals, would prefer to avoid them if possible. All this leads inevitably to an adversarial situation which is unfortunate because the licensing authority, the Medicines Division, the Committee on Safety of Medicines, the industry, the doctors and everyone else are all trying to get safe and effective therapy. It is rather silly that there should be these antagonisms but it is understandable that it should occur. There are problems related to these. One of these is confidentiality. The regulatory authority has a tremendous amount of data of which good use could be made were it not for a confidentiality problem. The volume of data that is stored by the CSM in the Medicines Division is enormous and would provide an excellent base upon which to make decisions and remove a great deal of the present imprecision. But nobody in the Division has the time to perform any kind of academic, scholarly appraisal of the importance or impact of particular types of data and nor is there anyone in the country studying this problem as an academic pursuit. It would be in industry's interest to support some such activity, but again the confidentiality problem would arise. Of course many of these problems between interested parties involve matters of trust, respect and confidence and these are very often dependent upon human contact and the appraisal of various actions that each of the parties take. One cannot theoretically think of any scheme to alter those factors.

Finally, there are a number of things which do not fit well into the categories already mentioned. Scientific standards in the industry vary and the problem of the lowest common denominator has been noted, but there is a similar problem that the regulatory authority frequently meets. That is the poor scientific standard, not of the work that is done but of the presentation and the submission of the results. It seems incredible that a company that has spent millions of pounds on developing a drug will not spend a few hundred pounds writing it up properly so that the results are understandable, properly analysed and properly presented. Anyone with experience of the workings of the Committee on Safety of Medicines will know about the appeals procedure and hearings. The fact is that many drugs get passed on these hearings without anything very essential or new being said that was not mentioned before at the original submission. This happens because data included in that original submission has been reconsidered by the company and re-presented in a way that makes it more understandable or acceptable and capable of removing the previous doubts of the Committee. This leads to an enormous waste of time, and it is hard to comprehend why industry cannot get it right first time. Certainly, the standard of presentation is often very low compared with that necessary for publication in the more reputable journals. It is in the medical director's interest to make sure that reports are of a high standard, but often he does not do so. No regulatory authority is tolerant of the brushing aside of adverse effects upon either animals or man. Unsubstantiated statements like, 'The rise in liver enzymes did not appear to be drug-related,' or, 'This non-steroidal anti-inflammatory analgesic agent was well-tolerated,' when in fact 10% of patients had nausea or vomiting, are totally unacceptable. Somebody has not bothered to give the matter any thought. If there is one regulation that should be introduced, it is one designed to improve the standard of the analysis and presentation of the work that has been done in industry.

References

1. Gross, F. (1977). Need for innovation in drug research and development. In Bankowski, Z. and Dunne, J. F. (eds.) *Eleventh CIOMS Round Table Conference on Trends and Prospects in Drug Research and Development*, p. 57, December 8–9, Geneva (Scrip)
2. Herr, E. B. (1977). Influence of statutory requirements   viewpoint of the pharmaceutical

industry. In Bankowski. Z. and Dunne. J. F. (eds.) *Eleventh CIOMS Round Table Conference on Trends and Prospects in Drug Research and Development.* p. 103. December 8–9. Geneva (Scrip)

3. Janssen. P. A. (1977). Prospects for innovative development – scientific aspects. In Bankowski, Z. and Dunne, J. F. (eds.) *Eleventh CIOMS Round Table Conference on Trends and Prospects in Drug Research and Development.* p. 76. December 8–9. Geneva (Scrip)

Discussion of Chapters 4 and 5

CHAIRMAN: Dr J. COOMBES

Chairman: I will repeat the question that Professor Grahame-Smith posed to Dr Newbould. What would you do differently if we all went away? Is no research director willing to stand up?

Dr E. S. Snell (ABPI): These research directors are too shy, but I think what they would do is to work to schedule, work to time, with known dates, which would be extremely helpful and efficient in a complete flow of events, without the delays in the administration of the submission and the uncertainty of knowing when it will go in and come out.

Prof. Grahame-Smith: That is fine. I agree entirely. In clinical trials certification one hopes that this is the sort of thing that we shall be able to promote. But what about the actual pile of data, the actual toxicological testing? There are grumbles about the cost of animals, staff, and so forth. It seems to me that the organization of it, although very important, is a fairly trivial thing. The main problem is the actual regulatory requirements, the toxicology, or the number of patients, or how long, and the monitoring and so on. Those seem to be the hard things that are difficult to decide. Organizing it is a fairly simple problem compared with the actual data production.

Dr E. S. Snell: It has two stages: the clinical trials certificate and the product licence certificate. We are talking of delays of 18 months or more. I do not think that such delays are a simple thing to get rid of. The authority has never got rid of it yet, and there are no signs of its going away. At the clinical trials certificate stage in terms of volume of data there should be a lot less, I would think, for trials in the UK. For the product licence stage there might well be as much because that data has to be generated for submission all around the world, and there are the other registration authorities.

Chairman: I think we appreciate the planning improvements that would be made, but perhaps we could turn more to the work that is done and the phasing that might be changed.

Dr R. W. Brimblecombe (Smith, Kline and French): Since Professor Grahame-Smith and Dr Newbould have given nine tenths of my talk between them I may as well give the other tenth now!

It is not that we are shy at answering the question, but it is an extremely difficult one to answer, which is probably why we are not doing so. Mainly because we have become conditioned by what has gone on already, it would be a very brave man who would stand up and say that he would do only 1 month's toxicology, or only 3 months' toxicology, or whatever, for the very reasons mentioned in Professor Grahame-Smith's paper – there just are no data. What I had intended to say, and I was very interested to hear Professor Grahame-Smith say, was that this data has to be winkled out some way or another. We really do have to get at the archives of the regulatory agency. We do have to stop being coy about allowing our data to be used. Until we have that information it is impossible to answer the question. I do not know whether we should be doing 1 month, or 3 months, or 6 months, or whether we should be treating 100 patients, or for 1 year, any more than anyone else does. I know that this is easy to say and much more difficult to do, but it is the only answer to it. The data must be got out somehow. It does exist, and I am fairly certain that the industry would be prepared to spend money on a method that would enable the data to be had.

It is a fair question, but it is really unanswerable. 'What would we do if the regulatory authority was not there?', so to speak. We should certainly do things faster, as everyone has said. Since it can be seen that we can do things more quickly by going to Sweden or somewhere, we can provide that part of the answer. But in terms of the content of the work that would be done, I do not know what I would do if the regulatory agency did not exist, to be perfectly honest.

Dr L. Z. Saunders (Smith, Kline and French Research): I should like to try to answer the question about how we might avoid doing the trivial things by addressing myself to something that is difficult to speak about and that some might even think dangerous. The reason we are doing trivial things is because bureaucracy is a growth industry. Milton Friedman says this, although David Ennals may well think that he should not have had the Nobel prize for economics. He thinks it is a growth industry, at least in the USA. Part of his evidence is that our regulatory authority managed to get several hundred inspectors put on board the FDA (Food and Drugs Authority) right under the nose of a politician just elected on a platform of how he would cut the size of the government. It is not only a growth industry; it is a very astute and clever growth industry that knows how to grow. The wasting of intellectual resources, which is what I feared when they proposed the Good Laboratory Practice requirements, which I testified against, is something that has come to pass. Those of us who might be making some of these data more meaningful are engaged in clerical activity because otherwise we shall be caught by a marauding band of laymen whose jobs depend on catching us.

Mr Ennals may be right that the bureaucrats in the UK do not dictate to the politicians, but in other countries they do. The USA is one of them. Unfortunately, other countries seem increasingly to take over what is happening in ours, which is the constant trivialization of science by requirements that have nothing to do with science.

That is one aspect. The other is that there is a basic premise, that has neither been touched on nor discussed here, upon which the whole superstructure of toxicology is built, namely, that it is possible to detect in animals those compounds that are safe and do not need to be regulated and to distinguish them from those that are unsafe and which will therefore need a lot of attention. This premise has never been established and the evidence we have from pharmacology is that the opposite would be easier to defend.

Nevertheless we have built the superstructure, and the reason those books are so thick is because agencies are demanding all this data. They are not asking whether it is telling them anything; they are demanding it. It is no use then, saying we do not have the facilities to cope with it when it is a self-created pile.

Prof. Grahame-Smith: Dr Saunders, referring to the regulatory authorities, says 'They are just demanding it'. The reason that they are demanding the data is what I have tried to explain in my paper. One is asked to make decisions about such things as the length of the period of toxicity testing in animals. One sits there and comes up with a factor that one thinks – if one was to have the drug oneself – would be a reasonable time to see it does not kill a rat. Or one decides according to precedents, in that one knows of data where after 6 months toxicity testing in this species, this class of compounds does so-and-so. Not at 3 months, but at 6 months. It shows up at 6 months. Therefore the regulation creeps in. It is not a purely irrational demand for requirements. There is a base to it. However vague that base may be, there is a base.

Dr A. Dayan (Wellcome Research Laboratories): My paper too has been given, and I can now produce my encore in advance. But, to back up something Dr Brimblecombe said, a serious point. There is already a lot of data available. The difference is between the habits of the different regulatory authorities, with no evidence of detectable harm to the populations that they claim to examine. It shows that most of what any one regulatory authority is doing, if I can blame Dr Grahame-Smith for all regulatory authorities, is absolutely useless; in fact it is harmful.

I strongly support Dr Brimblecombe in saying that industry should produce a great deal more data, and so should the regulatory agencies, so that we can confirm that fact. But, in the early days, e.g. of the European Society of Drug Toxicity, it did do some comparisons of that sort, and showed that a great deal of the information that was being forced out was of no beneficial value to anybody. I would accept the point there that precedent is very important.

There is another aspect, too, to the data that we are forced to produce; a great deal of it is duplicative, perhaps even of higher orders than single duplication. But that is something I can get back to later.

6
The effect on pharmaceutical research

C. N. CHRISTENSEN

To help assure that the benefit–risk ratio in the assessment of drugs is a favourable one. most governments have increasingly regulated the pharmaceutical industry. We have arrived at the point where we must examine some of the costs of this regulatory environment. For a long time the industry enjoyed a relatively supportive public. The great medical advances of the 1940s and the 1950s increased public expectations of the wonders that could be wrought by new drug therapies and took attention away from associated risks. Then. in the 1960s. fed by political cynicism. at least in the United States. and ignited by the thalidomide tragedy. public suspicion that the industry's profit motive was contrary to the public's interest in safety and effectiveness began to gain momentum. The current adverse regulatory environment is generally a product of this 20-year era of public disillusionment with 'riskless' drugs and the social role of big business.

In one regard I think we can welcome this change in public opinion about drugs. There is no drug that is completely safe. There are always medical risks associated with drug therapy that need to be weighed against the benefits. The public is now beginning to gain some appreciation for what successful pharmaceutical firms for many years have been weighing. in what I feel to be a very reasonable fashion. before they brought a drug to market. But in another regard. there are disturbing signs that the public cynicism embodied in our current regulatory environment is not serving the public interest in several respects. We do not question the objective of government regulation intended to assure the public of safe and effective drugs. We are concerned. however, that regulation is causing much unnecessary expense and significant time delays. The real penalty that ensues is falling on the public. The sick are being denied new therapeutic agents. New products that reduce the cost of health care by diminishing the need for hospital stays are being delayed, and financial resources are not being applied to efforts that will increase our economy's productivity and reduce inflation.

A first step toward eliminating these unnecessary costs to the public involves clarifying the costs and benefits of our current regulatory environment. If we are successful in this endeavour, we shall have a basis on which to help build a new social consensus on the drug safety issue that incorporates an understanding of these costs. The time is ripe. Evolving concepts of safety associated with improvements in technology and growing concern with the long-term effects of drug therapies, as well as growing recognition of the impact of regulation, are increasing the need for a new social consensus on drug safety.

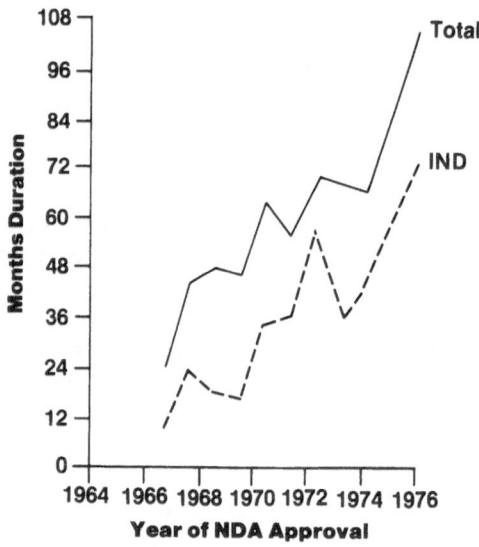

Figure 6.1   The worsening trend in IND times for US self-originated NCEs. From Wardell, W.[2] based on a sample of 39 self-originated NCEs

In the interest of helping to ensure that this new consensus is based on an understanding of the costs of our current regulatory environment, I shall devote the rest of the paper to exploring one area, namely pharmaceutical R & D, where we are only now beginning to realize the size and scope of the impact of current regulation. Academic and industry researchers have been making significant progress in understanding the compliance costs associated with such regulations, i.e. the costs to carry out regulatory requirements, and in understanding the full scope of what economists call the secondary or indirect effects of regulation on pharmaceutical R & D.

I shall speak in large part from a US perspective, given that is what I know best, but my comments will be found to be relevant because of the similarity of the regulatory problems that we face. and the growing interest in harmonization of regulatory patterns in the various countries.

First. I shall turn to what we know about compliance costs: direct costs of regulation on pharmaceutical R & D. Our best estimate now is that it takes 9½ years and nearly $70 million, including an adjustment for inflation, and including the implicit financial cost of capital from the time of basic research to marketing to discover and develop a new chemical entity in the US[1]. These data are based on a sample of new chemical entities supplied by 14 US firms for the 1963–75 period.

Data collected by Dr William Wardell[2] on development times for new chemical entities for the United States from 1967 to 1976 are shown in Figure 6.1. The trend line for IND times – the IND time being defined as the time from the start of human trials to the filing of a new drug application – for self-originating new chemical entities suggests the possibility of further deterioration of development times, not stabilization. Overall, the total time from IND filing to NDA approval – the top line of the graph – climbed to a high in 1976 of almost 9 years. The increase in the duration of the IND phase to approximately 6 years accounted for most of that increase.

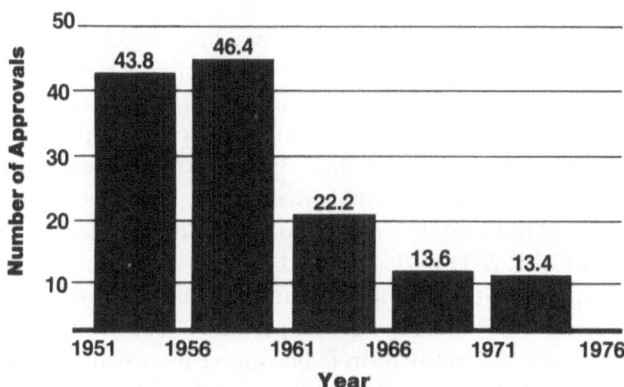

Figure 6.2 FDA approval of new chemical entities 1951–75. From Grabowski, H. G.[3]. Data excludes salts or esters of previously marketed drugs

There is no doubt that increased R & D times and costs have had a negative impact on the rate of pharmaceutical innovation. The most recent data confirms trends previously identified; a fairly consistent long. downward trend in all major classes of drugs being introduced into the new US market.

Figure 6.2 shows the average number of new chemical entities approved by the FDA by 5-year periods since 1950[3]. There has been a decline from an average of about 45 NCEs each year to about 13 in each of the last two 5-year periods: a matter of very real concern considering the therapeutic significance of many of these discoveries.

Another way of illustrating the negative impact of regulatory forces on drug innovation is to make a rough comparison of a measure of scientific discovery relatively less contaminated by regulatory forces, such as the number of drug-related patents that have been granted over a given period with the number of drugs approved in an appropriately lagged period. Between 1963 and 1975, the number of drug-related patents in the US increased at an average annual compounded rate of 5%. This trend would predict in a general sense some indication of a greater number of innovations reaching the market place beginning in the early 1970s. This has not occurred. Although other facts such as changing technology are also at work here in lengthening these times, it is fair to infer that part of this discrepancy between increased research opportunity and decreased new drug approvals is due to regulation.

At the same time that regulation has contributed to the increasing cost and decreasing rate of pharmaceutical innovation, other regulatory trends have been reducing revenues needed for R & D activities. Shorter effective patent lives and price regulation for indirect or direct purchases of drugs by the government have both combined to reduce revenues received by pharmaceutical companies from their marketed products. In the US the spread of state laws that require the substitution of generic lower-priced versions of drugs for trade name drugs and claims by governmental agencies of product identity on the basis of chemical equivalency have had a similar effect.

The effect of increasing R & D costs and declining revenues has been to lower significantly expectations of financial return from R & D. Several economists have reported on these deteriorating financial returns. Recently Virts and Weston[1] have estimated that three-quarters of new chemical entities may not even return their original investment, let alone a return on that investment. These data would lead one to expect the number of firms engaging in pharmaceutical R & D to decline and, in fact, the number of independent firms in the United States adding new chemical entities to the market place in the 5-year period 1954–8 and the 5-year period 1972–6 declined 20%: from 50 to 40 firms[1]. Similarly, innovation is becoming increasingly concentrated in few firms. In the 1957–61 period, the four largest US firms accounted for 24% of new chemical entities introduced into the United States. Twenty years later, the four top firms accounted for 48% of NCEs coming to market[3]. These are some of the direct costs, as we view them, of regulatory problems.

We now come to some of the secondary effects of regulation and the way firms are reacting to this adverse regulatory environment. We have no hard data about these kind of things, but it is possible from a number of sources to put together an informal list of the ways firms can be observed reacting and adapting to this regulatory environment. Since the R & D strategy of one firm may be quite different from that of others, each of these adaptive modes is not necessarily consistent with any other, although some may occur simultaneously in any one firm. These responses to the regulatory environment include efforts to reduce R & D costs and times, and they include the increased use of licensing as a way to diversify into new therapeutic markets; commitments to research agreements between high technology institutions that have complementary technologies to the sponsoring firm; the purchase of pre-clinical and clinical testing services in the market place instead of conducting such activities in house. This practice has given rise to a whole new industry in the United States – one can go out and purchase a clinical trial. Transfer of R & D activities to countries outside the US has occurred where the regulatory burden is relatively less costly. In 1961, US drug firms were investing approximately 5% of their R & D funds overseas, and by 1974 that figure had grown to 15%. A related development is the increasing tendency for US firms to first market their products outside of the United States.

There has been a shift of funds to developmental research and other projects with shorter payback periods instead of basic research activities. The amount of funds given to basic research has declined dramatically. New weight is being given to arguments for staying in familiar therapeutic areas where the fixed costs of establishing high-quality screening and modelling capabilities have already been incurred.

Lastly, we find firms favouring products aimed at large markets – this goes without saying. Many companies, including Lilly, continue to invest in socially-needed compounds, but there is increasing pressure not to do this kind of R & D.

We feel one of the more innovative of these adaptive responses is the development of cooperative R & D efforts – as I indicated. We have explored the possibility of reducing the time costs of basic research in rapidly expanding therapeutic areas by entering into research agreements with outside institutions that have established expertise in these areas. For instance, we have established a cooperative relationship with the Scripps Clinic and Research Foundation in California: a broad-based research organization with a world-wide reputation for its immunology programmes. Lilly scientists are working at the Scripps and are actively pursuing research aimed at developing new therapeutic agents in the area of immunology.

Other broad industry responses to the regulatory environment include efforts to create new management mechanisms. They include the use of formal project teams with broad representation to make decisions, rather than a group of scientists sitting down and looking at the problem to see what they could do about it. There is increasing reliance on other factors, such as the possible financial return, or the market orientation of a new research project. More and more we are finding in our research project groups people with financial skills and cost control and management skills. I am sure that some of this is good, but it does detract from the purely scientific approach to the problems.

The ability of firms, particularly the R & D intensive firms, to adapt to reduced financial return from R & D is not infinite. Thus we also find diversification of firms out of pharmaceuticals to non-drug related activities;

as previously noted. the disappearance of small R & D firms, often by merger, when they cannot adapt to reduced income from R & D; the growing market significance of firms dependent on the sale of generic drugs which do not conduct R & D activities and therefore do not have to recover these costs. We find an increasing divergence of time of top scientists to regulatory issues, which has a negative impact on the incentive of those who derive their motivation from scientifically productive endeavours.

As government regulations become more complex and the public's defi-nition of 'how safe is safe' changes to include more concern about long-term effects of drugs. firms spend more and more of their R & D funds in defensive research for drugs already on the market and for research to meet new regulatory demands that are brought upon these existing compounds.

Although no one can predict with certainty the implications of the current regulatory climate on the R & D strategy of various firms, and how those strategies will affect success in the market place. we still perceive a pharma-ceutical industry whose structure is still impacted by today's regulatory climate. Unless we are able to reach a better balance of costs and benefits than in the current climate. we predict we shall see an industry where even more new drug therapies will be delayed or lost completely to the public because of the impact of regulation. We see an industry where external financial and market-ing pressures will have increasing influence on the direction and priorities for our pharmaceutical R & D. Finally. we see that regulation will continue to affect the number and nature of firms conducting pharmaceutical R & D.

Because of the impact of regulation. any savings in time and cost that can be made in the new drug development process without jeopardizing public safety represent a very important opportunity. Lilly estimates that many millions of dollars per year could be productively employed if only excessive regulatory expenditures were eliminated. By excessive regulatory expenditures we mean those which in our judgement are not necessary to obtain the objective of safe and effective drugs. but are nevertheless required by the kind of regulation now in place. It is very difficult to define what is excess regulation. The question has already been posed. but to give a broad philosophical answer – that this is excess. and this is not – is very difficult. One can take small pieces of the whole regulatory process and say that this is redundant and should be eliminated. or that this should stay in place. but to fit the whole into a single. unified concept is difficult. Nevertheless. we estimate that every year of unnecessary delay for a new compound costs six to eight million dollars. This is based on the assumption that for every year of delay a firm could have been earning 8% in an alternative investment. and that inflation will raise prices at least 8% in that year. Thus the minimum total cost of a year's delay is 16% on each dollar invested.

To define such unnecessary regulatory costs. Lilly has joined with eight other pharmaceutical firms under the auspices of the Pharmaceutical Manu-facturers' Association to conduct a study in this area. The results of the study should be released some time this year. We hope to identify and to quantify excess regulatory costs. As one example I should like to cite certification requirements in the US for insulin and antibiotics. In the last 35 years, Lilly has submitted more than 5600 lots covering more than 700 million vials of insulin to the FDA for certification. The lots are submitted to the FDA only after they have passed – inside Lilly – all of the requirements that we know the FDA will impose on them and that the FDA might test them for. Of those 5600 lots, five have been rejected by the Food and Drug Administration. The rejections are interesting. For a couple of lots the pH was too high or too low. One had a slight excess of zinc. I would not think that the imperfections in any of the lots would have affected their safety or their effectiveness in any way. With our antibiotics we have had a similar experience. We have submitted 3400 lots of cephalothin since April 1967, representing 218 million vials, and by happenstance once again we had five lots rejected, and once again for relatively minor problems. The direct costs of these unnecessary certification requirements alone to Lilly is approximately $2.5 million a year; enough to finance a reasonably respectable research and development programme in a limited area.

I have mentioned that it is difficult to define precisely the excess regulatory costs. A large judgemental factor is involved. Nevertheless, by approaching the subject with great conservatism, we hope to identify in this study areas in which time and money could be saved. We encourage full support for the effort to make clear the full impact of regulation on the industry in terms of direct compliance costs, and also in terms of the indirect or secondary effects which such regulation has. Only in this way can we create a public awareness of the costs, as well as the benefits, of the current regulatory environment, and press forward for a much-needed new social consensus on the drug safety issue.

References

1. Virts, J. R. and Weston, J. F. (1979). Expectations and the allocation of R & D resources. To be published in *Drugs and Health: Economic Issues and Policy Objectives*. American Enterprise Institute for Public Policy Research, Washington, D.C.
2. Wardell, W. M., DiRaddo, J. and Trimble, A. G. (1980). Development of new drugs originated and acquired by United States-owned pharmaceutical firms, 1963–76. *Clin. Pharm. Therap.*, **28**, 270
3. Grabowski, H. G. (1976). *Drug Regulations and Innovation: Empirical Evidence and Policy Options*. American Enterprise Institute for Public Policy Research, Washington, D.C.

7
New-drug assessment in man: a clinical pharmacologist's view

A. M. BRECKENRIDGE

INTRODUCTION

One of the central roles of the clinical pharmacologist is the assessment of new drugs in man and in this respect he has a necessarily close relationship with the pharmaceutical industry. He is largely dependent on industry for the production of new chemical entities (NCE) but his independence of judgement must be preserved at all costs. Industry in its turn appreciates that competent independent arbiters of their new products are important for its prosperity. Currently both parties, clinical pharmacology and industry feel threatened by a third party, governmental drug regulatory authorities. The purpose of this article is to delineate problems currently faced by the clinical pharmacologist in new drug assessment and to suggest some possible solutions.

BACKGROUND

The assessment of a NCE in man progresses in four phases. In the first phase, the drug, already tested satisfactorily in animals, is given to human volunteers in doses initially too small to have a therapeutic effect, the aims being to compare the pharmacology of the compound with results previously obtained in animals and to examine how man tolerates it. In the UK (but not in the USA) phase I studies can be done without governmental permission, but clearly ethical consent is required. A Clinical Trials Certificate (CTC) must be granted by the Department of Health and Social Security (DHSS) before the drug is given to any patient in the second phase of its evaluation in man. Only a few patients (40–50) may be given the drug in this second phase of development, since the aim is to discover if the pharmacological effect discovered in preclinical testing has a therapeutic parallel. If confirmed, the drug passes into clinical trial – phase III of its development, in which many patients (let us say several hundreds) will be studied to compare its therapeutic effect either with placebo or with a well-established treatment for the condition. If all is still on course, the company will return to the DHSS at the completion of clinical trials and request permission to market the drug, for which they require a Product Licence. Once marketed, careful study of the safety record of the drug is paramount and this part of its development has been termed phase IV, or post-marketing surveillance, whose conduct is currently the matter of much debate.

PARTIES CONCERNED

Many parties are involved in these evaluation processes and each has aims and expectations which it hopes to achieve. Industry is intent on getting its NCE on to the market as quickly as possible. The drug regulatory authority, thalidomide sitting on its shoulder, attempts to license only safe and effective compounds. Medical science works to see its breakthroughs translated into therapeutic reality. The public demand more effective, yet safe drugs for disease, and look to the medical practitioner to prescribe them. The media monitor and report the moves of all parties.

THE PROBLEMS

Problem 1

Over the last two decades, the number of NCE given to man has decreased (Wardell, 1979) and there is some evidence that this decline has been more protracted in the USA than in the UK. Several reasons have been advanced for these changes. A fall in chemical inventiveness and a progressive decrease in understanding of human disease processes (the so called knowledge depletion theory) have been seriously advanced. But any reader of current medical scientific literature, assailed by the exponential increase in publications on both disease processes and the drugs to treat them would find these hypotheses hard to justify, although he would probably agree that most of the easy drug discoveries have now been made. One contributing and relevant cause is the increase in costs of drug research and development, when a fixed budget may well impose constraints on new drug research. Between £20 million and £40 million are now considered the realistic cost of putting a new drug on the market, before any capital return is made.

In the view of many people, one, if not the principle cause of the decrease in NCEs going into man is the proliferation of regulations at all stages of the drug's development.

Consequence 1

Whatever the reason, one possible result of a decrease in NCE going into man is a diminution in innovative drug use. Many important therapeutic uses of a drug cannot be ·predicted when the drug is first tested, and obviously, the earlier in the evaluation process the development of the drug is discontinued for fiscal or financial reasons, the less searching is the assessment of the ultimate value of that drug. Table 7.1 is a list of drugs and their uses which were only realized after the drug had been introduced into clinical medicine for other purposes.

Table 7.1 Major disease entities treated by drugs not intro-duced for that purpose

Drug	Condition treated
Propranolol	Hypertension
Sulphinpyrazone	Ischaemic heart disease
Diazepam	Status epilepticus
Phenobarbitone	Epilepsy
Chlorpromazine	Schizophrenia
Oestrogens/Progestogens	Contraception
Imipramine	Depression
Probenecid	Gout
Lignocaine	Arrhythmias

Problem 2

There are fewer NCEs available for clinical assessment and clearly, this situation also applies to the UK. But are there reasons why the situation in the UK might be more critical than elsewhere? Table 7.2 shows a recent estimate of times required to carry out the necessary tests on an NCE and to prepare reports in the form required for obtaining a clinical trials certificate, together with the time taken by drug regulatory authorities to process these reports in

Table 7.2 Duration of testing procedures prior to the start of clinical testing of a new chemical entity

	USA	Sweden	Germany	Holland	UK
Carrying out tests (weeks)	24–36	24–36	24–36	24–36	52–130
Processing time (weeks)	4	2	0	2–4	26–32

(Bayliss. 1979)

five countries (Bayliss 1979). Bayliss stresses that these times assume that the pharmaceutical company concerned is able to devote all its effort at one point in time to one compound (which is clearly rarely possible, but reasonable for comparative purposes). In the UK, regulations for completed fertility studies may increase the testing time to 52 weeks and should the compound be one of which the drug regulatory authorities require a carcinogenicity study (e.g. a beta adrenoceptor blocking agent) the period could be as long as 130 weeks before a single dose is given to patients.

Consequence 2

There would appear to be a great disincentive for industry to do its phase II studies in the UK. In practice this is true for when the medical directors of five British-based pharmaceutical companies were asked 'What percentage of your phase II (early clinical) studies has your company carried out in the UK in 1977—79', the responses (with comments) were as given in Table 7.3. The consequences of these findings for UK clinical pharmacology are clear. The testing of new compounds in patients is one of the most challenging aspects of clinical pharmacology, where difficult clinical decisions must frequently be made. Because of the small number of phase II studies being carried out in the UK, British clinical pharmacologists rarely have the chance to make these decisions or do this type of work. Since initial patient drug exposure usually takes place abroad, foreign clinical pharmacologists are rapidly gaining the expertise from testing new drugs produced in Britain by British companies.

Table 7.3   Percentage early phase II studies does in the UK, 1977–79

Company	%	Comments
A	0	Doing more and more in USA
B	0	Feel very guilty about it
C	0	Spent £60 000 on early phase II last year. Would have liked this to go to UK units
D	10	Doing more and more in USA
E	30	If quick data needed, going abroad. If long programme anticipated, some done in UK

Problem 3

The pharmaceutical industry appreciates that the standard of investigative medicine in the UK is of a high standard. Further, it is widely known that academic units are relatively starved of financial resources. Thus industry comes to specialist units, not for phase II studies but with the request to do phase III (clinical trial) work. Frequently they have already composed the protocols for these studies which are aimed at satisfying the specific requirements of one drug regulatory authority.

Consequence 3

The clinical investigator is immediately in a dilemma. He soon realizes that his scientific input into the project and also the scientific output may be very limited. He may have to employ a clinical research assistant or the equivalent specifically for the work. The calibre of a person prepared to take on this type of work may not be high, and thus the overall standard of the unit may fall. On the other hand, the money paid for this contractual work may solve some immediate departmental requirements. There is no easy solution to this.

Problem 4

Not all the ills that befall clinical pharmacology can be laid at the door of the drug regulatory authorities. There is a current tendency for pharmaceutical companies to do much phase I (volunteer) work 'in house' rather than farm this out to units in the NHS or universities. When the same five medical directors of British-based pharmaceutical houses were asked the question, 'What percentage of human volunteer studies (phase I) has your company carried out 'in house' in 1978–79?', the answers and comments given are shown in Table 7.4. There is only a small amount of phase I work being done in the specialist units, be they NHS or university-funded.

Table 7.4   Percentage of phase I studies done 'in house', 1978–79

Company	%	Comments
A	100	Better supply of volunteers than in academic units
B	95	Very convenient. No shipping of samples or methods
C	75	—
D	80	—
E	50	We are building up our facilities and hope to do more

It is relevant at this point to ask what are the necessary skills expected of a clinical investigator involved in new drug studies in man.

(a) He must be a competent clinician, trained in general medicine and in the primary area for which the new drug is intended, e.g. hypertension, rheumatoid arthritis, depression. Further, he must be able to deal expertly with any unforeseen event which may arise during the testing of the new drug.

(b) He must have a training in the methodology of clinical research. As Dollery (1978) has recently discussed this is one of the most difficult disciplines for the young doctor to learn, and without training, he performs extremely badly in clinical research.

Consequence 4

These trends, the decrease in phase II and phase I studies and the increase in phase III studies, all militate against the training of the competent investigator, be he destined for industry, academia or the NHS. Further, the less well trained he is, the less likely is he to light on unexpected therapeutic drug activity of the type mentioned previously (Figure 7.1).

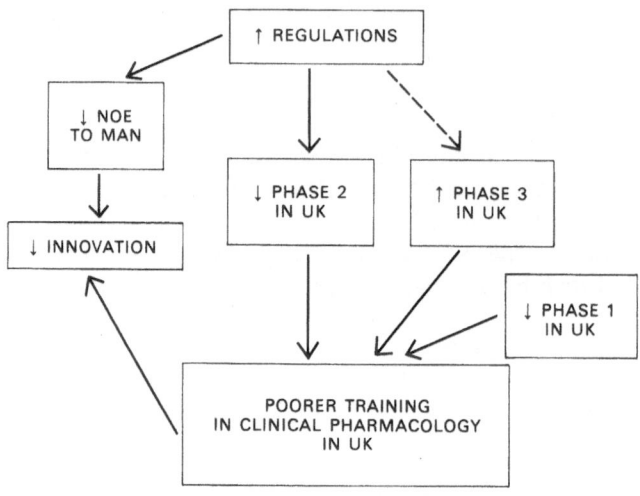

Figure 7.1   Influences relevant to the poorer training of clinical pharmacologists in the UK

THE SOLUTIONS

(1) Clinical pharmacology must be prepared to shoulder more responsibility. This does not only mean serving on the appropriate drug regulatory authority committees as individuals, but speaking as a discipline with a corporate voice on appropriate matters. Drug safety is obviously a political matter, but must be based on scientific principles. If there is little scientific basis for the proliferation of animal testing which prevents new drugs being given to man, then the scientist, i.e. the clinical pharmacologist, must say so.

(2) Clinical pharmacology must be prepared to collaborate more closely with industry. Many academic departments have members of the pharmaceutical industry working as part-time research fellows. The future may well lie in joint formal appointments, with the clinical investigator in training spending time both in industry and an academic unit. The CASE system for science postgraduates works well, why should we not try the same in cinical pharmacology?

(3) The public must be educated in their expectations by clinical pharmacologists. The demand for novel drugs cannot be satisfied without running the risk of adverse reactions. Prescription of any drug by a doctor is a clinical trial and not a guarantee of instant success. How far the individual patient should be drawn into the decision-making process of drug prescribing is a contentious problem, but the process of drug prescribing at present is too one-sided. These problems are clearly spelt out in the most excellent book *The Medicine you Take* (Laurence and Black, 1978) and the debates therein must be given more publicity.

CONCLUSIONS

The aims of drug regulations for the approval of new medicines would appear to be two: first to ensure a level of drug safety acceptable to the public, the doctor, science and industry and second, to allow the development of significant new medicines by stimulating both basic research and clinical pharmacology. The first of these aims should not be achieved at the price of the second.

These are some problems associated with new-drug development, their consequences, and possible solutions, as seen from the standpoint of one clinical pharmacologist. The drug regulator, the manufacturer, the public and the media will also have views on these matters.

Public Statement

From the European workshop held at Sestri Levante, Italy, 28th September, 1976

Medicines can never be entirely safe. Despite extensive testing and monitoring, unforeseen and unpredictable adverse reactions will continue to occur. The public needs to be aware that treatment with medicines always carries some risk. It is the duty of all concerned to maximize benefit and minimize risk.

Public concern was deeply aroused by the thalidomide tragedy, and in consequence drug regulatory authorities were set up or strengthened in many countries. Rules and regulations for drug testing were put forward and, in step with the laudable intention of increasing safety, the rules have proliferated. They now place onerous burdens on the manufacturers and investigators of new medicines. There is, however, little evidence that many of the rules do any good or actually protect the public from harm, while there is much evidence that they impede innovation.

There are still fatal and disabling diseases which lack effective treatment.

Mental disorders, arthritis, multiple sclerosis, psoriasis, and many kinds of cancer all await adequate treatment. Resources which could be used for discovering medicines for these diseases are being diverted to the pursuit of so-called safety, and the public are losing benefits they might otherwise have.

The present methods of testing for safety consume time, money, and man-power, without a corresponding increase in safety. Some of them originated soon after the tragedy of thalidomide and were the most promising which could be devised at the time. They have since been multiplied in the question-able hope that more extensive testing would achieve still greater safety. They have not been altogether successful in achieving their objective. Misfortunes have occurred; the latest, the case of practolol, happened in spite of all the activities of regulatory bodies. Practolol was submitted to, and passed, every known appropriate test which could be devised by its manufacturers or required by the authorities of several nations. It has, nonetheless, caused unforeseen injury to hundreds of patiens, though this number is a minute fraction of those who have benefited from the drug. In the present state of scientific knowledge, more extensive laboratory testing would not have pre-vented this misfortune.

In the opinion of this group of European scientists, it is now advisable to revise our methods of assessment of medicines. We must recognize that existing methods are unsatisfactory. We recommend more rational but less extensive laboratory studies, without unnecessary multiplication of detailed clinical trials before registration. Instead, we recommend much closer and more extensive surveillance of medicines after they are available for general prescription. Only by the careful study of medicines in everyday use can the greatest benefits be obtained from their administration, the untoward rare potential disaster be recognized at the earliest possible moment, and the ill effects be minimized. Absolute safety is unattainable, and its pursuit regard-less of other considerations is achieving more harm than good.

Reproduced from *European Journal of Clinical Pharmacology*, vol. II, pp. 233–278 (1977) by courtesy of Springer-Verlag.

References

Wardell, W. M. (1979). *More regulation or better therapies?* (Centre for Drug Development, Univ. of Rochester, Reprint Series)

Bayliss, P. (1979). Preclinical testing of new medicines. Presented at an *A.M.A.P.I. symposium*. London

Dollery, C. T. (1978). The end of an age of optimism: medical science in retrospect and prospect. Rock Carling Fellowship, 1978. Nuffield Provincial Hospital Trust

Laurence, D. R. and Black, J. W. (1978). The medicine you take. (London: Croom, Helm)

Discussion of Chapters 6 and 7

CHAIRMAN: Dr T. I. WRIGLEY

Prof. D. G. Wibberley (University of Aston): Dr Christensen has suggested that excessive regulatory controls, and to a lesser extent decreased patent life and price regulations, have resulted in a spectacular decrease in the number of new clinical entities. Surely this is an over-simplification. Is there not at least an equal possibility that other factors, such as the increasing scientific difficulty of drug discovery, the increasing cost of suitable models for diseases where animal models are no longer adequate, and the increasing demands of his own workers for safety in their laboratories and better scientific back-up are also responsible for this particular decrease?

Dr Christensen: I do not think that there is any question that the increasing technology has contributed to the decline in innovation, the decline in development, and all of these things. I alluded to it. How does one get at information which might reveal how much of a factor that is as opposed to the regulatory factors? I do not know. In an earlier discussion someone asked how much testing is enough before administering a drug to a human. Should it be 30 days? Or 90 days? What is the answer? I do not think that there are any clearcut solutions or clearcut answers to these questions.

I am convinced, however, that excessive regulation has played a very significant role in this. In the US over the last 2 or 3 years we have gone through a period of increasing concern with legislative and regulatory initiatives. In 1978 there was introduced to the US Congress a Bill known as the Drug Regulatory Reform Act, 1978. Fortunately it did not get through Congress, but that did not deter the legislators, who then introduced the Drug Regulatory Reform Act, 1979, in the same language but with a different year on it. There has been a steady decline in interest in that Bill because other things are interesting our politicians more at the present time than drug legislation.

The FDA has had in mind for a number of years that there needs to be certain reforms in terms of drug regulation. The '78 Act was largely written by the Food and Drug Administration. But the upshot of it is that they have decided that they can exist with the current law, the 1972 amendments to our Food and Drug Law, and simply revise the regulations. We are now engaged in a very large project, revising all the regulations governing the investigation of drugs, how they get on the market, and so forth, and also issuing a whole new bunch of guidelines for what we call a bio-research monitoring programme. About a year and a half ago, the FDA was allotted some 600 more inspectors to monitor bio-research activities. They are coming into the companies and going through records – in terms of Good Laboratory Practice – and I am afraid we shall soon be implementing the Good Clinical Practice regulations. These include regulations for institution review boards, for clinical investigators, and for the monitors and sponsors of drug investigations, that is clinical investigations.

Take, for example, one small thing, though it is a very small detail and probably I should not pick on things like this, but many regulations seem to get built this way. The Institutional Review Board Regulation, that is, the proposed one, has a requirement that when an investigator submits his protocol to the Institutional Review Board, the Board will advise the investigator in writing that it has been received and that the Board will act on it at an appropriate time! An unnecessary communication. But when the inspector comes in 2 years later and wants to see all the records, he will be looking for that piece of paper. It is just silly. (*applause*)

Dr Wrigley: And it is obvious that a fair number of those listening agree!

Prof. D. G. Grahame-Smith (University of Oxford): I hesitate to put my head in the lion's mouth. I can see the point that Professor Breckenridge makes, and it is a logical sequence to blame increases in regulations. What I have not seen is absolute evidence to show the kind of correlation between the increase in regulations, the increase in the amount of money that has to be spent in research and development, and the decline in the introduction of new chemical entities. I know that these things have occurred together, but things occur together for all sorts of reasons. The increase in mortality from coronary thrombosis agrees very well with the increase in the number of television sets; it is a well-known correlation and there may be cause and effect, but I do not know.

But I have not seen the evidence for this and I can think of many other reasons. Professor Breckenridge has said that he did not think that the cause was a decrease in biological understanding of disease, and to some extent I would agree with that, but what happened in the fifties and in the sixties may have been soaking up the knowledge that had accrued previously in the years since the war. As I see it now, and see what is happening around now, we are beginning to catch up with the biological developments over the last 10 or 15 years, and I would see the industry poised for a very large number of significant innovative pharmacological advances during the next 10 years. I think it is quite possible that the lie will be given to this by developments over the next 10 years. I should also like to see what happens if we are successful in altering the requirements for clinical trial certification in the UK and indeed, whether clinical trials might come back to the UK. In other words, there are ways and means of finding out whether what we are saying at the moment is true.

Prof. Breckenridge: Professor Grahame-Smith is quite right that there is no logical proof of what I said. When I was speaking to my friendly medical research directors, three or four of them made the point about the line going down, flattening off, and perhaps, as Professor Grahame-Smith suggests, being poised to take off. But, they said, only if it were allowed to do so by the drug regulatory requirements.

It may well be that I am over-stating the case, but I would nevertheless say that it is a very significant and important influence. More than that I would not claim.

Dr R. N. Smith (Hoffman-La Roche and Co): First, to support Professor Breckenridge. Just as somebody like himself, who left clinical pharmacology, and then the UK and industry, we saw the problem 2 years ago and he has documented it well. To me personally, it is still a sad fact that we remained here with the problem and nothing constructive has yet happened.

We have evidence from the US and from the UK. One could certainly say that the European and other countries are not placing work for clinical pharmacologists in Britain and for all the reasons that Professor Breckenridge has indicated for the United Kingdom companies.

There is no doubt that we all accept peer review by regulatory authorities. I do not think that that is in question, and I thought that Professor Grahame-Smith was being rather defensive when he spoke earlier. I would entirely agree with him that the standards being established between industry and the regulatory authorities are extremely valuable. We then heard a very clear documentation and a catalogue of the effects on innovation as seen by Eli Lilly, and I am sure that all the other major companies would echo word for word what Dr Christensen said. One interesting point there is that what we are trying to do in industry is to become more efficient. The change is in management systems, to make sure that we do make decisions within the company very quickly. But then we are thwarted as soon as we come to the regulatory agencies, and particularly if those standards are changing, or certain value judgements are being brought in which we did not anticipate and could not have anticipated 2 years before.

In his last comments Professor Grahame-Smith doubted whether there was a true correlation. I would say to him most earnestly that people outside the industry, and certainly those inside, accept the facts. In this first day we have had it so well documented that we really have to accept this correlation. Why not try the experiment of relaxing the regulations and seeing the benefits?

Mr M. Crawford (Sandoz Limited): As an ex-drug regulator may I counter that last proposal and quote as reason for it Dr Christensen's comments that 5 out of some 5 500 lots of drug A and another 5 out of almost 5 000 lots of drug B failed FDA quality control standards after they had passed Lilly testing to comparable standards. I take his point that the observed deviations were small, and probably not of clinical significance, but if the standards are abolished, less reputable companies have the chance of setting their own levels irrespective of their competence, and thus of exposing the public to much greater risks than those mentioned.

Dr Christensen: I am not proposing to abolish the standard, not at all. I think the standard should be established and that every product that is introduced to the market-place should meet it. What I am proposing is that the FDA does not have to do the duplicate tests that they are currently doing. Every test that we do on these lots is duplicated at the FDA. We can do the tests, send them down there and they can inspect them, but stop duplicate testing.

Mr Crawford: A follow-up question, then. Would those five lots have been detected by Lilly if they had looked at their own results again?

Dr Christensen: I did not look them up. I did a few months ago when I gave a similar talk. In duplicate testing they may have shown up.

Dr A. W. Peck (Wellcome Research Laboratories): I have been trying to think of simple examples which we might argue from. I thought of the discovery of cromoglycate by Dr Altounyan and the fact that at the time he made that discovery he used, I believe, 600 different varieties of inhalant over the years. He has calculated how long it would take to do that under recent requirements. Obviously that type of clinical pharmacology, a kind of human screening, would not be possible at all under current requirements.

Has Professor Grahame-Smith any comment?

Prof. D. G. Grahame-Smith: No, I have not. I do not want to be identified with what regulatory authorities do. I am concerned at trying to see my way through. I realize that there are problems about drug development. I am not arguing with that. I am trying to see what the causes are. Of course, industry will blame the regulations because they are an obvious thing to blame. It may be that indeed they are responsible for the cutback in innovation and so on, but I am not absolutely convinced. I believe that regulations can be altered without one necessarily being clubbed over the head every 5 minutes by the call that they are stifling innovation. In other words, it can be perfectly logical to alter regulations without necessarily invoking this rather emotional response all the time.

Dr J. G. Collier (St George's Hospital Medical School): Professor Breckenridge's list of important new applications for previously discovered drugs, all of which came by chance many years after the drugs in question had gone into production, represents a very important step in therapeutics. All of these could come to clinical pharmacologists. In fact, in conducting many of the initial trials one has a feeling that one is actually doing hack work for the very first studies. The major contributions in many respects are the sort of things illustrated in trials that come later.

Personally I feel that the initial clinical work should be done by people who are prepared to do it, and as quickly as possible. I do not object to its being done out of the UK at all.

Prof. Breckenridge: I am quite surprised at that. I stand by everything I said. The small amount of early clinical studies I have had the chance to do I can look back upon with pleasure, with excitement, to a special type of clinical pharmacology quite separate from any of the other more routine studies in which perforce we get involved. All I can say is that I disagree with that.

The other point which I would pick up, looking back at the first drug on that list, propanolol and hypertension, Brian Prichard made this observation, and it was only because the drug was in the hands of an astute cardiovascular investigator that the observation was made. Had it been in the hands of the kind of research assistant that would usually be employed to do a phase 3 study, the chances of that observation having been made would have been much much smaller.

Prof. C. T. Dollery (Royal Postgraduate Medical School): Professor Breckenridge summarized the problem quite beautifully and I want to support what he says. But, to add one point, there are two additional reasons for wanting to get into man quickly. The first is that for the great majority of disease entities, the animal models either do not exist or are really very poor. The chance is of overlooking useful drugs because they do not give a response to the animal models commonly used. I wonder how many people know how pharmaceutical companies screen for anti-depressants, for example, and the remoteness of the connection between that test, namely, reserpine-induced hypothermia and the relief of depression. And there are many, many other examples. Even for hypertension there really is no good animal model. There are plenty of animal models of hypertension but there is no really good model of human essential hypertension.

That is a very strong argument for getting into man quickly, because one very likely will not make good predictions from the animal tests.

The other reason, and this is to the credit of clinical pharmacology, is that we really are in a much stronger position now for making precise measurements of drug action in man. For a long time clinical pharmacology was rather bedevilled by a pharmacokinetic approach in measuring plasma concentrations and little else, which is one of the most unrewarding activities known to mankind, but nowadays, by a combination of physiological, psychological and biochemical techniques, we can get a very long way down the wards, precisely pinpointing drug action in man, by doing well-designed experiments. As for what Dr Collier said, all that I can imagine is that he has taken part in the dreariest kind of protocol research imposed from outside, and I suggest that in the future he refuses to do it.

Dr Collier: It is difficult to reply to that statement. Of course it is not at all dreary. Some of the stuff, when I have been involved in original work in man, has been absolutely fascinating: the converting enzyme inhibitor work, for instance.

A well-known adage says that there is never a hurry to get it right and to publish. I feel that careful science is useful. I do not see that we should be in a hurry to do the work. I absolutely agree with Professor Dollery that the faster the drugs get into man, in many respects the greater the benefit. I am arguing why there is no great need for it to be us in England. What is the enormous hurry for us to be doing it? Our expertise can be used as needed.

Prof. Breckenridge: I could not disagree more, but I think we should leave it there.

Prof. D. G. Grahame-Smith: I agree with Prof Dollery. From the point of view of going early into man, I would agree with that as well. This is the point of the negotiations that the CSM has been having with industry over the last year or so in regard to the regulations for clinical trials. I hope that when those are finished the clinical trials will return to the UK. I am not pessimistic. I think that they might well. But I do hope that they will, that is all, after all the work that is being put into it.

Dr Wrigley: I am sure we all share that opinion.

Mr F. Steward (University of Aston): I should like to go back to the question of the increasing time and expense involved in drug innovation. The figures that were shown were averages for the development time for innovation and I should like a little more information on the degree of variation in the length of time involved in innovation and the relationship this has to the particular types of drugs involved in the disease areas.

I should particularly like comments on the FDA's new approach adopted in the last couple of years. I think it is called a 'fast track' drug approval process, and it tries to give greatest priority in the regulatory system to those drugs that appear to offer the greatest therapeutic benefits.

Dr Christensen: I do not have to hand the information about the variations in drugs that relate to the timespan of the studies. Suffice it to say that these data are applicable to all the new chemical entities introduced into the US since 1963 and they cover all drug classes. We did have a unique situation in the US regarding cardiovascular drugs. Because of some special problems with the FDA there were no approvals for a 10-year period in that particular division of the FDA. But even since the cardiovascular log jam has been unblocked, the timespan has not shown any corresponding decrease. There is a lot of variation from one class of compound to another in terms of how long it takes to get through but the averages are there.

In terms of the FDA's fast track, they apply this to what they call Class 1A and Class 1B drugs. The numerical designation identifies it as a new chemical entity, a new molecule, and the A means that it is of considerable therapeutic advance whilst the B means that it is of modest therapeutic advance. All I can say is that the approximate time for approval of new drug applications in the past year or two for the 1A and the 1B drugs has gone to 25 months, while the time for the 1C and the lower classes of drugs has now increased. They have not decreased the average time it takes to process the 1A and the 1B drugs but they have increased the time it takes for the lesser classifications of drugs. The FDA's own figures for the last year show this. We do not think much of the fast track.

Another thing that bothers us about the classification system is this. Someone asked when we know that we have a really significant drug on our hands. We could make a guess, a very very poor guess before we go into humans. We could make a somewhat more sophisticated guess at the end of clinical trials, but I propose that no one really knows the value of a drug until it has been out there for a period of time and a lot of people have had a chance to use it, and a lot of people have had a chance to misuse it and all kinds of things like that.

Dr J. D. Coombes (Hoechst Pharmaceuticals): Can I amplify the point on the importance of getting drugs early into man: not from the point of view of selection of the drugs, but from the feedback to the research programme. If the feedback loop is overly delayed, it makes it that much more advantageous to use only well-validated animal models where the transition from animals to man has already been demonstrated. If one is more interested in innovative research, testing new biological hypotheses or testing new animal models, this can be so discouraged by a very long delay before being able to examine this model in man that one is forced to reduce the amount of innovative work and to take up what is sometimes called 'me too' research.

Prof. Breckenridge: In some respects I am perhaps arguing against myself, but there is a problem that we have run into – very interestingly – quite recently, when we have been approached to do phase 1 studies. Clearly we have gone to our institutional review board for permission to do this. In the past when we have been doing our dull phase 3 work they have been quite happy to rely on the Clinical Trials Certificate (CTC) that the drug already has, but when we confront them with a total new entity and data, toxicology data and the raw data from industry, which of course industry gives to us, many institutional review bodies really go into a whirl. It may well be that if the CSM do cause a change in policies with respect to investigating new drugs, our institutional reviews will have to gee up their thoughts as well.

Dr A. W. Peck: The point was made that the 1968 Act is really a very flexible instrument. Has Professor Breckenridge ever felt sufficiently strongly about investigations, and investigations about particular drugs, to take the exemption clauses and bypass the CTC?

Prof. Breckenridge: It is interesting that Dr Peck should mention that. We then come up against our institutional review boards or rather we have difficulties with them. The answer is that I have not. I have not directly. But we have discussed it. The approach has been made to us to do this, and after considerable discussion with our institutional review body we decided not to do it. It depends on the drug of course.

Prof. C. T. Dollery: Perhaps Professor Grahame-Smith should comment on that. There are two procedures that can be used. One can, as any licensed physician, give any patient any drug that one thinks their clinical needs require, so that if a physician wants to infuse concentrated nitric acid intravenously he can; and there is only the Medical Defence Union between him and his patient. But my understanding of the position is that this is not intended as a way of bypassing the clinical trial regulations, and that if it was systematically used in that way then some action would have to be taken to prevent it.

The second procedure referred to by Dr Peck is the exemption procedure, but the exemption has to be granted by the licensing authority. It is their practice generally to grant an exemption if there is no clinical trials submission in the works, nor likely to be. In other words, it is some kind of special procedure. There was an example recently at Hammersmith where there were people using a pyrogen, a more purified preparation of a pyrogen-inducing material. They were giving it pretty much on their own authority, and I suggested that they should try to get an exemption. But if there is a Clinical Trials Certificate in the works, then it is the view, quite properly, of the CSM that they cannot allow people to bypass it. Unfortunately quite often pharmaceutical companies do come along to people like myself and say 'Oh, go on. You can give the drug on your own authority'. It is not usually the British-based companies that do that. It is usually mainland continental companies. But if people are doing that, then that is simply outside the rules. People should not deliberately break the rules in that way.

Prof. D. G. Grahame-Smith: Perhaps this is neither the time nor the place to discuss whether the rules are right. But what Professor Dollery says is right. It is for a physician, if he wants to, to give a drug to a named patient. That is different from a clinical trial. On the other hand, by and large if there is a CTC application in house, then an exemption is not normally granted. Once there is a CTC one can get a variation. How quickly one will get that variation depends on a number of factors, but it is usually not as long as getting a CTC. But it is a problem once the CTC is in house, or is actually there, legally, to get permission quickly. I am sorry, but that is the law.

Dr R. G. Penn (Department of Health): Could I confirm what Professor Dollery and Professor Grahame-Smith have said. Exemptions should not be seen as a short-cut by the industry to clinical trials being performed. They are intended for the doctor on his own responsibility, and in his own interest, to do clinical trials on patients, and where there strictly speaking is no interest, to use the term loosely, in the compound on the part of the company. As Professor Grahame-Smith said, the exemption would not be given if a Clinical Trials Certificate for the same indication was in house, but it is then very easy, and usually very quick, to get a variation to the Clinical Trials Certificate. This can often be done by the licensing authority on its own initiative, without reference to the CSM.

But I do recommend that in any of these cases we are consulted at Market Towers, where we would be happy to advise on any problems in any particular case.

Dr J. F. Cavalla (Wyeth Laboratories): With the greatest respect to Dr Penn, I should like to point out that his belief that variations take a short while is misfounded. We – Wyeth – may be exceptional in having to wait 5 months for a variation certificate to allow use of a modified route of synthesis of a molecule which has already been approved for CTC.

Dr Penn: I did point out that this is where a doctor, a clinical pharmacologist, wishes to associate himself with a CTC already granted. Where there is a variation to, say, route of synthesis, this obviously has to go through our routes, which may be long and may be short. I appreciate and will accept that there are times when variations will take a long time, but in this particular case when a doctor wishes to associate himself with an existing CTC it need not be that long.

Dr Cavalla: I should like to come back on a general point. Professor Breckenridge pointed out that there were differences and if I may say so salutary differences, between a clinical pharmacologist and an ordinary GP. On the other hand, it has been pointed out to me by a very august member of the CSM that in his view, to requote Gertrude Stein, a drug is a drug is a drug, and that there can be no differences in the way one would reflect upon that particular entity. In my view this is not the case. A drug can differ, depending on the hands in which it finds itself. To that extent the degree of control which is required for a drug in the hands of a named clinical pharmacologist is less than that required for a drug which will be in the hands of literally thousands of general practitioners.

Having said that, I should like to point out for Professor Grahame-Smith's attention, and I am certain he realizes it, that generally speaking the data requirements for the UK Clinical Trials Certificate in toxicological and pharmaceutical terms, are currently identical with those for a Product Licence Application. This, I think, is most in need of change.

Dr Wrigley: We might conclude our discussion by apparently agreeing that regulations are adversely affecting innovation in discovery research.

On the question of elimination of delays as one moves towards the clinical phases of a programme, and the question of bringing clinical trials back to the UK, we are probably very happy to put ourselves into the hands of an energetic and practical man, such as Professor Grahame-Smith, who, we hope, will do a very good job for the industry.

8
The effect on choice of research

P. A. J. JANSSEN

Let us take two generally held principles that form the basis of civilized society, principles that are taught to our children at a very early age:

(1) Don't do unto others as you wouldn't have them do unto you.
(2) Don't expect others to do what you would refuse to do yourself.

In applying these general principles to the field of drug research, this would mean that

(a) It is ethically unacceptable to expect a patient to receive a drug that you yourself would not take in a similar situation.
(b) It is unreasonable to expect others to work under research conditions and constraints that are unacceptable to yourself.

And to make it even more concrete one must add that weighing the risks of the administration of a drug against its anticipated benefits is a matter of conscience which a doctor faces continually and from which he cannot escape.

It is essential for a doctor under all circumstances to treat his patient as if he himself were the patient. If there is no problem with the diagnosis, or if he is dealing with a well-known and rather common disease or syndrome, the treatment for which is readily available, effective and safe, then the doctor will find no major obstacles in carrying out his job. In such cases, the doctor's professional skill is his main asset. But if it is a rare condition of unknown aetiology and the treatment option ill-defined, then common sense will be more valuable than book lore and the doctor will have to take a calculated risk. In extreme cases, when a patient's life is at stake, his decision must come quickly and decisively.

Surgeons in particular are often confronted with such agonizing problems.

Doctors are of course individuals and there is no way of avoiding different doctors placing different interpretations on the same basic situation. Different interpretations will result in different courses of action, but always with the same objective – patient care. Thus a doctor may be expected to keep abreast of medical progress and be prepared day and night to take action to the best of his ability.

And what can be reasonably expected from those who are engaged in the search for better medicines? As much as possible, of course. But then, what is possible? What is reasonable or practicable, and where does Utopia begin? To what frontiers does science reach and where lie the limits of our economic possibilities, of the socially and economically acceptable? On the one hand, our world of 1980 witnesses the existence and development of a technologically oriented science, capable of quickly and efficiently unravelling and solving problems traditionally regarded as inextricable, and on the other hand it fosters a bureaucracy created and supported by public opinion and intended to protect society from unexpected and unwanted dangers which modern technology seems to entail. Fear of the unknown is a particularly strong sociological motive which politicians experience day after day. So where lies the real interest of the citizen in general and of the diseased in particular?

It is not my intention to give you a lengthy and possibly sterile analysis of the problem, but I would like to contribute to what may be a small but, in my opinion, important step forward. The benefits of any new drug must always be weighed against possible risks. The benefit–risk ratio will vary according to the condition to be treated. Thus in the case of common, self-limiting minor ailments, the benefits must always significantly outweigh the risks, as is also the case when effective and safe treatments are already available. However, in rare diseases, where the prognosis is poor and no effective therapy exists, it is justifiable to take great risks, but always with due consideration to the hazards of remaining untreated.

In the interest of the unfortunate patient who is suffering from a rare and serious, spontaneously irreversible and, so far, intractable disease, I propose that all those who are trying to find an adequate therapeutic solution for such a patient be well encouraged in their endeavours rather than demotivated by all sorts of bureaucratic red tape. The legislator who has set up the bureaucratic control systems of new drugs ought to finally be aware that there is a considerable difference in the risk–benefit analysis between a toothache and sleeping sickness. It is a matter for regret that too little attention is paid to diseases of rare occurrence and to typically tropical diseases that cause great damage to the Third World but are seldom diagnosed in thriving countries.

The main cause of this shortcoming is usually sought in merely economic considerations. It is quite obvious, indeed, that the financial risks of drug research in these two areas bear no acceptable relation to the potential market. From a purely economic point of view, these problems are very difficult indeed. Yet there are sufficient people in this world who would be willing to take that risk. Fortunately, there are still some idealists, even in the pharmaceutical industry. The government ought to encourage these people. It would be wise to deliver them from the bureaucratic yoke under which they are currently bending their necks. This deliverance would suffice to give drug research in the field of rare and tropical diseases new and vigorous impetus. And if, besides, the governments of many developing countries were able to set up a fair and sound patent legislation, this would, in itself, mark a considerable step forward. Whether there should be any direct support by the government remains a matter of controversy.

To conclude with a more general remark. Risk–benefit analysis in drug research is, first and foremost, the responsibility of the drug researchers themselves, and afterwards, it is a problem which the attending physician will have to solve in each individual case. In these matters, public authorities can play only a minor role for the protection of public health. They must, of course, track down any evil-doers and fight their ill effect upon society. But they do certainly not serve the interest of the public in general or the needy patient in particular by creating a dictatorial bureaucracy which rapidly loses sight of the real aims of its existence and unintentionally imposes a check on the real progress of drug research.

Creative people dislike an exaggerated bureaucracy and are, to a great extent, demotivated by it. To them nothing can be worse than the obligation to complete piles of paper with insipid data. That deadly dull sort of work will finally result in a loss of the creative capacity itself. Useless work drives out useful work, and who may benefit from that?

9
The relative worth of animal testing

A. D. DAYAN

The experimental use of animals to predict effects in man may be claimed to date from the soothsayer's practice of divination with entrails. The more recent mechanistic success of physiologists and biochemists in revealing body mechanisms has emphasized the value of the study of animals in explaining the responses of man in health and disease. In pharmacology, too, so many advances in basic knowledge and therapeutic power have come from animal experimentation that it has become accepted dogma to use the results of the latter to control development and toxicity testing of new medicines. The belief has gained ground, and is reflected in the legislation society demands, that extrapolation to man from studies in animals will always permit exact prediction of the desired and adverse effects of new medicines, i.e. that efficacy and safety can always be assured by animal tests, which must, therefore, be of the highest value.

The purpose of animal testing, once a substance with desired pharmacological actions has been identified, should be to define toxicity in terms of risk, that is a measure of the probability and severity of unwanted and adverse effects. That information can then be used to determine safety, in other words the degree to which a risk is considered acceptable under any given set of circumstances. The 'relative' worth of animal testing depends upon the qualitative and quantitative accuracy of its extrapolation to man, and on the direct and indirect costs of doing or not doing work in animals.

The weakness and intellectual poverty of a naive trust in animal tests may be shown in several ways, e.g. the humiliatingly large number of medicines discovered only by serendipitous observation in man (ranging from diuretics to antidepressants), or by astute analysis of deliberate or accidental poisoning, the notorious examples of valuable medicines which have seemingly 'unacceptable' toxicity in animals, e.g. griseofulvin producing tumours and furosemide causing hepatic necrosis in mice, the stimulant action of morphine in cats, and such instances of unpredicted toxicity in man as the production of pulmonary hypertension by Aminorex and SMON. The rapidly increasing interest in clinical pharmacology, and the drive to better means of making measurements in man, also reflect the uncertainty of animal experimentation and realization that the study of man alone can ever prove entirely valid for other men.

The value of animal work cannot be denied, but it is essential to realize that at best it can provide only partial information, on which it is risky to base any final decision unless there is prior knowledge of the predictive value of the particular test employed. The peculiar dilemma of the toxicologist is that ideally he would never be able to validate his work by reference to toxic effects in man, and yet it is the results of his toxicity tests that are used, at least in the first instance, to determine the circumstances of human exposure to a medicine or chemical. The worth of animal testing from the toxicological viewpoint depends, therefore, on comparison of the limited number of examples of adverse effects in man with the results of studies in animals, and on extrapolation from the very much larger number of examples in which a drug has been deliberately selected for development because it appeared 'non-toxic' in animals. As the majority of compounds that are toxic in animals at anywhere near the therapeutic dose are abandoned in the laboratory, there is no general experience of their administration to man to show the accuracy or otherwise of extrapolation of their effects from animals to man.

SCOPE AND NATURE OF ANIMAL TESTING

Experiments in animals may be considered separately in relation to research into basic pathophysiology, work to identify a chemical or biological material of therapeutic promise, or study of its desired and unwanted (side or toxic) effects. The worth of any procedure employed is strictly defined by the confidence with which its results can be extrapolated to man, as successful prediction underlies initial selection of a chemical as a candidate drug, it is of equal if not greater importance in evaluation of the probable significance of the drug's other actions, and, hopefully, it should be the sole arbiter in selection of toxicity tests. The ideal would be never to detect any novel toxic effect in man, as only those should occur which had been anticipated and which had been judged to be of acceptable nature and severity.

Basic research and the selection of candidate drugs are dealt with elsewhere in this book and this discussion will concentrate on toxicity and the detection and prediction of unwanted actions.

Comprehensive toxicity tests must employ suitable means to demonstrate any significant effect, be it an organic physiological response, a biochemical action, a histopathological lesion, or in functional behaviour. Their methodology, therefore, should be holistic or universal in nature, or comprise multiple specific methods, because the crux in the first instance is detection of any change due to the treatment. This should be contrasted with a conventional experiment, in which every possible influence is controlled, and only one effect is observed as a single factor is varied. A toxicity study is a more complex assay of innumerable variables in which the primary endpoint is alteration in anything that can be observed. Only at the second stage, when the mechanism of the toxic effect is to be analysed, can the technique be changed to conventional scientific practice. For this reason, efficient toxicity testing must often be based on multiple observations of complex systems, because it is only under those circumstances that the many types of toxic mechanism are able to operate and be detected (Table 9.1).

Table 9.1   Types of toxic mechanism

Type	Mechanism
1. Direct	action on target
2. Indirect	consequence of target effect
3. Secondary	activation to toxicant:
(a) local	affects activating tissue
(b) distant	affects distant tissue
Non-specific	'disturbed homeostatis'

Important types of test must be able to reveal many or all of these mechanisms and effects with minimum effort if they are to be efficient, i.e. within the experimental system one manoeuvre, administration of the substance, should lead to manifestation of the consequences in a fashion accessible to simple observation, and, if possible, it should also afford clues to the cause and consequences of the toxic effect. There is a hierarchy of importance here. First is detection of any effect, second, determination of its nature and third, decision about its importance. In many instances the third decision may take precedence over the second, because consideration of dose, route of administration, pharmacokinetics, etc., may show that the effect is not likely to be of practical significance. From this, it will be seen that the value of any toxicity test lies in its generality, and so in its ability efficiently to demonstrate secondary or indirect effects, as well as the primary action of the substance.

Because of the non-specific nature of primary toxicological procedures, although their sensitivity and reproducibility should be high, conventional criteria, such as specificity and precision cannot be employed. Many of the variables are qualitative (e.g. histopathological lesions), or at best quantal, so numerical analysis is often difficult. All of these factors affect the basic worth of animal testing.

TYPES OF TOXICITY TESTS AND THEIR ASSESSMENT

For convenience, the broadest range of toxicity tests is considered (Table 9.2), arbitrarily divided into functional, pharmacodynamic and conventional procedures, the latter largely being based on morbid anatomy plus a few parameters of life. Their value in development of a new medicine is examined to determine the worth of extrapolation of results from them to man, and with some consideration of alternative methods. The judgements of value presented are solely the writer's opinion, but it is hoped that they will encourage more critical evaluation of the place of toxicity testing.

Table 9.2 Value of animal toxicity tests

Test	Sensitivity	Specificity	Convenience	Predictiveness
Acute (LD_{50})	na	+ +	+	+
Subacute oral	+	+	+	+
parenteral	+ +	+	0	+
Chronic	+	+	+	+
Carcinogenicity	±	±	0	+ /0
Reproduction				
Fertility	+ /0	+	+ /0	+ /0
Fetal toxicity	+	?+	+	?+
Peri- and post-natal	+	?	+	?0
Short-term mutagenicity	+	+ +	+ +	?
Topical				
Irritancy	+ +	+ +	+	+ +
Sensitization	+ +	+ +	+	+

na = not applicable

Functional toxicity tests

These may be taken as examination of behaviour in all its forms, i.e. at rest and in response to specific stimuli (including sexual stimulation); 'higher' nervous activities, such as learning, memory, conditioned responses, natural rhythms of activity and sleep and social behaviour.

There is no substitute for an animal or group of animals if sophisticated functions are to be studied, because it is impossible to dissect their integrated behaviour into lesser fragments accessible to other techniques. The only exceptions are a limited number of highly restricted responses, e.g. the role of hypothalamic and gonadal hormones in governing sexual activity, but, by definition, their very specificity makes them inappropriate for general toxicity testing.

The predictive value of these tests can best be described as mixed, reflecting the inadequacy of present-day knowledge of psychological mechanisms and of their physical substrates. The lack of any well-founded theories against which to evaluate observations is a further handicap that reduces the experimenter to a phenomenologist ruled by precedent (experience). The information that can be gained is worth having, but gross effects alone are likely to be detected, and only simpler actions can be extrapolated to man, albeit with considerable caution.

Knowledge of many features of the social functioning of man, as an individual or in groups, is still inadequate, and these aspects do not have established parallels in animals, especially the more advanced and more precious intellectual powers. There have been and probably will continue to be drugs introduced on apparently good laboratory evidence, which have had subsequently to be controlled because of what might be termed 'social' toxicity, i.e. undesirable psychological or intellectual effects on the individual or on cultural groups. Examples of such substances are opiates, barbiturates and benzodiazepines. In this context only physical addiction can be predicted in the laboratory, so study of man must remain the sole means to detect such activity.

Although in no way restricted to this area of toxicity testing, many physical factors will influence any experimental results obtained. They include species, sex, strain, age and previous treatment or handling of the animals, the need in many tests to preselect only those animals that can be trained to perform in an appropriate manner, the physical environment (temperature, noise, lighting, etc.), diet (amount and presentation, adequacy), exposure to pheromones, the attitude and physical manner of the experimenter and·other variables, many only suspected and probably many others unknown. Standardization of any of these factors will help to control experimental variance and to ensure reproducibility of tests, but at the inescapable cost of increasing remoteness from the rich and uncontrolled variability of human life. The contradictory urges for rigid control of experiments for scientific reasons and the need to cover the diverse circumstances of real life run throughout toxicology and must always be in mind when evaluating the worth of any animal experimentation.

Overall, therefore, false positives and, false negatives are common and predictive potential is limited. It remains essential to continue to try to study in animals the complexity of integrated mechanisms which underlie individual and group behaviour if better founded techniques are to be developed. Techniques based on study of man are also required, as he must be regarded here as no less an experimental animal than the conventional laboratory species.

Pharmacodynamic toxicity tests

This division, which is artificial but of practical convenience, covers effects on specific physiological mechanisms, usually of an acute type and measured as a physical or chemical change.

Experience has shown a generally high predictive value for man of these effects, except for the more subtle changes in higher nervous activity, provided that there is careful selection of the species and circumstances shown by experience to be most relevant.

Pharmacodynamic actions may usefully be sub-divided according to the major systems of the body.

Cardiovascular system (CVS)

The complexity and capacity of the mechanisms that integrate haemodynamic responses are such that the final result of drug action can only be determined in the intact animal, e.g. blood pressure, heart rate and rhythm, etc. The detail of selected variables, either solitary (e.g. blood flow through a particular region) or as the resultant of a small cluster (e.g. baroceptor-mediated responses to a change in blood pressure), may be examined under well controlled conditions, but the need for work in the intact animal is inescapable.

The predictive value of CVS experiments is high, subject to the caveats mentioned above, provided that time is also taken into account, so that measurements are made over a period in which responses of diverse kinds may occur. Unexpected reactions in man appear to be unusual, and when they have occurred, hindsight has often shown that they could have been predicted from animal studies of appropriate quality.

Respiratory system (RS)

Here, too, the complexity of the ultimate physiological integration necessitates studies in animals, even though many of the constituent parts of respiratory mechanics, air flow, blood-gas exchange, etc., can be evaluated in isolated preparations. The latter statement must appear disingenuous, in that only known mechanisms can be so examined, and the importance of other, less well-defined responses cannot yet be properly determined, e.g. mucus secretion. This exemplifies a general problem of toxicity testing, namely use of a specific, restricted experimental system, in which only one or a few responses are possible, presupposes that no other effect can be of importance.

Gastro-intestinal system (GIS)

Certain pharmacodynamic responses can readily be studied in isolated preparations (e.g. motility, acid and saliva secretion), and some even in mechanical or computer models (e.g. lithogenic effect of altered composition of bile). Many cannot be examined outside the whole animal, probably because the pathophysiological mechanisms are too complex to be demonstrated or controlled in any other way, or because there is insufficient understanding of the way in which they work; for example, the production of gastric or duodenal ulceration by drugs.

Clinical GIS effects are commonly anticipated in animal studies, but there are exceptions, e.g. nausea. Particular types of action should certainly be sought in experiments in animals before undertaking a extensive development of a novel substance, including tests for emesis (in dog, monkey or cat), for effects on propulsion (rat) and for ulceration (rat).

Genito-urinary system

So much is now known about the mechanisms of renal function that it may well be possible to evaluate the direct action of a compound in an isolated preparation of the kidney, and this probably applies, too, to the ureters, bladder and parts of the genital tract. Such studies may not be necessary as part of general pharmacodynamic screening, and a simple effect on urinary excretion may readily be sought in animal without subjecting it to unusual stress.

Ignorance of the gonads, and of the functioning of the remainder of the genital system is more profound, and with limited exceptions *in vitro* studies are likely to be misleading. For example, the release of hypothalamic releasing factors can be studied *in vitro*, but their relative importance differs in different species, and luteolysis, too, is complex and great care is required in selecting a suitable model for man. Overall, the interrelationships of genital mechanisms are so complex that *in vivo* experiments alone will provide reliable data for extrapolation.

Nervous system

Even at a lower level, the complexity of many integrated CNS functions commonly defeats other than animal experimentation, although specific isolated effects can be obtained by simpler means. In the peripheral somatic and autonomic nervous systems there is more value in use of isolated preparations, as they have some predictive value, albeit less than that of corresponding *in vivo* systems.

Detection for the first time in man of effects on the central nervous system does still occur, but actions on the peripheral nervous systems are largely predictable. However, false negative results from animal and *in vitro* testing do occur, e.g. the ephemeral ototoxic effect of ethacrynic acid and other diuretics, neuromuscular blockade by certain antibiotics etc. Indeed, serendipitous clinical observation has been the source of several major classes of drugs acting on the nervous system, notably the antidepressants, although animal tests predict this activity in man are now available.

Conclusions

In general, pharmacodynamic tests have been well proven for many limited somatic or organic functions, for which their results are of high predictive value. Gross effects on the central nervous system are readily recognized in animal tests, but subtle actions on mentation and mood are less well covered, largely because of the lack of adequate models. The specificity of many techniques limits their value in any toxicological investigation of general effects.

Conventional toxicity tests

The boundary between these experiments and those belonging to the pharmacologist is arbitrary, and an efficient toxicity test must include assessment of acute and chronic pharmacodynamic actions as part of the desired and undesirable effects, to show whether an excess or prolongation of the desired action might itself have undesirable consequences.

In prolonged toxicity tests it is likely that indirect and secondary mechanisms will be expressed, and minor byways of metabolic activation may be brought into prominence by use of high doses. The enormous problems of species-specificity of xenobiotic metabolism, pharmacokinetics and response mechanism then become very important determinants of the value of tests on individual compounds in particular species, or under a specific set of circumstances. There can be no truly general rule to account for these entirely individual factors, which are unique to each experiment, but it is important to consider all of them in assessment of any toxicity test. Equally, it is essential to adapt each test to the properties and nature of the compound under examination.

Acute toxicity test ('LD$_{50}$')

By definition, this can only be done in animals, so the only questions to be answered are whether the information gained is worth having, and how it can be collected in an efficient manner.

The predictive worth of the information depends on whether man will ever be exposed to such a dose. From the several viewpoints of those who handle bulk chemicals and those who have to treat an accidental or deliberate overdose, there can be no doubt that the data are useful. What is most valuable, however, is not extreme arithmetical precision, because, like all drug actions, it varies with the experimental conditions, but some indication of the magnitude of the doses at which various effects occur, including death. The range of doses studied should be related to those to which man might conceivably be exposed. It is important that a full range of observations is made, as in the so-called 'Irwin test', so that no information relevant to the effects of the substance and their mechanisms is overlooked.

In general, the results of acute toxicity testing are of definite but restricted use, and they cannot be replaced by other information. They are relevant to abnormal circumstances rather than therapeutic use, but they provide information important to safety and hence to precautions.

Subacute and chronic toxicity tests

The current, almost universal convention of prolonged dosing of two species has arisen from prior experience, so it should be of proven value. In practice, little public attempt appears to have been made to demonstrate the predictive value of such work, so the only way to assess its importance is to point to the relative infrequency of adverse effects in man of newly introduced pharmaceuticals. That any serious effect occurs at all is some condemnation of present-day technique, although allowance must be made for individual idiosyncracy and hypersensitivity.

It is impossible to replace animals by other experimental systems, because of the limitations imposed by the latter in terms of the solitary or few endpoints or effects that they can manifest. Secondary and indirect activities would be missed and the crucial effects of pharmacokinetcs and metabolism might be omitted, resulting in an artificial situation in which the only detectable effects would be those which it was desired to detect. Experimentation *uberissima male fides* can have no place in toxicology.

The value of subacute and chronic tests is that they should indicate the probable nature of toxic actions and the dose level at which the latter are likely to occur. The principal determinants of their sensitivity include the numbers of animals employed, duration of treatment, handling of the compound administered, species used, and the investigative techniques employed. In addition, the previously mentioned factors of health, environment, diet, etc., must also be considered.

All these determinants carry inbuilt weaknesses. The number of animals is increased from time to time by regulatory fiat, but it remains a small figure relative to the number of people who will receive the drug, because of the impossibility of dealing with larger groups. This imposes statistical insensitivity on the experiment. Pragmatic decisions have been taken about the relationship between the duration of dosing of animals and the corresponding period of treatment of man. The selection of animal dosing for 12 months in the USA, but for 6 months in the UK, to cover prolonged administration to man, with no evidence that either period is unnecessarily prolonged or unsafe, shows how arbitrary has been the choice. The problem of xenobiotic metabolism in different species is too well known to require amplification, but the risk of non-linear pharmacokinetics must be emphasized. In the attempt to produce a detectable toxic effect, and thereby to define a dose/response curve, and also somehow to 'compensate' for the use of fewer animals than patients, it is customary to give enormous doses of test compounds. There is then a real risk of exaggeration of the importance of minor metabolic pathways with resultant effects of no more than 'academic' importance.

The range of investigative techniques employed is of considerable importance, because it will determine whether or not particular actions are discovered. For that reason it is customary to examine a very large number of
quantitative and quantal variables, and to record many qualitative observations of general behaviour and of the histological appearances of a very
large number of tissues. Multiple comparison of all these values in control and
dosed animals, before and after treatment, just by chance alone will result in a
number that differ at some arbitrarily chosen level of statistical significance.
Such arithmetical niceties must be interpreted in the light of biological understanding, but they do limit the sensitivity and resolving power of these tests.

It is important to be confident that the observations made are relevant to the
activity of the compound under test, as well as being of a general nature. It is
just as important, however, to be certain that the variables estimated are
biologically important in the animals used. For example, plasma alkaline
phosphatase is always very high in certain healthy primates, so it is useless as a
marker of liver damage, and conversely, hepatic transaminase activity is so
low in other species that its plasma level is just as useless for this purpose.
Many of the biochemical and haematological estimations done in conventional toxicity tests have accrued over the years, largely from experience in an
unrelated species – man. Their indicative or diagnostic value should be
reassessed, particularly as many are only an expensive reflection of other
variables that are also measured.

Subactute and chronic tests have become the unfortunate battleground of
regulatory manoeuvres, as ever more *ad hoc* requirements are introduced to
cover the latest problems revealed in practice or raised in hypothesis. The
point is forgotten that increasing standardization of experiments carries the
danger of increasing the irrelevance of their results in the real world. The
toxicologist requires more freedom not less in adapting tests to the specific
properties of individual compounds and therapeutic circumstance.

In practice, prolonged toxicity tests have had a fair measure of success, as
shown by the rarity of predictable toxicity in man, but there is a strong
impression that today's processes for weeding out potentially harmful substances are inefficient, and that potentially valuable therapies are also being
discarded for erroneous reasons. For example, pyrimethamine appeared to be
a very toxic compound until its very prolonged half-life was appreciated, and
furosemide was in jeopardy at one time because it can cause hepatic necrosis
in mice.

False negatives do occur. If idiosyncratic responses and reactions due to
metabolism, etc., unique to man are excluded, some remain as failures of
extrapolation. Some may have been due to failure to use appropriate
investigative procedures in animals, and others have come from hitherto
unrealized mechanisms of toxicity, such as the ototoxicity of aminoglycoside
antibiotics and the hepatotoxicity of paracetamol. Both would have been
detected in animals had there been prior knowledge to show the need for the

appropriate tests when these agents were first introduced. The considerable differences in responsiveness, kinetics and metabolism and in other ways between man and experimental animals are likely to outweigh any theoretical advantage of standardization of every pettifogging detail in a toxicity study. As a non-specific type of empirical examination, toxicological experiments must be left general in nature and unconstrained by the artificial rules of precedent based on probably irrelevant knowledge of other materials, even though they may possess superficially similar properties and actions. Previous regulatory experience of particular types of compounds, or of poorly designed experiments, must not be allowed to determine for evermore the nature and details of experiments on new substances with novel actions.

Carcinogenicity tests

As a particular case of chronic toxicity testing these deserve special attention because of their unique difficulties. The strengths of the current practice of carcinogenicity testing are that almost all known carcinogens can be detected, that limited dose/response data are sometimes obtained, and that although very prolonged and costly, the experiments are finite. Their particular weaknesses are that experimental conditions may have to be very considerably modified to suit individual compounds, their statistical resolving power is weak, excessively high doses have to be employed and their general cost and difficulty create considerable practical problems. Consideration of dose/response data has been very arbitrary, as the usual argument has been that any dose of a carcinogen must be regarded as liable to produce tumours, regardless of theoretical and factual information about non-linear pharmacokinetics, threshold dose and the relationship between carcinogenesis and the duration of treatment. Regulatory action has too often been hasty and based on unrepeated and sometimes unrepeatable results.

Assessment of the worth of carcinogenicity testing is impossible, because there is insufficient information about a representative range of pharmaceutical agents. It can only be said that the results have been interpreted to prevent or permit use of the same compound in different countries, with no apparent harm to the populace, other, perhaps, than lack of useful drugs in some countries. In relation to pharmaceutical agents, as opposed to chemicals in general, so much is known about their actions when they are released for general use in man that it seems most unlikely that a carcinogen would escape undetected until that stage. This does not exclude the possibility of failure to discover a promoter, or an epigenetic or co-carcinogen until that stage, but understanding of those activities is so limited that there are not yet any realistic tests for such activities.

Reproductive toxicity testing

Here, too, work in animals is paramount. Use of the few lower systems or other alternatives that have been suggested, would entail reliance on the dangerously restrictive assumption that the experimenter need be concerned only with the actions that his method can show.

The first of these tests to be discussed is the fertility test. The objective of the test is to demonstrate any effect on gonadal maturation, gametogenesis, transport of gametes, fertilization, and formation and subsequent implantation of the blastocyst. In practice, unless a multi-generation study is done, normal pre-natal development of the oocyte restricts the stages in the female open to influence by the compound. Despite the many processes involved, with the consequent possibility of biological amplification of an effect at any stage, the test is notoriously insensitive. Almost all substances that are effective in diminishing fertility appear to be overtly toxic, or to have endocrine effects, which are apparent by other means.

The fertility test has also been commended as a type of dominant lethal test for mutagenic action, in which a genetic (probably chromosomal) defect would be manifested as an excess of early intrauterine deaths. In practice, it is a very inefficient procedure for this purpose, because the pattern of treatment of the animals and the time of examination of the dams are poorly adapted to demonstrate such an effect.

Not only are there often considerable differences in kinetics between species, but the entire reproductive mechanism is also under a different set of endocrine controls. Extrapolation then becomes a very risky business.

The second of the reproductive tests is the fetal toxicity test. The primary objective of this test is to demonstrate induced abnormality in organogenesis. It is probably quite good at doing so, and in fact may be in danger of being too sensitive in at least one respect. The requirement that the top dose administered to dams should cause some maternal toxicity means that their fetuses develop under severe stress and possibly with no better than a marginal supply of, or real competition for, a variety of nutrients and endogenous factors. It should not be surprising that minor abnormalities are a common finding in fetuses from top-dose groups, the interpretation of which may be difficult.

A recent practice has been to test the effects of compounds on post-natal physical and behavioural development up to or beyond weaning. The underlying concept may appear reasonable, but what is to be tested and how?

Various schemes have been proposed, many bearing a suspicious resemblance to developmental assessment of human babies, but rats and rabbits are not scaled-down men. Much more investigation is required if this potentially valuable phase of testing is to give interpretable results. It exemplifies the danger of a regulatory requirement beyond scientific understanding, in which the standard of normality is unknown and any effect is likely to be uninterpretable.

Information about compounds active in the test is very sparse (aspirin can have definite effects), and there does not appear to be any correlation with an action in man unless there is gross maternal toxicity. At best, therefore, the method appears unproven and to be a potential source of uninterpretable data obtained at real expense.

Topical testing

There is general agreement about the value of animal experimentation in final assessment of a topical preparation, as there is no other reliable way to mimic potential irritancy of a substance, either direct or by an immunological mechanism. If anything, current methods may be over-sensitive, as a constant background of false positives is a common laboratory observation. The converse of topical damage in man not reproducible in an animal, does occur, and in most instances it appears to be due to hypersensitivity or atopy.

Short-term tests

Under this fashionable heading come methods still under development but claimed to predict carcinogenicity and mutagenicity in man. None of the most popular involve work in animals at an initial stage, although they may be used in the more difficult secondary or tertiary techniques.

Some attention has been paid to the host-mediated assay as a means to expose readily mutatable indicator organisms both to the parent compound and its short-lived metabolites by *in vivo* administration of the compound and the indicator organism. In practice, it has proved to be a tedious and relatively insensitive method, rarely if ever better in primary experimentation than use of metabolic activating systems in the test tube.

The secondary techniques include various cytogenetic methods, the micro-nucleus, dominant lethal, sperm morphology, specific locus and heritable translocation assays, etc. It is too early to determine the real value of any of these procedures. In their favour is that being performed *in vivo* a positive result ought to indicate a definite risk of an effect in man. Against them on scientific grounds is their apparent insensitivity, which is more likely to reflect the natural protective mechanisms ignored by *in vitro* work, and perhaps the restricted range of actions that can be studied.

A tentative opinion at present, although in the absence of adequate data, is that short-term techniques may one day prove a useful adjunct to other methods. They require much development before their predictive value for man can be realistically assessed. The pharmaceutical industry and regulatory agencies have a duty to publish sufficient information about test results to demonstrate the relative value of the techniques that are coming to be required.

Additional significant weaknesses and problems of animal testing

At the scientific level, animal experiments are done in a small, healthy, relatively homogeneous population, which differs from man in those and many other respects. This often results in poor sensitivity and resolving power, which it would be naive to assume could be overcome just by increasing the number of animals or the size of the doses employed. The risk of creating additional difficulties by the latter manoeuvres has been clearly shown by the notorious failures of mega-mouse experimentation, and by occurrence of non-linear pharmacokinetics.

Animals chosen at random cannot be used to mimic or predict events in patients with an idiosyncratic response, be it due to a genetic difference in metabolism, e.g. slow acetylator status, or to immunological hypersensitivity, There are such differences in immune reactivity between individual members of all species examined, reflecting nature as well as nurture, that it is not possible now, and may well never be, to predict such bizarre problems as the auto-immune side-effects of procainamide and hydrallazine, and the unique response of a small proportion of patients to practolol.

What is the real worth of animal testing?

In developing medicines for the treatment of disease, the worth of animal testing lies first in its ability to predict an inevitable toxic effect of the therapeutic dose of a substance, and so to warn against administration to man; second, to predict probable or conditional toxicity, i.e. an adverse action under certain circumstances of treatment, and so to aid the clinical decision of when to employ a particular therapy; and third, to show the nature of toxic activity, thus indicating what should be closely monitored in man. The fourth and final role is to suggest or even to show the mechanism of toxicity, so that it may be avoided by fresh chemical synthesis or by pharmaceutical means, and a potential therapy made into a treatment of practical value.

The particular worth of animal experimentation is that it affords a holistic view of many effects of a substance, provided that appropriate observations are made. By comparison with more specific experimental techniques, such as isolated organ work, enzyme assays, etc., it offers less sensitivity and statistical accuracy, but not at the unacceptable price of being able to demonstrate only one or two responses. As the latter techniques require that the nature of the effect sought be determined prior to the experiment, they are entirely unsuited to toxicological experimentation, in which the objective must be to seek any effect at all. Animal experimentation is also the only realistic way to detect indirect and secondary toxicity, and disorders of physiological integration, and to take cognisance of pharmacokinetic factors.

Animal experimentation as commonly described carries the burden of a small number of experimental units, and of considerable and incompletely controllable variation due, for example, to environment, diet, social interaction etc. The high intrinsic variance adversely affects sensitivity. There is also the barrier of extrapolation across species when the results are applied to man. In turn, as man, too, is a highly variable species owing to innate and exogenous causes, the risk of extrapolation is further increased.

Prediction of activity in man, especially toxicity, from data obtained in animals is constrained by limited knowledge of the dose–response relationship. The precision of animal results may be poor and it is often difficult to predict the shape of the curve under conditions of low-dose human exposure from high-dose experiments in animals. Consider, for example, the Sisyphean controversy over the dose-response relationship for low doses of carcinogens. This represents an extreme case of the quantitative uncertainty of extrapolation from animals to man, and yet objective risk–benefit analysis can only be done on the basis of quantitative data. In practice, information about the consequences of exposure of man to hazards is commonly qualitative, or at best quantal, and this only aggravates the difficulties of the would-be analyst.

Improvement will come from more rational animal experimentation, in which less attention is paid to the minutiae of peripheral or minor factors, and instead there is encouragement to demonstrate the pattern of actions of a compound by broader experimentation under a wider range of conditions and in more species. The ingenuous expectation of greater quantitative rigour of animal toxicity testing by a simple increase in the numbers of animals employed must be restrained by the understanding that any practicable size of experiment will give only a derisory increase in statistical confidence in relation to the numbers of patients that will be treated. Allowance must be made for the problems of non-linear kinetics, inter-species differences in metabolism and responsivity and of interaction with environmental factors.

A problem of a different nature is how to deal with the information obtained in toxicity tests. The simple extreme cases are easy, e.g. severe toxicity in several species at a dose level very close to that producing the desired therapeutic effect, or no untoward activity at many times the likely human therapeutic dose. But, what about the more common circumstance, when there is some toxicity at a low dose in one species and none, or a different type of damage, in a second animal species? Or, how can anyone try to assess not just the risk of a toxic effect in man, but to balance the clinical distress caused by different types of toxicity, e.g. what should be done if one candidate therapy for a severe illness was likely to produce liver damage and another was to cause peripheral nephropathy? We lack a calculus to evaluate the confidence of extrapolation of risk, and we are also unable objectively to balance qualitatively different risks.

A popular illusion about animal experimentation, as of toxicology as a whole, appears to be the unfounded belief that as toxicity tests should confer safety, so ever more tests should afford absolute safety. This is false and no scientist or regulator should further such a belief. The real need is for more critical experimentation based on rigorous analysis of the unique properties of each compound, and not on thoughtless expansion of a regulatory checklist applied equally to all compounds and therefore probably suited to none. Precedent must not insulate regulation from reality.

The relative worth of animal testing lies in the demonstrable help it has given in preventing administration to man of unacceptable toxic compounds. But it is not a universal panacea, and its real limitations and costs are such that search for alternative techniques should be encouraged, provided that they permit the holistic assessment that is essential in general safety studies.

The toxicologist must be permitted to direct his work to the practical problems of real compounds, and especially to discovering the mechanism of adverse effects, for their avoidance should result in safer medicines. In this way the toxicologist, who is criticized by society for the inadequacy of his advice, and by his employer for its cost and delay, could fulfil his scientific conscience by making discoveries of real value.

10
The prospect of product liability

J. D. SPINK

In attempting to assess the prospective changes of product liability law in the terms of a risk–benefit analysis one faces some formidable difficulties. The first is that one can only speculate at this stage on what the ultimate law will be as only a draft of the EEC directive is available and even when it is finalized there will be a degree of flexibility in how it is implemented in UK legislation. The second concern is that, in expressing any benefit at all the author does not renege on the view that strict liability on medicines is one of the most damaging things that has ever hit the long-term prospects, not only of the pharmaceutical industry, but of the entire practice of therapeutic medicine. The views expressed here are the author's own and not necessarily those of the Association of the British Pharmaceutical Industry (ABPI) although there is no disagreement of which the author is aware. This paper will examine the important features of the EEC directive, and then assess the significance of the main differences between the first and second drafts. Finally, it will attempt to develop some kind of cost–benefit analysis. The word 'cost' is preferable to 'risk', as risk has a particular meaning in the context of insurance.

EEC DIRECTIVE ON PRODUCT LIABILITY

The basic proposal of the directive is to make industry strictly liable for injuries arising from defects in its products, without the need to prove that the manufacturer was negligent. Defects can be of two main types; manufacturing and design defects. A manufacturing defect is one which occurs when a product is not manufactured in accordance with its specifications, and a good

example in the pharmaceutical industry would be an injection product contaminated with living micro-organisms. A development (or design) defect, on
the other hand, occurs when a product is manufactured precisely in accordance with its approved specification but the drug contained in it is found to
have some intrinsic feature of its chemical structure which gives rise to serious
adverse reactions. With a design defect the pharmaceutical industry has a
further problem in that it may remain latent for several years during which
time it could have been building up, unbeknown to the manufacturer or
anyone else, a pile of damage amounting to several million pounds.

The majority of manufacturers would undoubtedly be willing to accept a
situation of strict liability for manufacturing defects and indeed have already
done so in effect for generations. If a mistake is made in manufacturing a
product, such as a failure of sterility, or an error of identification of an active
ingredient, or the inadvertent doubling of its proper content, and an injury
results, no amount of pleading of high standards maintained or circumstances
beyond his control is likely to affect the outcome of a case against the
manufacturer. Inevitably therefore he settles out of court. It is when the injury
is caused by an adverse reaction which has not been detected in the course of
development of the product and is intrinsic to its nature in the pure form of the
drug that the problem of strict liability really causes concern. And when it is
the case that it could not have been detected by any means known to science at
the time that the product was put on the market strict liability becomes a blunt
instrument lacking in any semblance of justice.

Another expedient in the directive is that strict liability extends to importers
notwithstanding that they have little or no control over the safety of many
products they handle, simply because the manufacturer is outside the juris-
diction of the country in which the claim is made. This is, however, both
justified and manageable as it is open to the importer to make his own
arrangements for his protection with his supplying manufacturer. Producers
of so called 'own brand' goods are also liable notwithstanding that they do not
'put the products into circulation' but this also is not unreasonable.

An important provision of the directive is that it reverses the burden of
proof in regard to the defence that the product was not defective when the
manufacturer put it into circulation. However, while the need to prove a
negative places an onerous burden on the manufacturer, it does not provide a
commensurate advantage to the plaintiff as most cases are settled out of court
at a point before the need arises to prove the case either way. Thus, if a
manufacturer denies liability on plausible grounds this, in effect, re-reverses
the burden by forcing the plaintiff to dispute those grounds.

Finally, the directive places limits on times within which claims can be made
and an overall limit on the extent of a single manufacturer's liability in terms
of money. There is a limit of 3 years placed on the time within which a claim
can be made and this runs from the date that the injury is attributed to the
product, which is in line with our own statutory limit. Much more contro-

versial, however, is the period of 10 years which is fixed as the time, after marketing the product, within which it can give rise to an actionable injury. This is indeed a blunderbuss and despairing sort of provision which does not attempt to take account of either the difference in the working life of different types of goods or the difference of useful life between different qualities of the same type of product. However, so far as we are concerned the limit is of little relevance as few of our products have a purported life of more than 5 years let alone 10. It does, however, suggest that all medicinal products should be dated as, in the absence of an expiry date, liability could possibly be held to extend to 10 years.

The most controversial limitation of all is the maximum of 25 million units of account, which amounts to about £17 million, for which a producer can be liable for any one incident and it appears that an incident is to be regarded as the aggregate of all the injuries arising from a single cause throughout the Common Market. This creates all kinds of questions which have yet to be answered in relation to catastrophes where the sum involved exceeds the limit. Is the limit to operate on the first come first served principle so that any claims decided after the limit has been reached go uncompensated? If it is we would very soon be back into the situation of 'trial by newspaper' in which the manufacturer is forced by public opinion to pay in excess of the limit. Alternatively, if the sum is to be evenly distributed over all those injured in proportion to the extent of their injuries this would mean waiting until all claims had been heard before any could be compensated. In the case of latent injury this would be even more intolerable. Aggregate claims in excess of the £17 million limit are surely a case in which governments must step in with their support to ensure that justice is done to all alike.

CHANGES PROPOSED IN SECOND DRAFT DIRECTIVE

I only propose to consider changes between the first and second drafts insofar as they affect liability for death and personal injury. Several of the proposals relate to damage to property which we believe should anyhow be excluded on the grounds that the present law and facilities for the insurance of property are already adequate.

The first difference is the exclusion of primary agricultural products. This is of little significance to us except to note that it will not exclude drugs of vegetable origin since these are invariably processed by one or more industrial operations which has the effect of barring them from the exclusion.

The second is the exclusion of craft and artistic products. This is interesting as it has been suggested that this could enable pharmacists and dispensing doctors to escape liability for the preparations they dispense. The attitude of the industry to this is that, while we do not suggest that simple operations such as the counting and re-packaging of tablets in suitable containers or the dilution of products in accordance with our recommendations should attract liability, all persons who engage in the actual preparation of a medicine should be equally liable. Otherwise there would be an insupportable discrimination between the rights of patients suffering similar injuries from dispensed and manufactured products. Even more important in this context is that non-commercial institutions such as hospitals should not be excluded from liability on the grounds that their small-scale manufactured products are not 'industrially' produced, or not put into commercial circulation.

Next we have a welcome change. This is in the definition of defect which now only applies to products when used for the purpose for which they are apparently intended. Thus, if they are misused there is no liability for resultant injury. However, a disturbing point to note is that the official explanatory memorandum states that the use of the word 'apparently' means that the use is determined by public opinion and not by the producer.

The new provision for liability for contributory fault up to the full extent of the damage is also to be welcomed as this will protect from loss arising from the failure of patients to use products correctly.

Less welcome is the addition of non-pecuniary damage, such as pain and suffering, in the factors comprising 'damages', as this is one of the most controversial and most often misapplied elements of damages in injury cases.

Finally, we have a rather sinister looking change which is the one giving powers to the Council to raise or even eliminate the limit of total liability of the producer. If this power is used only to adjust the limit in line with changes of exchange rates in order to keep it at the same level in real terms, it is reasonable. If on the other hand it is used to raise the limit in real terms it will have the effect of increasing the level of uninsurable risk attaching to high risk products such as our own.

Before leaving the matter of changes in the draft directive we should take note of two changes which were recommended by the European Parliament but did not find favour with the Commission, as these were of particular importance to the pharmaceutical industry. The most important of these was the proposal to allow the 'state of the art' defence. The rejection of this means that we will be fully liable for development defects, including latent defects, even though we could not have detected the defect by any means known to science. The second rejection was the proposal that the liability of the producer, who discovers a defect after he has put the product on the market, could be mitigated by taking all reasonable steps to withdraw the product from the market and to warn those likely to use products already purchased. This means that the producer has no means of reducing his liability in respect of products distributed beyond his ability to recall them, or by directly warning those who have them in their possession.

Summing up the significant changes between the first and second drafts there are two to the producers' advantage, three to their disadvantage, one neutral, and two big ones that got away!

DISADVANTAGES OF STRICT LIABILITY TO THE INDUSTRY

The risk of uninsurable liability must be the greatest of the 'costs' with respect to the continued viability of companies. Faced with an uninsured claim of the magnitude of thalidomide all but five or six companies in the industry would go to the wall and this would lead to a loss of investor's confidence in the whole industry. It would also mean that those injured by that company's product would go uncompensated. The question therefore arises as to the extent to which the industry can cover itself by insurance, and here there have been some rather bland assurances from the insurance market that they can handle these needs and are preparing to do so, albeit at a price. In a recent report to the Department of Trade in which the British Insurance Association gave estimates of premium increases to take account of strict liability in a wide range of industries they refused to give a figure for the pharmaceutical industry but said it would be in excess of a three-fold increase whilst other estimates given have been as high as five- and six-fold. But this does not necessarily mean that cover will be available for everyone even at these prices and there is reason to question the insurers' statements that they can meet the industry's needs, quite apart from the fact that there is no way in which they can give cover for unlimited liability at any price. These misgivings are supported by the recent disclosure of an extract from the evidence of the British Insurance Association to the Pearson Commission. This extract is very significant and it reads:

'In addition we must also enter the caveat that there are certain products, such as vaccines and drugs, with a potential for injury which is:
  (a) to a degree inevitable (for example, the known incidence of brain damage arising out of smallpox vaccination) and/or
  (b) beyond the bounds of present human knowledge (for example, the ultimate effects of ingesting a new drug over many years).

To impose on producers what is close to a strict liability in respect of injury caused by such potentials is, we submit, fraught with problems. We appreciate that we are entering into a very difficult area of definition and interpretation, but unless any change in the law relating to liability for injury recognizes these special features of certain products, we have reservations as to the extent to which producers and their insurers will be able to provide the financial support on which any system of liability ultimately depends. Special measures such as those discussed later in this memorandum may be necessary.'

These special measures are not identified as the full evidence submitted to the Pearson Commission was not published. It would not be surprising, however, if at least one of them came very close to the partial government support to cover catastrophe risks, that was proposed in the ABPI submission to Pearson.

Another very disquieting and also recent development on the question of insurance prospects is that an important firm of brokers who carry quite a lot of product liability cover for medicines have just informed their policy holders that they will not in future be prepared to underwrite liability for eight named drugs, and these include some of the most widely used. Judging from the identities of these drugs in relation to published horror stories it would appear that the documentary evidence on which the exclusions are based has been derived from the *Daily Mirror* and the BBC 'Nationwide' programme, and perhaps *Reader's Digest* thrown in to give the evidence international authority! However, this is not a joking matter, as it is representative of a problem often found in dealing with insurers on questions of drug risk assessment, which is that their skill in actuarial science is not matched by their understanding of medical subject matter. Attempts to communicate with laymen are impeded by the fact that the drug industry is an interested party and they do not too readily accept the explanations and assurances that are given.

The next point in the list of 'costs' is the further escalation of safety testing that will follow on the heels of strict liability and the monetary costs that will go with it. After a certain level of safety testing has been reached further safety is only achieved on a rapidly diminishing return, and I would say that we have already passed the point at which the cost and time involved in further testing could more usefully be applied in the interests of the community to the search for new drugs. Government is as well aware of this as are the manufacturing companies but when claims start rising under strict liability, as inevitably they will, and the media start going to town on them, government will want to show that they are doing something about it. It is then that they will turn to more mandatory safety testing to demonstrate their concern and require an extra year here and an additional animal species there.

As a direct consequence of the additional safety testing will come a further erosion of patent life on new chemical entities, and looking at this in purely financial terms it is probably the most worrying of all the 'costs' in regard to the future viability of the pharmaceutical industry. Companies are already using up something approaching half the 20-year life of a patent in developing the average new product and in some cases considerably more. As each further factor delaying the marketing of a new product arises so their capacity to utilize monopoly protection to recover research and development costs is further depleted. There is obviously a critical point in time during the 20-year life of a patent at which research can no longer be self-financing, and let us be under no illusion that at that point the private sector pharmaceutical industry in its present form dies.

Next, there is likely to be a sharp deterioration in the relationship with the medical profession, particularly with general practitioners, through their un- avoidable entanglement in the manufacturers legal problems. When liability becomes strict and the manufacturer is denied the defence that he has taken all reasonable care, and he is legally prevented from relying on the fact that the state has given him an official seal of approval in the form of a Product

Licence, the defence that we have given due notification of the hazard which caused the injury will assume a greatly elevated importance to us. The problem is that the hazard is notified to the doctor through data sheets and other literature but it is the patient who is injured and will claim the right to have been warned. How this communication gap is to be bridged and indeed whether it is in the patient's interest that it should be bridged with all the information given to the doctor is already the subject of controversial debate. The selective notification proposed by the Department of Health in the draft revised Data Sheet Regulations is not an answer which will be acceptable to the industry. By advising doctors which warnings they should pass on, one is in effect advising them which they need not pass on, and there is no more lethal instrument with which to commit corporate suicide in a situation of strict liability. However, if some satisfactory solution is not found to the problem of patient information it is inevitable that doctors will be drawn into product liability suits through having frustrated the manufacturer's defence by not having warned the patient of the hazard which caused the injury. Whether manufacturers like it or not they will be forced by their duty to their shareholders, or by their insurers who have a contractual right to conduct their defence, to serve a third-party notice on the prescribing doctor. This is the legal device by which a defendant sucks in a co-defendant who he believes may have contributed to his liability, and it is not calculated to improve relationships between the profession and the industry.

There will probably be an expatriation of the early marketing of new products, since this is the period when latent defects are most likely to become manifest, to countries where their legal system is less adversely disposed against the innovating manufacturer. This will undoubtedly be associated with an increase in the rate of the flight of clinical pharmacology and clinical trials from the UK, which is already well under way because of the extraordinarily suffocating controls in the form of the Clinical Trial Certificate. This will not be because of any change in legal liability for clinical trial injuries, as the pharmaceutical industry already effectively accepts strict liability in this area for both moral and self-interested reasons. It will rather be because the launching of new products will become more of a progressive evolution from clinical trials to first marketing, linked by the bridge of some form of post-marketing surveillance, than two separate operations divided by a launching date, and it will simply be more convenient and efficient to carry out the two operations in the same overseas country.

My final point on the negative side for the industry is that manufacturers will become much more involved in litigation. This does not necessarily mean that there will be a lot more court cases as the industry will undoubtedly continue to pursue its sensibly pragmatic policy of settling claims it finds itself unable to reject. But undoubtedly there will be many more claims, which will involve legal staff in a large amount of executive time in preparing defences. They will also involve persons like those from research in equally large amounts of time in collecting, and feeding their legal colleagues with the necessary scientific evidence and then explaining it all to them! However, there is one comfort in that it will never be as bad over here as it is in America. Leaving aside some of the apocryphal stories such as poodles being cooked in infra-red ovens, which have probably arisen from rejected claims having graduated to decided cases through repeated hearsay, there are three extra-ordinary features of American civil law which happily we do not have over here, though one of them does exist in Ireland. The first and probably the most important is the contingency fee system which gives the plaintiff's lawyer a cut of anything up to 30% of the damages won in a successful case and nothing if he loses. The effect of this is that a prospective plaintiff can embark on a case with nothing to lose and everything to gain subject only to the lawyer's confidence that he has a case. The second feature is that product liability cases are tried in most American states by juries who also decide the level of damages, and it is well recognized that juries respond readily and remuner-atively to a silver-tongued attorney. In the UK, but not in Ireland, such cases are tried by judges who tend to be less responsive to tear-jerking rhetoric. The third difference is in the award of punitive damages over and above the value of the injury damage as judged by the court. These damages, which are awarded amazingly to the plaintiff rather than the state, are really based on the measure of the fury against the defendant company into which public opinion can be whipped by the news media, and they can be extremely heavy as occurred in the Ford Pinto case. While it is unlikely that these three legal Americanisms will be imported into the United Kingdom there are two other transatlantic developments which give a little more cause for concern. The first is the development of the concept of class actions. These are cases in which suits are brought against multiple defendants on the basis that whilst no member of a group can be individually implicated all the members are jointly implicated on the grounds that being engaged in the same enterprise each of them, but for chance, might have caused the damage. The classic precedent is the case of a shooting party in which one member was injured by being accidentally shot by another member who could not be identified, and all the members were successfully sued by the injured member and shared equally in the payment of damages. This concept has recently been extended into class actions against all the manufacturers of a generic drug in which the actual manufacturer of the product which caused the injury cannot be traced. The other worrying development is discussion which has now been going on for some time on a possible convention on the reciprocal enforcement of judge-ments, whereby judgements made in American courts would be enforceable also in English courts and vice versa. In the light of American civil legal practice such a convention would be much more worrying to us in the UK than to Americans but the many forms that the convention could take, if in fact it is adopted at all, are so varied and controversial that it would be premature to lose any sleep over it at this time.

However, the situation remains that strict liability will bring with it a substantial increase in demands on legal services. Lawyers specializing in drug cases will be at a premium, so perhaps the best course for anyone who is bright enough to graduate in two professions will be to become a barrister/toxicologist!

ADVANTAGES TO THE INDUSTRY

I propose to deal with the possible benefits to the industry more briefly as they are much more speculative than the 'costs'. First, there will be an acceleration of the transition from bulk to original pack dispensing which has been gaining momentum over the last 25 years. This is because as few people as possible will want to become involved in anything which might be regarded as an interference with the manufacturer's product, which might thereby attract part of his liability. This is not only a matter of purity or contamination through handling or storage but also what is said about it on the pack, or some other feature of its presentation. In the definition of a 'defective product' in the second draft of the EEC directive account has to be taken of 'all the circumstances, including its presentation'. Consequently, any changes made in the presentation of the product, particularly in the matter of warnings passed on, or not passed on, could become a legal issue in a liability case. Also, original packs provide a better identification of the manufacturer of the product than dispensing from bulk into packs bearing only the dispensing pharmacist's name.

This leads on to the second possible benefit which is that there could be a slowing or even a reversal of the trend towards generic prescribing on the same grounds that the prescribing of specialities identifies the manufacturer not only at the time that the product is supplied and used but also in the memory, and possibly the records, of both the prescriber and the patient. One of the main weaknesses of strict liability from the consumer's point of view is that while it removes the need to prove negligence against the manufacturer it does nothing to help the plaintiff to identify his defendant. Bearing in mind that records are hardly ever kept of the makers of products used to fill prescriptions, and that the maker could be different for successive prescriptions of the same drug, a product prescribed by its trademark could provide the evidence needed to establish a claim. Consequently, there could well be patient pressure for more prescribing by trademarks rather than generic names, and it could well be in the doctor's interest to respond to that pressure.

Subject to clarification of 'business purposes' and 'industrial processing' as qualifications of products attracting strict liability, there will probably be an ending of small-scale manufacture of anything but the simplest preparations in hospitals, and a return of the business to the industry. Hospital manufacture has already been hit by the Department of Health's policy of requiring hospitals to conform to the standards of the Guide to Good Manufacturing Practice, and strict liability could well put paid to it altogether.

The limit of total liability at £17 million could be said to be a benefit to us as this is well below some of the total settlements that have been made, here and in the U.S.A., but this is overshadowed by the new power to raise or eliminate the limit as mentioned earlier. Also, it will not stop the media from persecuting companies for more in cases where the limit is reached.

There will probably be a reduction in the unorthodox use of pharmaceutical products for fear of the doctor attracting the manufacturer's potential liability to himself. Doctors will probably be advised by their professional bodies and protection societies to be more circumspect in prescribing products outside the range of the manufacturer's recommendations whether by way of dosage, purpose or against published contra-indications. There will also probably be an end to such things as prescriptions for equal parts of Actifed and Benylin Linctuses.

CONCLUSIONS

Some conclusions can be drawn from the problems outlined and these suggest matters to which the pharmaceutical industry should now be directing its attention and whatever persuasive influences it can bring to bear. It has fought hard to persuade those who will have the last word that strict liability will bring to society more losses than gains when it is applied to medicines. In this the industry has a number of influential supporters such as the Royal College of Physicians and the Medicines Commission but largely due to influences from other EEC countries, strict liability will probably have to be accepted as a fact. Medicines are unlikely to be excluded if only because the pharmaceutical industry is blamed as the trigger of the movement towards strict liability. However good their arguments may be and however much support they may have for achieving it, the exclusion of medicines will probably prove to be politically unacceptable. The manufacturers should therefore now turn their attention to means of coping with the problems strict liability will create and try to secure such modifications as will avoid some of the worst of the long-term disadvantages.

The first problem to be answered is how to cope with the uninsurable catastrophe if government will not buttress the top layer of the risk and insurers cannot be persuaded to provide cover at prices which more reasonably reflect the actual risk than the premiums they now contemplate. If adequate cover cannot be had or the costs or other conditions and exclusions are so onerous as to render the insurance unacceptable the industry will be driven to turn to some other means of protecting themselves. One possibility to be considered is to set up a 'captive' insurance organisation, staffed with both insurance and scientific experts and funded by the companies who insure with it. There are many successful examples of this and it is well known that one or two of the largest firms in the pharmaceutical industry already run their own 'captives'. Another possibility which is being tried in America is the grouping together of companies to negotiate block insurance schemes direct with the insurance market thereby spreading the risk over a broader cross-section of an industry, hopefully at a lower cost. Yet another is the formation of 'risk retention groups' whereby a number of companies group together to provide mutual cover funded from their own resources and backed by pledges in the form of contingent liabilities against their own assets, without the formality of setting up an actual 'captive'. This device is now being so seriously pursued in the United States that new insurance law is being considered to regulate the activities of 'risk retention groups'.

The next most important problem to be solved is the highly controversial question of how much information should be properly transmitted to patients and then to ensure that the EEC directive is implemented in such a way that it does not leave anyone in a legally untenable position. Those in the industry have argued, on good grounds, that their duty ends with the provision of sufficient information to the patient to ensure that he knows how to take the medicine correctly and safely. They go on to say that any disclosure to the patient of adverse reaction hazards is a matter for the discretion of the doctor, and the manufacturer's duty ends with the disclosure of this information to him. This is surely reasonable but in a situation of strict liability, in which hazard notification becomes all-important to the companies' defence, the doctor will be faced with an impossible burden. To lay it on his shoulders without modification will inevitably lead to doctors being involved in litigation between patients and manufacturers and will result in the practice of defensive medicine. In the House of Lords debate on product liability, Lord Smith said, 'A doctor who feels so unreasonably threatened that he might think first of his own protection and only second of the best interests of his patient is a bad doctor and we must do nothing to encourage such a situation'. It seems that there is no other answer to this problem than to provide an express exemption in the legislation to excuse the doctor passing on anything he considers in his own discretion is not in the interests of his patient to pass on, and for the manufacturer to be excluded from liability if he has given notification of the hazard in question to the doctor. Such a solution would be anathema to the consumerists who are determined, it seems, to have all the information they need to work out their own risk–benefit analysis on every treatment they are prescribed. This being so, perhaps the sooner the pharmaceutical companies get down to the job of persuading them that this is against their own long-term interests the better it will be for all concerned.

Finally, it is society alone who will determine how much safety it really wants and is going to have. The pharmaceutical industry must therefore do all it can to make society aware that drugs are inherently unsafe, and that the pursuit of safety into areas of unattainability reaches a point at which the risk–benefit equation yields a loss in terms of the alleviation of human suffering.

Discussion of
Chapters 9 and 10

CHAIRMAN: Dr T. I. WRIGLEY

Mr A. J. Clarke (Fisons): Dr Dayan appears to have an unreasonable bias against the use of animal experimentation. I was surprised at his pessimistic attitude, and at the poor contribution he appears to feel that his profession is making to safety evaluation. He seems to suggest that if it was not for regulatory bodies, he would not bother to do any animal experiments.

    The extrapolation of data from animals to man is difficult, and it is not 100% successful. Nevertheless, there have been considerable benefits from animal testing in reducing the risk to man. Had Dr Dayan presented some numerical data, this would have been more supportive. One of the contributors has recommended papers published some years ago in the Proceedings of the European Society of Drug Toxicity which give more support to the use of animal testing.

Dr Dayan: I am sorry if I have given a wrong impression. I am not decrying the use of animal experimentation. Far from it. But I am decrying the unthinking use of the multiplication of numbers and types of testing beyond what I would regard as being sensible limits. I did refer to the European Society's publications but they are now some years old. If one looks for further information in the literature. I am sorry to say that it does not exist, with the exception of two papers from the NCI showing the direct predictability of action of cytotoxic agents between animals and man which is hardly surprising. It is a very restricted form of toxicity testing indeed.

Prof. C. T. Dollery (Royal Postgraduate Medical School): I very much enjoyed Mr Spink's presentation.

    For the last few months there has been a study group at the CIBA Foundation, which includes a member of the Law Commission, looking at this issue largely from the standpoint of the effect it would have in a research context, including clinical trials after the drug was marketed. The sort of things that perplex one are these. Suppose a trial takes place and let me take as an example the clofibrate trial. I do not know whether participants are familiar with it but I shall briefly sketch out the two questions that arise. This was a trial of the use of clofibrate to try to prevent myocardial infarction. When the results came out they showed increased incidence of gallstones in those who had had the drug. That was already a known or suspected effect of clofibrate. But let us take for argument that it had not been previously known and it had emerged from that trial. There was also a placebo group and there were gallstones amongst them as well, but there were about three times as many gallstones among the people who got the drug. I suppose under a strict liability situation all of those who got the drug and developed gallstones, not having been previously warned against or having previously known (we shall assume) would have been compensated, although the reality is that probably only about two-thirds of them really had got gallstones because of the drug. The other one-third had got gallstones because they would have got gallstones anyway. But there is no way known to medicine of discriminating between gallstones that were caused by being predisposed to gallstones and gallstones caused by clofibrate.

That question is difficult enough, and in a sense perhaps one would say that one would have to compensate everybody. But also in that trial there was a hint that the overall mortality of the treated group from many causes was increased. Would that mean, if it was taken to be true, that everybody who was treated with the drug and who died could be compensated? Inherent in the idea of strict liability is that cause can be established. But in many instances of real or apparent toxicity, to establish causality is extremely difficult when the toxic effect mimics an existing disease.

Mr Spink: As Professor Dollery has referred to a clinical trial product, if the product is not yet on the market strict liability will not apply. The directive refers only to products put into circulation, that is, into commercial circulation.

Prof. Dollery: It was in commercial circulation.

Mr Spink: Fair enough. I make that point because it is relevant to the issue of clinical trials. But perhaps not so relevant for another reason I shall mention in a moment.

The second point is that if a product is commercially available and it is subject to the directive, then we have to consider what the directive does. All the directive does, and all strict liability means, is that the need to prove that the manufacturer was negligent in order to establish a claim against him has been removed. The position regarding the establishment of causation is precisely the same, and although I do not understand technically the example that Professor Dollery gave, I can see that it is the sort of example about which lawyers would just love to get together and spend days fighting to thrash out whether it was the drug or the other possible causes that had led to the injury. I would say that the situation will be no better for the individual than it is now under negligence liability. He will still have to prove cause. This is not one of the parts of the new rules, so to speak, in which the burden of proof is reversed and thus the situation will be very little changed.

Having said all that, I said in my paper that manufacturers have been prepared to accept strict liability for a very long time, if not ever since they have been in the business of doing clinical trials. But there is a moral aspect here. If patients volunteer to be guinea-pigs and they get hurt, one must do something about it. It is not a bit of good, and certainly not morally right that one should be able to plead that one was not negligent. If one did, one would not just be persecuted by the press, one would be crucified by them. This is perhaps not unreasonable.

Prof. Dollery: While I agree that what Mr Spink says is eminently fair and reasonable, and it is easy to implement in a case of a study in normal volunteers who are relatively healthy people, unlikely to suddenly die or get seriously ill, where there is therefore a fairly strong presumption that if they do so during the course of an experiment, that this is in some way causally related to it. It is not the case when trying out treatments for people who are desperately ill. The example that comes to mind would be that of a drug designed to prevent an arrhythmia of the heart action in a patient who has had a heart attack, where there would be quite a high mortality, perhaps as high as 10 or 15% over a period of a month, and one knows that drugs used for that purpose could as part of their action quite often produce death by themselves causing an arrhythmia. One can see almost limitless opportunities for agument there, with it being impossible to show decisively, one way or the other, whether the drug was responsible.

Mr Spink: I can understand this and that there could be cases where patients were actually killed by a drug. But such patients would have died anyway so it was a fair risk to take. This is the sort of thing that would be taken into account by a court in awarding damages, if any. But let us face it. We as a company would not allow such a case to come to court. We would reach a settlement between ourselves and the patient, probably with the guidance of the governors of the hospital. I believe most hospitals have Ethical Committees which deal with the problems that arise from clinical trials. I think a settlement would be a sum that would be acceptable all round, and fair in the circumstances, taking account of the point that Professor Dollery has made.

Dr L. Z. Saunders (Smith, Kline and French Research): I should like to support Dr Dayan, which means opposing Mr Clarke. I did not think Dr Dayan said we should stop animal testing, but he is the most outspoken example I have seen amongst the small fraternity of those of us who do test in animals, who is modest and shows the proper humility about what we can actually deliver. Part of the reason that the whole process of drug development is being held up is because, for reasons I find inexplicable in medical history, somebody has over-sold the notion that we can deliver and has got a lot of people to believe him. The public believes it. The press believes it. Many politicians either believe it or feel that they can get elected by pretending to believe it. And we are now in a position where those few tests that Dr Dayan showed on the board whose limitations are great – and nobody is more aware of that than those of us who are involved in the work – hold the key to safety. It is a product that everybody wants and I think reasonably. But we do not hold the key to it and no more do the tests.

Dr Dayan said, too, that he does not want to regard toxicology as pure morbid anatomy. That implies to me that in the UK some people do. I am a morbid anatomist. I regard toxicology as having a higher calling. It is really pharmacology done at higher doses and for longer periods than most pharmacologists use.

We had an example. Professor Breckenridge showed a table of drugs that have very important applications which were not dis-covered until they were put into the hands of the clinical pharma-cologist. These were drugs that had already been in man. I am not sure, but I think most of them had not had the second action predicted in animals at all. Most pharmacologists identify useful actions in animals. They are happy if 30% of those turn out to have the same action in man. So in pharmacology *per se* people are humble. They do not expect that every rat will be the key to a new useful agent in man. Yet in toxicology, which if my definition is accepted is only pharmacology at higher doses, the expectation perversely is the opposite. If we could find out how that arose, how well-meaning but misguided colleagues come to place so much faith in us, perhaps we could do something to reverse the trend. I too feel very guilty about the increasing percentage of the research and development budget that is being thrust on my department, and I feel it could be better spent in almost any other part of the research process than in drug safety evaluation.

Dr Dayan: I am very grateful to Dr Saunders for his support and very honoured to have it, and I accept everything he says except for the definition of pharmacology. Pharmacology to me is such a transient ephemeral state – (*laughter*).

Dr L. Z. Saunders: If somebody says do something that is socially useful, the burden of proof has to rest with whoever makes the contention. I cannot be manoeuvred into a posture where I have to do something, merely because I have been asked, that I think is of limited value. I shall not say worthless, and Dr Dayan did not say worthless, but, rather, of very limited value. Merely because I have identified it as being of limited value, no one can say we have nothing better so let us do it anyway. That is precisely how we got into this mess.

Since I find there are a few bureaucrats in the audience, which I did not realize this morning, I should like to reassure them that bureaucracy does not just exist in government. It exists in pharmaceutical houses, of all places. There are plenty of self-serving toxicologists who have foisted these tests off, they have promoted them in public. The pamphlet to be found at the registration desk, *Trends in Pharmacological Sciences*, has a leading article by Professor Bucher of the university of Basel, who puts the finger right where the blame is. It is people like ourselves who have thrust those things on us, and people like Professor Grahame-Smith who get stuck with the results. He gets blamed if his committee says to do several unsubstantiated mutagenicity tests. There are a lot of people who would like to give themselves job security, and they are by no means all in government.

Mr M. Crawford (Sandoz Ltd): Could I take up the gauntlet put down by Dr Dayan and Dr Saunders in that a proposed regulation should define the objectives and not the means of testing. I endorse this statement very strongly as an ex-regulator. Let me try to put up what I regard as a satisfactory aim for toxicity testing, which would have been acceptable to the Australian authority when I was there, and may be a useful guideline for other authorities.

I submit that the primary aim of toxicity testing is to predict the likely problems, the likely target organ problems in man, and I further submit that secondary to this one approach is to endeavour to define in animal studies the ratio of the pharmacologically effective dose to the toxic dose of a new drug in a species, one species, with a comparable metabolism, and preferably comparable pharmacokinetic handling of the drug, as man. This requires some re-phasing. The first clinical pharmacology in man will obviously have to be run concurrently with the pharmacokinetic experiments in animals and with the metabolic experiments in animals. But given this re-phasing, may we not be able to define a more sensible and shorter programme, and yet one which will be acceptable to the authorities as well as to ourselves?

Dr Dayan: I would certainly accept the broad principle of what Mr Crawford describes. Yes. We can quarrel about numbers, but that is immaterial, perhaps.

Could I amplify a point I passed over rather lightly. That is the difficulty or at the moment, I believe, the impossibility of attempting to quantify certain phenomena. I am aware of a drug at Wellcome that I am mulling over at the moment. It will be used, potentially, for the treatment of a particularly unpleasant disease in which the serious effects become apparent maybe 5 or 10 years after the inception of the complaint, and which may cause death in perhaps 20% of sufferers after another 4 or 5 years. I am speaking of a very chronic disorder. The existing treatments for the disease are poor. They have perhaps a 30–40% success rate at the very best, and they are associated with very severe, quite crippling – literally crippling – side-effects. The drug that we are looking at, or that I am thinking about, may be more effective if judged by animal tests, but it will have to be given as a dose that will be very close to that, which may well cause a degree of liver damage. How on earth can one balance the risk of liver damage, the risk of crippling side-effects of existing treatment and the risks of that slowly progressive disease? That is the sort of circumstance where I do not know what one does. Does one throw the papers to the wind and see which way they come down, perhaps!

11
The effect on world medicine

J. F. DUNNE

Within a healthy, vigorous, socially-conscious society drug safety can readily be portrayed as a highly evocative subject, but those who are sick or debilitated are likely to take a more indulgent view. It is inevitable that biologically active substances administered in pharmacological dosages will possess a potential to inflict harm as well as to offer benefit. Indeed, the prescribing doctor is not only required to balance as rigorously as any drug regulatory agency the benefits and risks of the drugs that he uses, he also needs to remain constantly alert to the possibility of unanticipated reactions. In turn, the community has to accept a measure of risk as the price of therapeutic advance, although it has every right to expect that professional skills will be dutifully applied to minimize the dangers.

Few would deny that on balance, society has been exceedingly well served by the pharmaceutical industry over the past forty years. In the affluent regions of the world bacterial diseases and their latent sequelae have been eliminated as major causes of mortality. The management of tuberculosis has been transformed. Wound sepsis is no longer a scourge of surgical wards, while advances in anaesthetic and immunological techniques have considerably broadened the scope of surgical practice. Not least, new classes of psychotropic drugs have revolutionized the treatment and understanding of mental illness. The morbidity related to the psychoses, the mortality of depression, and the need for prolonged hospitalization of many afflicted patients have each been impressively reduced.

In less privileged regions, however, much remains to be achieved. The population explosion which is estimated to have placed an additional 1000 million individuals in the world over the past 15 years is destined shortly to outstrip available food supplies unless radically new approaches to contraception can be devised. Despite the availability of a variety of effective anti-malarial drugs and concerted efforts to control mosquito vectors, malaria continues to claim more than a million lives each year. Resistant strains of the parasite are liable to threaten the utility of effective compounds as soon as they are developed and the disease is again encroaching into many regions from which it had been successfully eradicated during the time that widespread use of DDT offered an acceptable means of vector control. Unless a satisfactory vaccine against the disease can now be developed, little amelioration of the existing situation can be expected.

Indeed, wherever new irrigation schemes enter into operation in the tropics in a determined effort to raise food production, water-dependent diseases tend to escape from control. Schistosomiasis offers the most persuasive example in that more than 200 million individuals are now estimated to be infected. The recent development of a number of effective anti-schistosomal compounds offers the prospect of more efficient treatment in this instance, but the management of other serious diseases, including onchocerciasis and trypanosomiasis, has remained essentially unchanged for the past 40 years.

The prospect for adequate control of leprosy remains similarly bleak. The number of dapsone-resistant cases is estimated to be increasing in some areas by as much as 3% annually, and whereas rifampicin and clofazimine may offer therapeutically-effective alternatives, their cost precludes their use in community-scale management of the disease in endemic areas.

Admittedly drugs and vaccines do not offer the only viable approach to the containment of transmissible diseases in developing countries. Undernutrition, poor housing, overcrowding and contaminated water supplies all contribute in important measure to the general health problem. Nonetheless, the availability of specific, effective therapeutic and prophylactic agents could reasonably be expected to transform the prospects for their ultimate control. However, the reality is that, although more than 2000 million US dollars are invested each year in drug research, work on the chemotherapy of tropical disease has dwindled to the point of extinction in most companies. Whereas a few do maintain an active interest, only a small number of the new compounds currently synthesized within the pharmaceutical industry are systematically screened for activity against these diseases.

The situation is particularly ominous since, through no particular design of its own, the research-based pharmaceutical industry has created a virtual monopoly in the development of new drugs. It alone now commands the technology and resources required to undertake this work. But, as economic pressures bite upon individual companies, the range of research options regarded as practicable progressively diminishes. Many factors contribute to these constraints, but central to the issue is the fact that at a time of rampant inflation, the amount of developmental work required to place a new product on the market in the industrialized countries has tended to increase. It is, of course, understandable, in the absence of reliably predictive animal models, that regulatory guidelines for safety testing of new compounds should tend to expand to match the capacity of the pharmaceutical industry to respond. But it is also inevitable, as long as development costs continue to rise and the effective patent life of new products is further eroded, that the industry should respond by adopting a less ambitious attitude toward innovative research. Real health needs are at risk of being disregarded, effort is increasingly directed to capture stakes in well-established markets, and close competitors are forced into aggressive and damaging competition.

The developed world, in which bacterial and parasitic diseases have been so effectively controlled, is better placed to accept the consequences of this situation than the developing regions, but we should all be aware of some of the more serious implications of current trends. At a time when interest in the possibility of successful vaccine therapy against some of the major parasitic diseases that are endemic in the tropical world is gaining momentum, and when the World Health Organization is launching an expanded immunization programme throughout the developing world, several major companies with long experience in the development and manufacture of vaccines are discontinuing all activity in this field as a result of reduced profitability. Of similar concern is the constraining effect of current onerous long-term toxicity requirements applied to new steroid contraceptives by many of the established regulatory authorities at a time when further research into injectable contraceptives is a matter of highest priority in many developing countries. An injectable contraceptive is regarded as the corner-stone of family-planning policy in many developing countries. The only product of this type that is as yet commercially available, is not considered suitable for routine contraceptive purposes by regulatory authorities in many highly developed countries, but, within communities in which fetal and maternal mortality are greatly in excess of those prevailing in the affluent world, it has found wide acceptance. This situation has been interpreted by some as indicating that a double standard of safety has disingenuously been applied to products destined for the developing world. However, having regard to the realities of the situation, it is, perhaps, more constructively regarded as an illustration of the need to consider the risks and benefits of drug use in relation to specific community requirements rather than abstract or idealized global standards.

In this connection it is also relevant to recall that clioquinol, despite its undoubted implication in the SMON epidemic in Japan, is still widely used in the treatment of amoebiasis. It is by far the cheapest of the luminal amoebicides, and its apparent utility in a potentially dangerous condition is considered, particularly in the least-developed countries, to outweigh any recognized dangers. Similarly, reserpine, because of its low price, remains a popular treatment for hypertension in less affluent countries, regardless of doubts raised over the past few years that it may have marginal carcinogenic properties.

In those countries where almost half of the sadly-deficient health budget is already allocated to drug procurement, the choice for the individual patient frequently rests between economical treatment or no treatment. We may, in fact, be perpetrating a sad disservice in the developing world by attempting blindly to apply standards of drug development that were never intended to subserve its needs. The importance of exploring new approaches to contraception, or of introducing a vaccine against malaria is simply too pressing for the work to be geared inexorably to a 12-year development programme, which might well now be required to register such a product in a highly developed country, and the capital required to underwrite such programmes is clearly not likely to be forthcoming from private sources alone.

In order to meet this contingency many governments and independent funding agencies have been persuaded to offer generous support to two specialized programmes for which WHO functions as the executive agency. The first, relating to human reproduction is now well established, while the second, co-sponsored by the United Nations Development Programme and the World Bank, and directed to research and training in tropical disease, has attracted funds in excess of US$25 million in its fourth year of operation. The aims of the tropical disease programme obviously stray away from the commercially attractive areas of development that are of crucial importance to the survival of an independent research-based industry. Private institutions cannot be expected to survive by philanthropy, nonetheless an effective input from scientists within the pharmaceutical industry is likely to be critical to any success that may be achieved, and WHO is committed to fostering an integrated effort that will embrace private as well as public interests.

If collaboration between the pharmaceutical industry and WHO can provide the stimulus for improving facilities for the clinical testing of promising compounds and for co-ordinating the basic research effort, these programmes are likely to pay handsome dividends. Once the dual problems of population control and transmissible disease are ameliorated in the third world, all countries can expect to benefit from the economic development that would surely ensue.

12
Preclinical requirements

R. W. BRIMBLECOMBE

There is a regular debate, which recently has become somewhat more intense and wide-ranging, concerning the amount of information on a potential new medicine which should be available before it can be tested in human subjects and then before it can be marketed. The universality of this debate is exemplified by the fact that in Scrip of 9 February Mr Patrick Jenkin, the UK Secretary of State for Social Services, was quoted as expressing 'his concern at the drain of clinical evaluation work on new drugs away from the UK to other countries because of the very lengthy pre-CTC testing requirements'. Five days later in *Nature* of 14 February the leading article was entitled 'A dearth of new drugs'. This was a well-balanced article and it may be invidious to quote from it out of context but one particularly telling sentence read, 'There may be a case for cutting back on animal testing but if so, it is only on quantity in a limited number of respects and not at all on quality'.

Against this background of contemporary attention it is difficult to make points which have not already been discussed at length. However, there are some fundamental principles which, if agreed among all interested parties, might enable a fresh look to be taken at preclinical requirements and thus allow a package to be devised which will enable innovation to proceed without undue restriction but at the same time not expose patients to unacceptable risk. The main protagonists in this debate have been traditionally those who are responsible for developing new medicines, i.e. the pharmaceutical industry, and those who have the authority to permit their use in man in clinical trials or as marketed products, i.e. the regulatory agencies. However, at least two other groups have, or should have, an equal interest in this subject and those are the prescribing physicians and their patients. It is, then, these four groups who should agree on fundamental principles from which detailed recommendations or requirements could emerge.

The first principle is one with which few people would quarrel, i.e. that new effective and safe medicines should be made available to those who require them as expeditiously as possible. The second principle is, perhaps, not as readily acceptable, especially to laity, and that is that no medicine can be completely safe and completely effective. However, if the second principle is accepted it leads on to the third which involves the acceptance of a risk–benefit ratio which will vary according to the nature and severity of the disease to be treated, the availability of alternative methods of treatment and the nature and likely incidence of the risk.

These principles may appear trite and are certainly extremely familiar to all involved in the discovery and development of medicines whether in industry, academia, the clinic or the regulatory agencies. They are probably not as familiar to politicians or to the public and their acceptance by these groups may be essential if reasonable data requirements prior to testing of potential medicines in man are to be formulated.

There are some other principles, equally familiar to the cognoscenti but probably not as unanimously accepted among them, which need to be enunciated and agreed if any radical changes are to be made to existing preclinical data requirements. They are:

(1) Potential medicines should be tested in man at the earliest opportunity compatible with reasonable safety.

(2) The risk of unexpected adverse effects appearing (i.e. those which cannot be predicted from available preclinical data) increases as the population to which the medicine is administered increases in numbers and in variety but this is offset to a greater or lesser degree by increased experience with the new medicine in man.

(3) If principle 2 is accepted it follows that the initial tests on man in strictly controlled, carefully monitored studies with low doses probably represent the safest stage in the testing of a new medicine and thus it should be possible to carry out such studies with a minimum of preclinical data.

It must be recognized that of the investigations carried out, these early studies in man, be they in volunteers or in patients, represent the most critical checkpoint of all in the history of the development of a new medicine. Many compounds are discarded earlier than this for a variety of reasons but once this stage has been passed successfully resource allocation to the compound will increase incrementally so that it is to the benefit of all, including the potential patient, that this checkpoint be reached rapidly and most of the points made in this article address themselves to that issue although reference will also be made to requirements for later clinical trials and for marketing approval.

This leads on to principle 4 which states that the total package of preclinical data, whatever it is agreed to be, will not be required in toto until approval for marketing is sought and that lesser packages will be fed in to regulatory agencies step-wise through the various phases of the clinical testing of a new medicine. However, the fifth principle which is proposed states that data requirements must be based on validated scientific evidence rather than on intuitive feelings that more animals, more species and indeed more tests will lead to greater safety.

It is not the purpose of this article to debate in great detail the specifics of the various tests which should or should not be required but rather to raise some general issues and make some general proposals which may form the basis for agreement on specific tests. To summarize what has been stated so far, the main points are:

(1) Complete safety and complete efficacy are unattainable goals.
(2) Risk–benefit considerations should play a major role in defining pre-clinical requirements for new medicines.
(3) Tests in man should be carried out as early as possible.
(4) Early tests are probably the 'safest' tests and so should require a minimum of preclinical data.
(5) Data for extended clinical studies and for marketing approval should only be required if valid scientific reasons exist and emphasis should be placed on meticulous appraisal of data from *man*.

At this point it should be stated that the views and ideas expressed below are those of the author and not necessarily those of his company or of the industry in general but it is probable that a large number of individuals in the industry share at least some of them.

To begin with requirements for single dose studies. The object of such studies should be to obtain at least preliminary information on the pharmaco-kinetics of the compound, on its absorption, distribution, metabolism and excretion and, if this is feasible, on its efficacy. Historically the incidence of serious adverse reactions in such studies has, to the knowledge of the author, been very low indeed. Acute toxic effects, with some exceptions, tend to be species independent so that careful dose-ranging studies carried out for limited periods, over a wide range of doses, in, say, two species – a rodent and a non-rodent may well be sufficient to warrant administration of the compound to man. There appears to be little evidence that addition of other tests with consequent loss of time and increased expense adds appreciably to safety. This raises two important points. The first relates to access to evidence. The evidence comparing results of animal tests with subsequent experience in man lies to a limited extent in the archives of individual companies but to a much greater extent in the records of the regulatory agencies. It is the belief of the author that these agencies have a duty to produce this evidence and to make it available for analysis. Confidentiality is often used as an argument against producing such evidence but this could easily be overcome by preserving the anonymity of companies and compounds. The second objection is that to carry out such an analysis would be immensely expensive in terms of money and manpower. It is so much in the interest of the pharmaceutical industry to obtain this evidence that it seems highly probable that they would be prepared to give financial support to enable such an analysis to be carried out.

The second point concerns the value of carrying out additional tests at this stage in the development of a new medicine. An example of considerable interest at the present time is the use of so-called short-term or mutagenicity tests. The fact is that these tests have not been validated adequately. There is confusion about whether they are predictors of mutagenic effects or carcinogenic effects. No one appears to be very sure what constitutes a 'positive' result with a given compound and little account appears to be taken of the eventual human dose in interpreting results of such studies.

These tests are mentioned to exemplify a typical situation and to enable a suggestion to be made concerning the way in which industry and the regulatory agencies might work together to develop sensible and valid tests. The situation is typical in that an upsurge in interest in these tests, especially in academia, has drawn them to the attention of both the industry and the regulatory agencies. They have a superficial attraction, at least, to both parties in that they can be carried out relatively quickly and cheaply. The cost to industry in money and time is relatively small and equally the regulatory agencies feel that they are not imposing expensive and time-consuming procedures. These, however, are not really the important issues. The only valid question is whether the pursuance of these tests will give additional protection to patients in clinical trials or when the product is marketed. The answer to that question will take many years to emerge but in the meantime an arrangement could be made whereby companies would agree to supply to the agencies results from such tests on the understanding that *in the absence of other evidence to contraindicate the use of the compound* positive results would not necessarily bar the compound from clinical trial or even from the market place. To be specific, if the results from a three-generation fertility study and a life-span carcinogenicity study were negative these results would take precedence over results from short-term tests.

It is recognized that several studies have been completed, or are in progress, in an attempt to validate these tests but they tend to be carried out on biased samples of compounds, known carcinogens or mutagens or familiar compounds which have proved to be negative in conventional tests. What is not known is how predictive the short-term tests are for novel compounds and unless companies have some reassurance that results will not be used arbitrarily they have little or no incentive to volunteer to carry out such studies.

It is fairly certain that in other areas of toxicology a similar arrangement could be made. The fact is that the people most likely to develop more relevant tests are mainly in the pharmaceutical industry but their reluctance to work on such tests or to publish results from them is indicative not of a cavalier, irresponsible approach but of a fear that results might be misinterpreted and compounds rejected before adequate experience has been obtained with the tests. The request would obviously not be for a complete moratorium, regulatory agencies are always free to make any decision they see fit, but rather for a period of grace and for encouragement to experiment with novel test procedures.

Turning now to data requirements for later clinical trials and those required before marketing, these tend to be somewhat less controversial areas. The reason for this, however, may be that once a compound has been identified as a really viable candidate medicine in the animal studies, the pharmaceutical development and other preclinical requirements tend not to be rate-limiting and so are accepted perhaps with less questioning than they should be. Again there must be a mass of information in the files of regulatory agencies which, if extracted and analysed, could conceivably answer questions which are being asked and which result in different requirements by different regulatory agencies round the world. Typical questions would be:

(1) What should be the maximum duration of toxicity studies – 6 months – 1 year? Evidence is required to ascertain whether adverse effects detected in animals treated in excess of 6 months have been of relevance in subsequent use of the compound in man.

(2) Is the use of two species in long-term studies really justified? Is there good evidence that if a species metabolizes a compound reasonably similarly to man that human subjects gain any additional protection from adverse effects by testing in another species?

Other examples of questions of this kind could readily be quoted. The point to emerge is that companies obviously feel a need to be able to market medicines as early as possible and patients requiring these medicines would also welcome early availability. In the phases between early clinical studies and marketing, animal studies, though often not rate-limiting in terms of time, are expensive and resource-consuming and are carried out non-critically in the sense that their validity has not been evaluated using the mass of data now available. It is highly probable that the money and time spent on such studies would be much more relevantly spent in post-marketing surveillance schemes in which human subjects were scrutinized more carefully than is sometimes the case at present but certainly far less stringently than the rats, dogs and primates in chronic toxicity studies.

Thus, the main point to emerge in considering modification of preclinical data requirements are:

(1) Initially single-dose studies in man should require a minimum of subacute toxicity studies in two species.

(2) Preclinical data requirements for subsequent clinical studies and for marketing should be phased and should be subjected to scrutiny in the light of the mass of evidence now available in the files of regulatory agencies.

(3) Industry should be encouraged to develop possible new toxicological procedures without the fear that they will be imposed as requirements without adequate validation.

(4) During the period of clinical trials and post-marketing, meticulous attention should be given to results obtained in man. Given that only finite resources exist some of these could be diverted from animal studies of dubious validity and predictive value.

13
Post-marketing drug surveillance

W. H. W. INMAN

INTRODUCTION

It is regrettable that the term 'Post-marketing Surveillance' (PMS) has become synonymous in many minds with certain types of prescription-based monitoring, proposed during the last 5 years[1-5], to the exclusion of other methods that have been in effective use for many years. The yellow card system, 'monitored release' organized by manufacturers, case-control surveillance and scrutiny of the literature all make valuable contributions to PMS.

Although much criticized for its apparent failure to identify the practolol problem, the yellow card system has provided many effective early warnings during the past 16 years. Although only one report of conjunctivitis was received during nearly 4 years of practolol marketing, because doctors failed to recognize or report the reactions they were witnessing, once the problem was noted, the yellow cards rapidly proved their value. Many hundreds of reports flowed in and the CSM was able to make a rough but very useful estimate of the incidence of complications, which turned out to be unacceptably great. So we must not assume that new methods will replace the yellow cards.

Whatever new methods are introduced, whether the patients are studied prospectively or retrospectively, whether ascertainment is by the Prescription Pricing Authority, retail pharmacists or doctors, a number of barriers have to be overcome. No single method will be suitable for all drugs and so a variety of methods must be tested and we must be prepared for failures.

OBJECTIVES OF PMS

The ultimate objective of PMS is the assessment of the relative risks and relative benefits of drug therapy. I use the word 'relative' carefully because, for two reasons, it is rarely possible to measure risks or benefits in absolute terms. First, it is almost always impossible to distinguish adverse drug reactions (ADRs) from conditions which can occur spontaneously, and secondly PMS should be conducted under conditions which do not differ appreciably from those of normal medical practice. Impressions about safety and efficacy gained during clinical trials, often in highly selected groups of patients, may be misleading.

PMS should introduce a minimum of interference with prescribing and record keeping and it should not compromise the prescriber's legal position or impose an excessive burden of extra work. If it does any of these, it may deter a doctor from using the drug we wish to research.

Another objective is long-term surveillance. Increasingly we become concerned about carcinogenicity or mutagenicity and about the influence of drugs on the incidence of other diseases such as diabetes or coronary disease which would not normally be suspected to be ADRs.

To obtain scientifically impeccable results we may require controlled experimental studies. On the other hand, we must not assume that useful information can be obtained in no other way. Simple, non-experimental observational techniques can yield valuable results provided we remember that the apparently significant differences we see from time to time may be due to biases we are unable to account for or are even unaware of.

LIMITATIONS OF VARIOUS METHODS

There have been many reviews of the various types of PMS and I shall not attempt another. I shall simply assume that, by one means or another, populations of patients will be studied prospectively or retrospectively after they have been identified by means of a prescription or other record of drug exposure. Each method will tend to vary in its ability to generate or test hypotheses and we must be quite clear about its limitations.

Spontaneous reporting systems generate hypotheses but can only very rarely be used to test them. There are only two examples where the yellow card system was used to test an hypothesis. In 1969 it was able to show a possible relationship between oestrogen dose and thromboembolism[6] and, a few years later, it was possible to test the theory that frequent exposure to halothane increased the risk of jaundice[7]. The Retrospective Assessment of Drug Safety (RADS) proposed by the CSM could not do more than generate hypotheses and other techniques will be required to investigate any potential problems that may be signalled by it. Case-control surveillance conducted by the Boston Collaborative Drug Surveillance Program can both generate and test hypotheses. Many epidemiological studies which start with the selection of patients who have experienced an event and work backwards into the drug history, are specifically designed only to test hypotheses.

We must be very clear about the power of any system to detect abnormal events. However carefully controlled, a clinical trial in a few hundred patients is only likely to detect ADRs that occur in more than a few per cent of them (Figure 13.1). Unless a very unusual event such as aplastic anaemia is reported it is likely that a conventional clinical trial will miss most serious ADRs. At the other end of the scale, spontaneous reporting systems based on large populations may, because they attract reports from astute physicians, identify

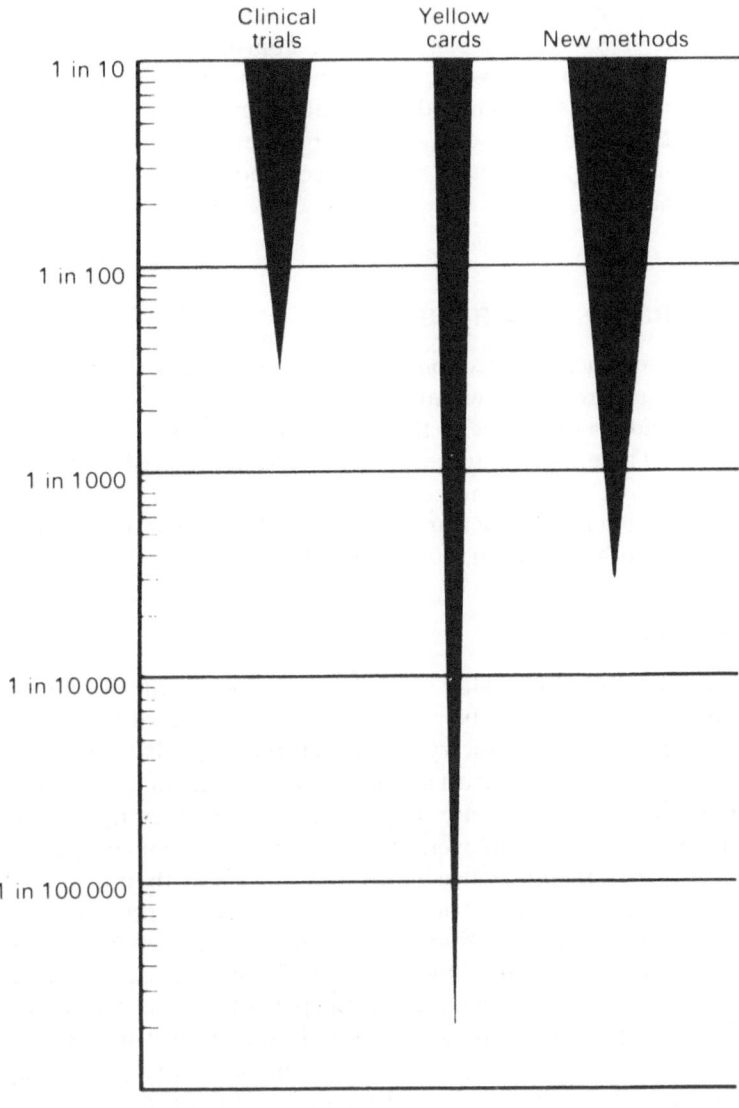

Figure 1.13

extremely rare events occurring perhaps in less than one in 10 000 treatments. It is likely that spontaneous reporting such as the yellow card system or reports to journals, will remain the only economically feasible method by which events of this rarity will be routinely identified. New PMS systems should be aimed at detecting frequencies in the intermediate range, for example those that occur more often than one in 1000 treatments. This will involve studies in up to 10 000 patients treated with each product. Similar numbers treated with a control drug will be required for comparison.

Finally, we must consider what types of drug can be monitored by each method. RADS, for example, would be appropriate for drugs used on a medium to long-term basis (e.g. more than 3 months). There would be little point in enquiring several months later, about events which followed a 5-day course with an antibiotic or a single exposure to an anaesthetic. For such drugs, short-term case-control surveillance of hospital in-patients is probably the best choice.

BARRIERS TO PROGRESS

Numerous technical and economic problems, beyond the scope of this paper, will be encountered when we attempt to improve PMS, but none in my view are as difficult to overcome as those I described last year as the three major 'barriers'[8]. These barriers to progress arise from the need to preserve confidentiality, from popular misconceptions about the safety and efficacy of drugs, and from increasing fear of litigation. They are intricately interwoven one with the others but can, nonetheless, be discussed individually.

Confidentiality

Doctor-patient confidentiality is essential for the practice of medicine, but unfortunately it creates a barrier to the epidemiological research which is intended to be of benefit to everybody. Doctors and, probably to a much lesser extent, patients tend to distrust anybody who becomes in some way a party to the mysterious secrets that are supposed to exist between them. This person may be a relative, an employer, an official, a drug-company physician or a research worker. If approached by any of these people, the doctor may sense a potential adversary. Paradoxically he is usually quite prepared to reveal a patient's diagnosis on a certificate which may be handled by relatives or lay officials and he will record the most intimate details in hospital notes which are clearly marked 'not to be handled by the patient', an open invitation to the curious and especially the patient himself. Few doctors will bother to ask the patient for permission to record such details in this way yet, increasingly, they tend to make this a condition of release of data to research workers who are the least likely to make improper use of them.

Ideally research records should be anonymous but if patients are to be followed up they must obviously be linked in some way. It would be useless, for example, to make an initial report of an ADR if the patient cannot subsequently be traced so that its outcome can be determined. It may not, however, always be necessary for the researcher to know the identity. Responsibility for record linkage may be left with the patient's own doctor by creating a system of codes through which doctor and researcher can communicate. This is a common practice in clinical trials and may be satisfactory in the short term but it will not work in long-term studies where the patient must be traced to other doctors or hospitals or identified in documents such as death certificates.

The only real safeguard is a guarantee of confidentiality. The Committee on Safety of Medicines is proud of the fact that, over 16 years, the guarantee given by Sir Derrick Dunlop to doctors who submit yellow cards has meant that no doctor has experienced medicolegal embarrassment as a result of his report to the committee. Although a lawyer may, quite properly, be able to gain access to the records of an individual patient for whom he is acting, there must be no 'right of discovery' of records of other identifiable patients which have been assembled for research purposes.

We must also look at confidentiality from another angle. Perhaps the greatest threat to PMS or indeed to any form of research is the pressure that may be exerted by the media and by politicians or consumer activists. This may lead to premature analysis and publication of misleading results. Premature publicity may introduce bias or destroy the chances of completing an investigation. It may also cause serious harm if patients become afraid of continuing with treatment. The CSM's record in this respect is also excellent, though it has frequently been criticized for apparent slowness to act. Research workers must publish their results when, and only when, they are convinced they have something worth publishing, and their scientific integrity must not be compromised by public or political demands. If subsequent work produces strong evidence that their conclusions were wrong they must be free to say so. It is admirable to be proved right, even more so to be proved wrong and to admit it freely. The public have a right to know about risks, but they also have a right to expect that the information released to them is accurate and meaningful. It is very easy to publish 'early warnings'. The agency gets the credit for its detective skill and also covers itself in the event that the hypothesis is confirmed. But if it is not confirmed an 'all clear' may be ignored by the media. Courage and experience are required to delay publication until solid evidence has been assembled.

Although at one time publication of unedited computer print-out of reports received by the CSM appeared to be justified on the grounds that the profession should be able to view the same 'radar screen' of alleged ADRs as the committee itself, and that critical perusal might reveal clues to toxicity that the CSM's monitoring staff had missed, experience has shown that this is not the case. On the whole, the risk of misinterpretation outweighs the advantages. Trained monitoring staff may be able to distinguish reactions due to the suspect drug from those which occur spontaneously or are due to concurrently administered drugs, but many false impressions have been gained by inspection of these unedited lists.

More sinister is the abuse of data of this kind by the litigious. A recent example is the suggestion that Debendox may produce limb deformities. Relatively more cases with limb deformities have been reported to national agencies than would be expected from their usual distribution among children with congenital abnormalities, but this can be readily explained by the fact that Debendox is used mainly for the treatment of vomiting in pregnancy and that limb deformities were the most striking feature of the thalidomide tragedy. It is to be expected that such deformities would be reported selectively and that relatively more would appear in lists of reactions to this drug. It is tragic that such data are being used to support claims of compensation and that they are being publicised in such a way that hopes of enormous rewards are being fostered in the minds of women who have used Debendox. In the CSM's study, which included 836 abnormal births and the same number of normal controls, 76 mothers of abnormal babies (9.1%) and 88 of the control mothers (10.5%) had used products containing doxylamine, mostly in the form of Debendox (which also contains dicyclomine), during the first trimester of pregnancy. The use of meclozine was also greater among control mothers. Forty-one (4.9%) controls were so exposed, compared with only 34 (4.1%) mothers of abnormal babies[9].

It is difficult to decide how best to achieve security of case records and research results. Possibly a change in the law is needed, though public opinion would undoubtedly favour relaxation rather than strengthening of security. Education of the public and especially the media to the dangers of hurried research and premature publication must be a major objective of all concerned in research and regulatory affairs.

Popular misconceptions

It may seem superfluous to say that the public does not appreciate that all effective therapy, be it chemical or surgical, carries some risk. Even when ADRs have been confirmed it is usually impossible to determine in advance which patients will develop them. The public demands total efficacy and total safety and it is our duty constantly to remind them that these ideals will never be achieved. However meticulous the manufacturers and regulatory agencies, accidents will continue to happen and all we can hope to achieve by premarketing tests and PMS is to minimize them. We need to remind the public that the greatest danger in essential therapy is not the risk of serious injury caused by treatment. It is the risk that patients will cease to comply with treatment, that doctors will be afraid to prescribe it or that manufacturers will be forced out of business by litigation. We must somehow exorcize the septic poltergeists who hover around the beds of those who have suffered adversity and make a good living from the pickings.

This leads us to the last of the three 'barriers'.

Litigation

The greatest of the three barriers is the increasingly litigious environment in which medicine is practised. Proposed changes in the laws of liability or the defects in existing legislation will not be discussed here. Given that some risk is inevitable it seems that some form of social security insurance rather than litigation should look after the small minority of people who suffer serious ADRs. They should receive the same high standard of care that can be expected by any person injured by accident or disease. This excludes, of course, the victims of malpractice who may seek just retribution in the courts. However, the victim or his relatives should not be entitled to astronomical sums of money in circumstances in which nobody has acted improperly just because injury has resulted from an ADR. To repeat an often quoted phrase, we must not create an 'elite' of drug-disabled people.

Japanese law does not distinguish between the statements 'drug X is *a* cause of disease Y', and 'drug X is *the* cause of disease Y'. Neither, it seems, does the majority of the public, or of the politicians. When the injury has been to a child or a previously healthy individual, there is no way in which patients or grieving relatives will accept that the illness or deformity was likely to have been due to factors unrelated to treatment. Once they have heard about a possible association with a drug they demand compensation. When, as in the United States, the stakes run into millions of dollars, they usually have little difficulty finding lawyers who are more than willing to collect their contingent fees in successful cases. There can be few activities more destructive of the human spirit than the long struggle for compensation. It leads to bitterness, depression and sometimes to avarice. As soon as an injury occurs, patients must be reassured that they will be properly cared for, and this assurance must be given without waiting for proof of cause. Even in negligence cases, care should not be delayed for years until settlements are agreed by the courts.

THE FUTURE OF PMS

It is to be hoped that these barriers will be overcome or at least diminished, but this will take many years and no one must be distracted from the need to develop new methods immediately. We should explore more thoroughly the concept of monitoring 'events' rather than merely suspected adverse re-actions. This concept is not new for it was proposed by David Finney before the CSD came into being. Any new symptom or sign, any new diagnosis, any , changes in the ability of a patient to conduct his life in a normal way, even a motor accident, is an event. It may be due to underlying disease, it may be due to treatment or it may be purely coincidental. An important advantage is that the recording of an event need not involve any expression of opinion about its causation and there is no reason why the reporter should be legally compromised, as he may be if he reports an ADR and his report is interpreted as an admission of responsibility as the prescriber of the drug. Since no medical opinion need be given it follows that it is not essential for a doctor to be involved in the subsequent documentation. He must make the diagnosis, since this requires medical skill, but once a diagnosis or other clearly defined event has been recorded, there is no reason why pharmacists, nurses or suitably trained lay people should not be involved in the collection and processing of the data. Indeed this is done successfully by nurse-monitors in the Boston scheme and by clerical staff who process records collected on yellow cards.

In some situations it may be possible for patients themselves to assist in PMS. Usually this is only appropriate in small-scale clinical trials. An example might be a comparative study of oral contraceptives. In most PMS systems, however, patient self-monitoring on a large scale is impracticable and it could even be counter-productive, causing anxiety which might lessen compliance or the reporting of imaginary complications. It also seems rather unlikely that doctors would be prepared to issue identical report forms to thousands of patients taking other drugs who would serve as controls.

SUMMARY

We must explore many new techniques for PMS, not in the hope of eliminating risk, for this is impossible, but in order to hasten the process of detection and to facilitate appropriate judgements of risk and benefit, We must protect research workers from the pressures that lead to hasty conclusions by educating the public about the unavoidable risks of effective therapy. We must instil a greater sense of responsibility among those whose power to do harm, however unintentionally, may greatly exceed their ability to do good. We must remove the enormous financial incentives from those who profit from other people's adversity and we must ensure that all injured people are adequately and fairly cared for, irrespective of the cause of their injury. This care should be provided by social security insurance rather than the law courts and indeed one suspects that strict product liability may prove to be the greatest threat to medicine and to patient-care to have emerged in the twentieth century.

References

1. Inman, W. H. W. (1978). Assessment of drug safety problems. In M. Gent and I. Shigematsu (eds.) *Epidemiological issues in reported drug-induced illnesses – SMON and other examples.* Hamilton, Ontario: McMaster University Press

2. Inman, W. H. W. (1977). Recorded Release. In Gross, F. H. and Inman, W. H. W. (eds.) *Drug monitoring*, pp. 65–78 (London: Academic Press)

3. Dollery, C. T. and Rawlins, M. D. (1977). *Br. Med. J.* **1**, 96

4. Lawson, D. G. and Henry, D. A. (1977). *Br. Med. J.*, **1**, 691

5. Wilson, A. B. (1977). *Br. Med. J.*, **2**, 1001

6. Inman, W. H. W., Vessey, M. P., Westerholm, B. and Engelund, A. (1970). *Br Med. J.*, **2**, 203

7. Inman, W. H. W. and Mushin, W. W. (1974). *Br. Med. J.*, **1**, 5

8. Inman, W. H. W. (1980). The barriers to effective post-marketing surveillance. Presented at the *Kyoto international conference against drug induced suffering (KICADIS)* 14–18 April, 1979. *Excerpta Med.*, pp. 79–84 (in press)

9. Greenberg, G., Inman, W. H. W., Weatherall, J. A. C., Adelstein, A. M., and Haskey, J. C. (1977). *Br. Med. J.*, **2**, 853

References

Discussion of Chapters 12 and 13

CHAIRMAN: PROF. C. T. DOLLERY

Dr J. Davoll (Conservation Society): The question of nuclear power came up again in Dr Brimblecombe's talk. It is not a very good comparison to make. For one thing, the nuclear power risks are so much more difficult to deal with. But, as the subject was raised, I was surprised that Dr Brimblecombe had been convinced by a nuclear engineer that the risks were vanishingly small, whatever that means. I certainly would not recommend that the drug industry tried to do the same for drugs, because it may get its own version of Three Mile Island. The point about Three Mile Island was not that people were injured by it, which probably they were not, but that the people who had been so confident about the risk quite obviously had not the faintest idea about what was going on inside the reactor. It is better not to approach this by trying to convince people that there is no risk, which seemed to me to be the implication.

Secondly, as a relatively detached observer, I would not have noticed from many of the contributions that the drug industry is actually in business to make a profit, and this does matter in any talk of risks and benefits. Not of the critical life-saving drugs, but as we go out through the spectrum of things, those recommended for increasingly trivial reasons, and in particular, the benzodiazepines. In many of these cases the risks, although they may be small, are real, but the benefits are extremely questionable. This fact should be recognized by the drug industry. It should not get paranoid about people criticizing it because it is rich, because it *is* rich and it is in the business to make money. As a result the public will expect it to be surveyed by some impartial body.

That said, I have a lot of sympathy for the points which have been made, but I do not think more sympathy will be gained by overstating the case.

Dr Brimblecombe: I did not say that I had been convinced by the arguments of the nuclear power people. It is irrelevant whether I am convinced or not. I was repeating the point that I thought Mr Maddox made in his paper, namely that the nuclear power people, presumably in the sincere belief that what they said is true, have gone out and carried out a campaign to educate the public and to say that there is a risk but there is also a benefit. We can quibble about whether it is vanishingly small, or just how big it is, but nevertheless they have gone out and they have made an attempt to put their case fairly before the public and I believe we should do the same.

On Dr Davoll's second point, I did indeed make specifically that point, that risk–benefit ratio is not a constant ratio, and there are many factors that have to be borne in mind in weighing or in deciding what this ratio should be. I do not want to say what I think it should be for the benzodiazepines. It is clearly different for the benzodiazepines than for cytotoxic drugs. Nevertheless, I did make the point, quite specifically, that it is different for different classes of drug, depending on a number of factors.

Dr P. Johnson (Smith, Kline and French Research): We have to keep reminding ourselves that the topic of the conference is risk–benefit analysis. One of the factors we have to consider in trying to push that ratio in the right direction is that of pre-clinical testing in laboratory animals. This brings me to the question raised by Dr Brimblecombe concerning how many animal species are meaningful. The question should be restated in the form, 'How many meaningful animal species are there?' Here I would echo the point of the need to proceed rapidly into man for early pharmacokinetic and metabolic studies so that meaningful comparisons with animals can be made at an early stage, and this will then allow a rational, or at least a more rational choice of species for longer-term toxicity studies. I do feel that in this respect both industrial toxicologists and the regulatory authorities themselves have done a disservice to drug development. We have had a too ready acceptance of the rodent and non-rodent principle, which in practice too often boils down to the use of rats and dogs. The problem is that if we are to avoid exotic intravenous studies in the osprey, or balance studies in elephants, we really do have a limited choice of species. I would say that it would be untenable for the species requirement to ever rise to a number greater than two, but that those two should have some rationale and be meaningful. In order to achieve that, we must be allowed to get the compound into man at an early stage so as to make the necessary comparisons.

Prof. Dollery: Dr Brimblecombe does not wish to comment on that, but I have a brief comment.

While I agree, I would not pitch my expectations from pharmacokinetic, and particularly drug metabolism studies, in man too high. It was a stage we went through about 12 years ago, when somebody said, as somebody indeed said at one of our earlier sessions, that we should find out what the paths of metabolism in man are and choose a species where those paths and rates are virtually the same for the animal toxicity tests. The problem is almost always that 'there ain't any such species', and so although there are some reactions known, like the lack of ability of felines to conjugate paraminobenzoic acid and things of that kind, there are only a relatively small number of toxic effects in man where we can say that any species would be an inappropriate or an appropriate predictor.

The point about kinetics is a fair one. One would like to know that the concentrations that are being used in man and the animals are relevant. The apparent margin of safety based on dose is often much smaller when one gets down to compare actual concentrations. But it would be dangerous to say one could select an appropriate species on that basis. I am doubtful about that.

Perhaps Dr Johnson might care to argue on the other side?

Dr Johnson: I think we have to try.

Dr D. Jack (Glaxo Holdings Ltd): I am very glad that Professor Dollery has made that statement. In my experience the range of choice of animals for toxicity tests is relatively small, even when one has done the various metabolic studies.

But, what exactly had Dr Brimblecombe in mind when he said that industry should be encouraged to develop new methods for toxicology? At least we have some notion of where we are with the existing framework of toxicity testing. New methods? What did he mean?

Dr Brimblecombe: That is exactly the problem. I do not know precisely what I do mean. It might be easiest if I give an example.

We are asked, in the Guidelines for Reproduction Studies to ensure that the animals, the progeny from these studies, show no neurological or behavioural deficit. Nobody quite knows how to do this. There are a number of people in industry who would have some ideas as to how to devise tests which could be meaningful, perhaps wholly meaningful. They are reluctant, I think, to talk about them too much because they might be difficult to carry out. Not everybody would want to carry them out. But if people are willing to devise such tests, and submit their compounds to them for a few years, and then see whether or not any data emerges that appears to be valuable, then that is a useful thing to do.

What I am trying to get at is a situation where we do not automatically accept the traditional toxicology. We have got to get back to what the accountants call zero auditing. We must start again. Dr Jack is absolutely right in saying we know more or less where we stand with the current studies, but I suggest that it is less rather than more. We think we know where we stand rather than knowing where we stand, and I should like very much to be in a situation where if someone has a brilliant idea for some short-term test he should be allowed to pursue it, and attempt to validate it, get his colleagues interested, without having the fear all the time that this will immediately be imposed on everybody in sight without any good reason.

I think I am saying that the present tests are well known to us but that does not make them good. There may be better tests around, but we have no incentive whatsoever to look for them at the moment. In fact, quite the reverse.

Ms R. Clarkson (ICI Pharmaceuticals): Dr Brimblecombe pointed out that quality was perhaps more important than quantity, and I would agree. But is it perhaps another barrier to post-marketing surveillance that people are getting rather carried away by quantity and forgetting the other factor of quality. They are counting reports, rather than looking at and looking into them. If, in fact, the story that we hear is true, and if there is no other explanation for that particular patient, and there is a positive re-challenge and a physiological explanation, and if the time before the onset of an event in relation to the time of the beginning of treatment is fairly constant in a small group of patients, then that surely must be more evidence supporting a whole field of sources of information that many people – not the speakers – many of those who think in terms of post-marketing surveillance seem to forget. They seem obsessed with 'P', but pedantically, 'P' does not apply where there is no random sample. They seem to be getting more and more tied up with the number of bad reports rather than trying to push for an increase in good reports.

Dr Inman: I entirely agree. One of the safety valves of the CSM system over the years has been our ability to follow up on reports. We have a large team of field workers, 100 of them, who have been able to validate the reports. On the whole, in something like 80% of the reports we followed up there were likely adverse drug reactions. Whether they were all neatly tied up with regard to the criteria Ms Clarkson has suggested I would not know. The yellow card 'tip of the iceberg' represents the reports in which the doctor is fairly sure that this is an adverse reaction when he reports it.

But I agree that we must not fall into the trap of playing a numbers game. People are getting excessively concerned about exceedingly rare side-effects and forgetting all the other things about the quality of life, and the quality of what is left for the patient when he has had an adverse reaction. They forget, for example, that the greatest danger to a patient on essential therapy is that he will stop taking the drug, and this far exceeds any risk of an adverse reaction.

I am not sure that I have completely answered the question, but I agree that quality is more important than quantity.

Dr C. N. Christensen (Eli Lilly): I was glad to hear Dr Inman say that existing systems of post-marketing surveillance have given us good information and have been able to identify risks in certain cases. In some of the programmes that have been suggested or talked about, in the US at any rate, I have been concerned that they were trying to accomplish too much, and that because of that they would fall before they started to walk. I am a little concerned about new systems that might be overburdened by trying to accomplish too much. In one of his early slides, Dr Inman said that one of the objectives of PMS should be the assessment of risks and benefits. I have the feeling that to try to get information about effectiveness out of a PMS system is asking too much.

Would Dr Inman comment?

Dr Inman: I should have qualified this. There are one or two ways in which benefit could be easily assessed, for example, in patients on hypotensive therapy. As long as they are tagged, and identified, we should at least be able to find out how long they live, and of what they die. Those sort of data could be used as a measure of benefit. But I would not envisage as a routine asking people about whether their grip has improved if they are arthritic, or whether their blood pressure has gone up or down. I agree that simplicity is the essence of these things. In fact, in the sort of recorded release scheme that we envisaged there were only four questions.

(1) What did the patient complain of?
(2) Did the patient have to be referred to hospital, or for another opinion, or was the patient admitted to hospital?
(3) Did the patient die?
(4) Did the patient have to stop the drug for any special reason?

If one can get the answers to those four, plus the NHS registration number so that the patient can be traced later, one has gone a long way, but it is nevertheless crude.

The other point that is worth making here is that practically every signalling system will generate huge numbers of hypotheses, so that considerable judgement must be exercised about which ones should be followed up. This is why one cannot talk about all these hypotheses or the press will pick up every single one. But on practically every occasion, an *ad hoc* study will need to be designed to investigate any particular hypothesis. A lot of people expect PMS to be a blunderbuss system that will give the answers to everything. Certainly it will not. All that it will do is perhaps be a marginal improvement to the yellow card system, giving a more complete recording of events and a faster detection of any hazard.

Dr A. B. Wilson (Llandeilo, Dyfed): If we are thinking about monitoring for efficacy, there could be difficulties, as another questioner said, of making it excessively burdensome. But that is probably in the context of the efficacy for which the drug already has its indicated use. We might be able to look very simply for unexpected efficacy, and in many ways this could be more valuable. We have seen a list of such instances where, during clinical use, a new indication had emerged which proved to be extremely important. Perhaps a fifth question on Dr Inman's questionnaire would give us the answer to that.

Dr Inman: Agreed. It is worth a try.

Prof. Dollery: Dr Inman said one thing in his presentation that bothered me a great deal. When I was a member of the CSM, I, along with one or two others, had campaigned to publish as much of the information as possible, and not just adverse reactions. But the only success we had was that the adverse reactions registers were eventually made available. They were not exactly published, but they were widely circulated. I think it a terribly retrograde step to go back on that and I can see no justification, I am horrified.

Dr Inman: This was a decision. It may only be temporary, and it was to some extent influenced by the enormous pressure on the secretariat. We just could not cope with the job of handing out extracts from the registers to everybody.

But, with respect, even some committee members have misinterpreted the lists publicly. It is so easy to do. To take one simple example. One may add up the reports of thrombosis listed against progestogens and those listed against oestrogens, when in fact any result should be divided by two. Little things like that have led to a lot of misunderstanding. And of course, the press, I am afraid, gets hold of these things. Large numbers of coincidental effects, or effects that are due to different drugs from the one under which they are listed, get widely quoted.

I agree it is a very debatable point, but marginally I think I am in favour of not publishing them widely.

Prof. Dollery: But it goes against the general tenor of what has been said here, namely, that we are more likely to succeed in the long run by taking the public into our confidence and convincing them that what we are doing has a solid justification than by cloaking things in secrecy and only letting out things of which we are certain. That would leave many intelligent people to believe that there are a lot of other things that are almost certain which are hidden in the woodwork, and which they would like to know about.

I can see that it may have been a lot of work for the secretariat to send out, as they used to do when an adverse reaction was reported, that page of the register. The information was nice to have but I would not have been too sad if that practice were stopped. But to cease to make the register available is less acceptable. In fact, I was about to write to the Committee saying that my copies of the seven yellow volumes seemed to be very old now, and was there an updated set because I should like to have them. But apparently if I wrote that letter the answer would be that I could not.

Dr Inman: For an *ad hoc* inquirer such as Professor Dollery himself, a medically qualified person, or a doctor working for a pharmaceutical company, there would be no difficulty in feeding back the information. I am not objecting in any way to that, although I would probably send a covering letter, if it was diazepam for example, saying, 'Please ignore the four or five reports of venous thrombosis because they all apply to people who took diazepam while taking the pill'. In other words, on an *ad hoc* basis, and provided that there is a certain amount of time available, the user can be helped not to misinterpret what he sees. But to have it available in every pharmacy, where inexperienced doctors and lay staff can go and look at it, may on the whole be more of a disadvantage than an advantage. But I agree that it is extremely debatable, and it took me a long time to change my mind: and maybe I was wrong.

Dr R. N. Smith (Hoffman-La Roche): Many of us listening to Dr Inman's presentation were appreciative of his professionalism, cool and academic response to the very difficult situations which he and other members have encountered. It is probably a very appropriate time to say that with his departure to take up his new venture in the University of Southampton, many of us will miss his counsel, although we know it is now available outside the bounds of the CSM.

To pick up one point he mentioned, which is very relevant to what Professor Dollery just said. It is very important that we do not allow ourselves to release information prematurely until there has been a full scientific and professional assessment of it. This is a slightly different point to Professor Dollery's. He is advocating that the documentation, once it has been assembled and the opinion has been formulated, should be available to the profession.

But what worries me is that in this trio of the company doctors, the doctors practising outside, and the doctors in the agencies, we do get premature release. We have seen examples recently, and this is very unfortunate, particularly when investigators present data that has not been put into the scientific journals, that is not available to the company doctors, that is not available to the agency doctors. This then gets media exposure, quite wide exposure which then produces pressures, tremendous pressures for someone to say something, and they do. And they do so prematurely without consulting those who are deeply involved in it. That, I think, is very unfortunate, and it is something which, as a professional group, we should try to avoid. I know some people will transgress, and that is up to their own personal conscience and beliefs, but if we do get ourselves galloping into situations that we cannot control, where key investigators particularly are not asked to present their opinion and their data fully to the agencies that are reviewing it, we shall come into more problems and eventually lose the confidence of the public – not just those of us in the companies but also those in the agencies themselves.

Dr R. G. Penn (DHSS): To extend what Dr Inman has just said and perhaps make Professor Dollery a bit happier, I should like to point out that there is certainly no intention of not letting people know what is on the register. But as Dr Inman said, the Committee were worried that misleading prints were being sent out, and they wanted to have another look at it to see whether a print could go out that gave the proper information rather than misleading information.

Secondly, and this is no plea for sympathy but a statement of fact, over the past few months we really have been absolutely fixed with shortage of staff for sending these out, and sometimes it has been a question of making the choice between recording the stuff, or doing some of our other public relations work that we would like to do. But we shall start to send out prints as soon as we can be certain that they are not misleading, and they give the correct information.

In the meantime, we do answer any inquiry as soon as we can get to it on the pile.

Prof. Dollery: This is a private argument to some extent, but I should have thought that that is the wrong approach to the problem. Obviously the opinions of the professionals at the CSM on the interpretation of the data are of very great importance, but at the same time, if the original purpose of making these documents public is to be served, that is to allow a wide access to them, and I would say it should be an unrestricted access, then other people can also form opinions. If, for example, some people say stupid things based on the data and I agree that that will happen – it will happen anyway. These days it is impossible to keep anything secret. The invention of the Xerox machine was the end of secrecy. But it means that other people also, more responsible people, will have access to the information and can answer it, whereas if they do not they are left completely up in the air.

Sir Edward Pochin (National Radiological Protection Board): The proper study of this type of information is very much in line with the proper purposes of our meeting – to get some evaluation of both risk and benefit. it has been repeatedly pointed out, and quite rightly, that there are very few estimates of benefit. Dr Inman said that the estimates could only be crude ones. That does not matter as long as crude means inaccurate rather than subject to bias. One cannot use risk estimates to any very great precision. One needs an approximation. Approximations to benefit from particular sources, particular patterns of treatment, particular drugs, will be of the greatest value, and there is plenty of room for better evaluation of risk.

Dr Dayan said that there was difficulty, and there obviously is difficulty. If the risks would come out as a group of different animals such as risk of death, risk of induction of certain diseases or loss of health things might be easier but even then it would be difficult to know what one could do with the data if one did obtain them. He suggested that one might write the results on paper, throw them into the air, and see how they fell. I agree with that, but they might fall in a very revealing way. When a study was made of the loss of working time from various occupational causes, including minor and fatal accidents, it was clear that for many of the more hazardous industries, the absolute loss of time in years from occupationally caused death was greater than the total loss of time from recorded absences from work from non-fatal accidents and diseases. If so, one can immediately say that as long as greater weight is attached to a year off work through being dead than to a year off work through having several minor accidents, then the index based on death is an overriding factor in terms of size, and the other is a second-order correction.

One may gain information simply by getting into a situation and seeing what comes out.

Mr J. Spink (Wellcome Foundation): Dr Inman referred to the suggestion that claims might be settled by insurance rather than litigation. The object of what he is saying is extremely good, but it is not really feasible in practice in that way. Insurance and litigation are not mutually exclusive. Indeed, most insurance policies on product liability restrict the right of the insured to have his claim settled unless legal liability is actually established. If litigation is to include the pre-court proceedings of pleadings, negotiation, and so on, then that sort of thing is bound to go on even if the matter is eventually settled by insurance. Probably it is not a bad thing that it is that way. If it were too easy, misuse would be encouraged, with avaricious, even fraudulent claims.

The only way in which litigation can be avoided in these matters is by a no-fault compensation scheme. One of the big advantages that was inherent in the ABPI proposals was that this would take the adversary proceedings out of the situation, where a patient needed compensation, inasmuch as the tribunal could be set up to deal with this matter without either party having to go to law about it, and the tribunal would be completely free of any commercial interest. What Dr Inman has said is a plug for the ABPI scheme.

Dr Inman: I realize I was being excessively naive. I felt that if I broke my leg I should like to have it put in plaster and to be brought a cup of tea straight away, and not have to wait until we had decided who was responsible for my having broken my leg. I agree that this is far too simplistic.

Dr C. C. Cowan (Fisons): Dr Brimblecombe suggested that perhaps industry could be persuaded to provide the money and the resources to analyse the data in the DHSS files. This is data, for a large part, on drugs that appeared safe by the safety testing methods used, but then went on to further clinical work. Clearly we would not be looking at data on compounds that appear unsafe. We could be in a situation where we are looking at drugs that appeared safe and were subsequently found not to be so. We are not addressing ourselves to drugs that may have been very active but that were indicated by earlier testing to be somewhat unsafe.

Would there be any advantage in trying to set up a co-operative scheme in industry where all the data that had been produced by preclinical testing were evaluated in some way?

Dr Brimblecombe: I take the point entirely. It is a one-sided situation in that if the toxicity studies that we currently carry out tell us that the drug is apparently unsafe to give to man, we do not give it to man. Therefore we have a biased sample of data. I do not quite know how to get around it. It would be a brave man who, if he did see some process in the liver of his rats or something equally adverse, would then push that drug into man simply to make the point that the rat was not predicting what was going to happen in man.

I do not quite know the answer. Certainly the data which is in the files of the regulatory agencies could be of use. But, equally, if Dr Cowan is suggesting that the data that we, collectively, have in our own files would be of use, then I agree with that.

There is a scheme afoot to set up a unit under the auspices of the ABPI – to persuade companies to give up data from their own files and records which would not perhaps be in the files of the regulatory agencies, because it would not have reached that stage, and from that, hopefully, some sense might emerge.

It is exactly as Sir Edward was saying: there is a lot of data around. We do perhaps have to throw it in the air and pummel it around and analyse it in one way or another, and something might emerge almost by chance. It is certainly much better than doing nothing and that is for sure. And I think the money is much better spent that way than doing some of the things we are doing now.

Dr A. B. Wilson (Llandeilo, Dyfed): Assuming such a unit ever came into being, would it be a better forum for the collection of the data on mutagenicity to which Dr Brimblecombe referred to earlier? There is now a strong feeling among the experts themselves that the validation of this data has not yet been really established. I am not perhaps as sanguine as Dr Brimblecombe that the collection of such data under the auspices of the licensing authority would give us, that is *us*, including the public and all the people who are interested in the problem, the right outcome.

I say this because it could be very embarrassing for the licensing authority if it collected data to the point where it looked as though there was a need to start requiring it from everyone. If at that moment in time the media put pressure on to them, they would find it very difficult to resist, whereas if the information was being collected elsewhere, we could reach the stage for which Dr Inman pleaded, of having it scientifically decided that the end-point was a proper one.

I would put in a personal view into this context, relating to what Professor Grahame-Smith said when he exemplified the precedent aspect of accretion of regulations, and gave the example of how many patients should be included in a long-term study, should it be 50, etc., and we all know we landed up with 100 for 1 year. Industry, by providing examples of the work that they are doing, often create the climate for requirements to be set, and in this regard I would suggest very strongly that because there is no legal requirement at all to submit mutagenicity data in the UK and in most countries of the EEC, it is foolish for companies to submit such data in their files unless they were to get a positive result, in which case they have other procedures to undertake to satisfy themselves that the drug is safe. But if it is a negative result, it is very foolish to submit such data to licensing authorities.

Dr Brimblecombe: I would agree. The mutagenicity example is a good one. But unfortunately the world is not quite as simple as that. If one is dealing with compounds that are subject to an IND in the US one has to submit the data to the FDA whether or not it is submitted to the CSM. But that is a procedural matter, and I agree in principle with what Dr Wilson is saying. If the regulatory agencies would be happy with a situation where we were generating data that we were not submitting to them, that would be fine, and if we could submit it to such a unit as we are talking about for them to analyse anonymously if we wished, or however we wanted to do it – that is exactly what I was trying to get at.

I am still slightly unhappy about the answer I gave to Dr Jack. I do not think I answered his question in the way I meant to answer it. I am not suggesting, in case this is the impression I have given, that we should do more tests simply to add them on to the existing tests. I am suggesting we try to find more sensible meaningful tests to substitute for the present tests. Although we are familiar with the present tests, that does not mean that they are good ones. There may be better tests around that we simply do not know about because nobody is looking for them. I know there is a limit to the amount of time we can spend on doing that sort of thing, but in the long run we might all be better off if we can produce better tests, whatever that means, shorter tests, less tests and tests that make the patient much safer than he is now.

14
The influence of the media

S. LOCK

I have just heard a rather anguished voice saying 'Patients come to their doctors to get well, not to sue'. Of course, the speaker was quite right. That is exactly what they do. And yet the curious thing is that a few do sue. I think we have to ask why.

The reason has been obvious over the last 2 days. Part of it at least must be the influence of the media, and the influence of campaigns, of community activists. We are all unhappy about this, and it is my duty to suggest what things are wrong and what things could be put right.

If one looks up *media* in the *Oxford English Dictionary*, there is no entry. If one looks in the supplements that are now being produced, there is still no formal definition. What one will find is a series of quotes illustrating how the word is being used in practice. All of us here know what we mean by media: the radio, the television, the newspapers. But, because there is no definition, I should like to extend it to include my own journal and the medical journals, and to discuss the role of the medical journals as well as that of the orthodox media.

Medical journals – most would agree – have quite a responsibility in providing accurate information about drugs. The Sainsbury Report showed this, reporting that 76% of GPs thought that articles in journals were a good way of getting to know about the existence of new drugs; just slightly worse than drug representatives, who scored 78%. When it came to getting to know about the efficacy of new products, articles in journals scored the best: 83%, compared with 61% for drug representatives.

The *BMJ* deals with the efficacy and existence of drugs in two main ways. It has regular review articles, either unsigned as leading articles or signed in the *Today's Treatment* series. It also accepts original articles about new drugs. Here it is very important to follow the traditional editorial process, or peer review. Most articles that have any chance of being accepted have to go to at least one expert referee. When they come back, and we hope that they come back within a fortnight or 3 weeks, any potentially suitable article for publication is discussed by an editorial 'hanging' committee. This is to take the concept of corporate responsibility perhaps rather farther than the editor is usually thought of as doing, but it is important to have four people, two outsiders and two on the editorial staff, all of whom have read the article and all of whom sit round and discuss it.

Next, any article that is to be accepted is sent to a statistical adviser if it contains any statistics at all. The statistical adviser has a particular interest in the methodology of clinical trials.

After this, most articles are then modified by their authors in the light of all these comments, not only from the original referee, but also those from the hanging committee and the statistical assessor.

Finally, even then our sub-editors will do rather more than cross the t's and dot the i's when they come to style the article. The aim is to rewrite any passage that is not entirely clear; perhaps even to reshape the article and to get the clarity and the implications absolutely clear.

This is a very smug account, and editors are very smug people. It sounds as if I think that we end up with perfect articles. Of course, we do not. There are many articles with many obvious defects that pass the editorial net, which we hope has a relatively fine mesh.

I was recently rung up by a professor of clinical pharmacology who said that he would like to photostat an article we had recently published and use it for his class. 'Fine', I said. 'What a compliment'. 'It is not a compliment', he said. 'This particular article breaks every rule in the clinical trial book!' That is what it is about. There is a final safety net, and on this occasion the safety net was invoked. The safety net is the correspondence column. Any letter that is not personally objectionable, libellous or obscene – and there are quite a number of letters that are – any letter that is serious really deserves to be printed, and it is often a very good way to get a debate going.

One thing to be noted from this description is that the process is rather dull. I am afraid that the outcome is rather duller than the brighter articles with unsubstantiated claims that came in initially. Even so, peer review is the only responsible way to treat new information. The literature is too full of obvious howlers over which a lot of time and money are then spent once the article has been published. Only the other day I read an article in another journal that could not possibly have been assessed. It had important national implications. The study group was selected. There were no control groups. The blood levels of a particular metabolite had not been estimated. The claims made were grossly exaggerated, and so on and so forth.

But, perhaps, you say, this refereeing does not really matter. I would agree, provided the debate could be kept within the medical family. But, of course, it cannot. The media people are on the lookout for any scandal, and, even within medicine itself, many subjects now are such an extended family that somebody at one end – say, working on the molecular genetics of diabetes – does not really understand the population studies of diabetes at the other. That is not to say that they do not have a broad appreciation of the whole field of diabetes, but what the editor and his audience are after is somebody with a rigorous expert knowledge of that particular bit of diabetes which enables him to assess an original article in a particular way.

Because many articles in journals – in fact most articles in journals – are contributions to this debate and are not the final answer, it is very important that editors should make this clear to their readers, because readers include lay people as well as experts. This can be done in several ways. If it is a particularly extreme view one can choose a heading such as 'hypothesis' or 'for debate'. We routinely get the authors not to overstate their case. And, as the *New England Journal* often does, and the *BMJ* will sometimes do, we can run an accompanying leading article to emphasize what the implications of this particular original article are, what it does say, and what it does not say.

The reason I have described this editorial process in such detail is for its importance for the 'primary prevention' of distorted treatment in the lay media. It is very important to try to get the message right: to try to have extrapolations from the data which are fair, and no more.

The secondary prevention is to review the media itself; something which is beginning to evolve and which was started by the *New Scientist*. One also sees such reviews in the *British Journal of Hospital Medicine*, and we have recently been doing it in *Medicine and the Media* in the *BMJ*. We have got to analyse how the media people are treating medical stories: their over-simplifications, their distortions, their plain misunderstandings. It is not their fault that they necessarily get things wrong. Many of us, particularly on this side of the Atlantic, won't speak to them. Correspondents in the US tell me that it is very much easier for them to get hold of any expert, rather than the selected few, as pertains in the UK, and, of course, any selected few often tend to be at one end of the spectrum with extreme views. So we owe it to the media people to educate them by reviewing what they are saying. There is no correspondence column for putting things right on television, which is why the journals should be reviewing the media more and more.

I should like to emphasize that no one must imagine that I am saying everything on the radio, or on television, or in newspapers is wrong, or that they are wrong all the time. They are not. I should think that between 80% and 90% is accurate and very valuable. But if we come to try to develop some cost–benefit analysis, we really cannot; so one has to depend on one's solar plexus. The harm done by 10% of articles or programmes may be such that on balance I believe that the cost–benefit is not on the positive side.

Many of the speakers have been allowed a short commercial. Mine is for Bill Inman's book, to which I am a contributor. There are no royalties for any of the contributors, but it does contain a lot of useful material. One of the particularly interesting articles is by Oliver Gillie, the medical correspondent of the *Sunday Times*. It is a very interesting account of the process of journalism, and sometimes of the outcome. Some might be tempted to conclude that he regards himself as a bit like Alan Ladd in those films at the end of the war, when pretty well every battle in Japan was fought and won by one person, but he does dilate on the new style of journalism. We realize that in the last 10–15 years most of us have been getting our news from radio and television, and not looking at our newspapers so much for news. So we have got this new style of crusading journalism, which most of us here do not really like. 'Popular writing in science and medicine', Gillie says, 'has moved away from the simple popularization of expert knowledge towards analysis and criticism.' It is this investigative trend that we have been discussing over these 2 days. It arouses a lot of disquiet among us as professionals. Why? I suppose no professional likes his ideals, his ideas and his principles being questioned. No expert really likes not being used as an expert, and instead being treated as a hostile witness.

The third thing to which we object is that to most journalists everything is black and white. As scientists, we hardly ever use such words as 'never' or 'always'. Even with something like rabies, we cannot do this any longer. There is some justification for this sort of journalism. The thalidomide episode has been hanging over the entire meeting. But that is a long way in the past. Journalists tend to see scandals under every stone, and not just in medicine: open any paper and one can see banking scandals, nuclear scandals, agricultural scandals, as well as medical ones. Doctors and drug companies must not get too paranoid. I equate this emphasis on the negative as part of the flight from science, the non-trusting of the expert. It is part of a general theme.

As far as medicine is concerned, it has had a very bad effect. John Spink mentioned trial by newspaper. I am talking about trials by television; trials by television of a reputable form of treatment, such as ECT, which had no mention at all of the other side of the equation, the natural history of depression that Aubrey Lewis described before the introduction of ECT, when people killed themselves. One can remember Virginia Woolf finally drowning herself after miserable episodes of depression. Nothing about that on television at all. Just a sheer campaign on *Panorama* for 45 minutes, admittedly later admitted by the BBC to be misguided (which is quite an admission from the BBC), but nothing on the other side at all. A totally unfair programme to which ordinarily there was no reply whatsoever. We have seen a similar trial of a beta blocker, practolol. Obviously some grounds for disquiet, but the way in which this was handled, again on *Panorama*, made a lot of us very unhappy.

To me the worst instance so far has been the campaign against pertussis. Immunization against pertussis has been attacked with virtually no shred of published scientific evidence known to me. As far as I know West's syndrome does not exist in the most litigious country in the world, i.e. the United States. It has not been seen in Sweden. Such prospective studies as have been done in

North London have not shown the condition to be associated with immunization against pertussis.

One can perhaps understand the campaigners, their sincere motives. One can understand the case for moving to the New Zealand system of no fault liability, or the modified no fault system they are developing in Sweden. But for a government that should base its decisions on reason to give into a campaign because it is continuous and strident, because it tugs the heartstrings, because it is led by somebody for whom one feels great sympathy but for a reason totally unconnected with pertussis immunization, strikes me as a total negation of what education and civilization are all about. It is rule by demagogy.

I have used pertussis as an example because it is fairly clearcut. Many of the drug examples are less black and white, although the principle is the same.

So far I have been rather negative. I should now like to turn to the positive side; what we can do to put right this appalling problem. First we must put our own house in order, by which I mean the industry. We can all here name drugs sold over the counter or on prescription which seem to us to have no advantages and a lot of potential disadvantages. Why are they still available? The simple answer is that they are there to make money for the shareholders – that it is a capitalist ploy. I suggest that another reason is out of a sense of pride by manufacturers who do not want to admit that they are wrong, or perhaps there may be lawsuits pending, and if these drugs were withdrawn that might seem to be a tacit admission of 'guilt'. I believe, too, that manufacturers must tighten up their standards in the Third World. We know very well that drugs are being promoted for indications that just would not be allowed in the West, and why do we have these two standards? Sometimes the appearance of two standards may be necessary. In his splendid paper, John Dunne has gone into the difficulties. Of course, there is the political difficulty of seeming to say to a Third World country that it can have second best drugs, but that is not true. We all know, for instance, that Indian women do not develop pulmonary embolism as much as their Western counterparts, so there are indications, perhaps, for giving them some cheaper form of oral contraceptive, with a higher oestrogen content and so on. Again, chloramphenicol, with its known risks, is cheap and effective – and obviously preferable to nothing.

In putting our own house in order, the industry needs a stronger corporate identity. Things seem all right at this meeting, where we are one big family, but the reality is that you represent a large number of competitive firms each trying to cut each other's throats. We need better press releases, and I mean those from the government in particular. Our problems and difficulties cannot be hidden. When we are dealing with intelligent medical correspondents, we must anticipate all the questions that they will ask and what they are likely to write. I have no wish to criticize any individual, but I wonder whether a better press release about Debendox – which David Ennals read out in an earlier session – would not have been something more explicit. I have pencilled down a draft of what I would have said had I been allowed to by the lawyers. Would not the following have been better?

> The Committee for Safety in Medicine has been following the American court case closely. Despite the verdict, it does not believe in withdrawing Debendox for the following reasons:
>
> First, it has no reports of similar abnormalities occurring in Britain;
>
> Secondly, vomiting in pregnancy may be a serious and distressing condition, both for doctors and pregnant women, and they need to have an effective drug for stopping vomiting;
>
> Thirdly, trial by jury is no way of settling such complex issues, and in any case, both the legal case in the USA and the debate in general are far from finished. Even so, the CSM is meeting urgently to consider its policy.
>
> In the meantime, as always, both doctors and patients should weigh up risks and benefits in their own minds, given that no drug or medical procedure is, or ever can be, entirely free from risk.

Something like that might have stopped a lot of the rubbish we read in the press, which I thought was very frightening and very ill-judged.

My second suggestion for making things better is that we must get together with the media people to tell them about the problems: how there are always risks with drugs; the vast amount of work that is done to find out these effects before the drugs are marketed; and the disservice that is done to society if it is deprived of a valuable and life-saving drug for a period as long as 10 years, which is half of its patent life. We must have some sort of forum for regular meetings with the media, so that we can get across this concept of risk, and the proceedings and the place of any forum need planning very carefully. It will have to be a long way away so that the correspondents do not spend all their time on a telephone and cannot leave when we have heard their point of view but they have not heard ours. The trouble is that none of these decision makers ever listen. A good example is Mr Ennals, who had presumably put out his speech to the Press Association tapes before he came here. It was on the radio within 2 hours of his making it. Any modification of his views – which might have been total – by the audience could not possibly have been fed into that system.

Even so, I am slightly encouraged because the problems with nuclear power have now been explained to the population, and good articles are now appearing in the press about the comparative risks. Brian Silcock did a first-class article comparing the risks of nuclear energy with those of riding motor-cycles or of smoking 20 cigarettes a day, not wearing seat belts, and so on and so forth. There was another excellent article recently in *The Economist*. So far we have not applied this approach to drugs, and we must. Personal contact is the only way of doing this. Books are not much good. With great respect to the publishers, I cannot think that anybody outside this gathering will read these proceedings. We get at least 50 books a week at the *BMJ*, ten of them reports of conference proceedings, all adding virtually nothing to knowledge. I believe that Bill Inman's new unit at Southampton could play an important part in starting a dialogue between industry, the medical profession and the media.

One final and important point. We have got to adopt the opposition's own tactics, by using emotion. All of us here are old-fashioned enough to believe that we can solve all the problems of the world by reason, as did George Moore or Bertrand Russell. But, of course, we cannot. Professor Dollery put his thumb on it when he was talking about John Maddox's paper on shared responsibility. Maddox's ideas were fine for the Hampstead intellectual with his Rover 3000, his hi-fi and his *New Statesman*. They were no good for the social class five Glasgow dockers. What is more, if we go along with the idea of shared responsibility, we have to remember that Dave Sackett has shown that no matter what one tells patients, how one tells patients, and of what social class they are, such a process does not necessarily increase compliance. I do not honestly see why John Maddox's proposals should be any better.

I was interested to read in *New Society* in March that the West Coast of America has spawned a new theory of decision making which is known as positive political science. I suspect that this new discovery is a bit like the character who was told in Moliere's comedy that he had been talking prose all his life. The first group taking part in positive political science are the bureaucrats and technocrats, who believe in reason. The second are the public, the electorate. On the knife edge in the middle are the politicians, poised uneasily between the electorate on the one hand and their advisers on the other. Now most of the electorate are apathetic, and if there are no major issues it does mean that the third group, the community activists, can get going and can influence elections. So we have a minority of community activists who are laying down policy on emotional issues. We saw a good example of emotional pressure here this morning. Mr Ennals was all for stopping the licensing of Debendox until we had some more information.

We shall have to fight in the same way as the community activists, using emotion to get out points across. After all, in 1979, Britain had the worst epidemic of pertussis since the 1950s, and no fewer than 12 children died. Why not a society for compensating the parents of dead children who had been scared of giving them pertussis immunization because of the campaign? The tragedy is that a government gave way on a compensation issue because of emotional pressure and not because of scientific reality.

We shall have to get across the fact that new drugs are better than nothing where serious illness is concerned. We shall have to get across that the preventable childhood fevers are distressing, dangerous, and even lethal. The industry will have to come out of its shell and say that its aims are directed towards the relief of suffering and not towards its shareholders. It needs to point out what the alternative is, and where I think we are going unless we rapidly do something. It is only a few hundred miles as the crow flies from Canterbury to Prague, to a stagnant society where there is no progress and where the only development is in officialdom. As Mr Spink illustrated, this development is already happening in the West.

A final thought. The Lord's Prayer has 56 words; the Ten Commandments have 297; the Declaration of Independence has 300. There has just been a new EEC directive on the import of caramel and caramel products. To say this, it needs a total of 26 911 words. Need I say more?

Discussion of Chapter 14

CHAIRMAN: PROF. C. T. DOLLERY

Prof. Dollery: When an article appears, such as the series that appeared in the *Observer* on Debendox, some of which seemed to me to be the most irresponsible smear journalism that I have ever read, is there any way of trying to answer the questions raised promptly? A delayed answer has no effect because of the ephemeral nature of these things. Is there something more that we ought to do?

Dr Lock: Journalists are very wary of the Press Council but it moves so slowly. I used to think that until a journalist had actually been reported to the Press Council once or twice, he was not fully-fledged, and that it was like going hunting and getting blooded. But not a bit of it. They are very scared of it.

Acting quickly? I think not. I do not know what we can do. We can report it in *Medicine and Media* and indeed we did. We are slightly limited by the laws of the land and there it is. It is very difficult when a case is going on.

Prof. A. Breckenridge (University of Liverpool): Would it not be appropriate to have a press release made from this meeting?

Dr Lock: If Professor Breckenridge will write it!

I do not know that pious press releases really do much good, because they have to be very general and very waffly. I would much sooner get one or two selected correspondents, whom we could all name, in a bar and talk to them. If they did appreciate the number of animals that were being used and the amount of bureaucracy involved, we might have gained something. We need a new medical Jonathan Swift or a satirist like Beachcomber to go into this medical situation. On the whole, I am not sure that a press release from this meeting would do much good. And we would spend the whole afternoon drafting it.

Prof. Dollery: David Ennals put his manuscript, or at least a release, to the Press Association. Dr Lock did not. Why?

Dr Lock: Nobody asked me!

Prof. Dollery: Of course many politicians issue speeches, or a release based upon them, to the Press Association, often trying to catch the weekend newspapers as well. It is not just the release that is important, but also the timing of it.

Dr Lock: The great pity is that he's got us; he's won already. This is 40:15 or game, really, because no correction that we can make, even supposing we were to write to the *Telegraph* today, would be effective. It will be Tuesday before it is looked at and by then it will be dead news. This is the trouble. Corrections are never news. These people win all the time. It is exactly the same with every campaign there has been. It is very difficult to get over the truth. And anyway how many people would be interested? This is an intellectual point and though we are interested, the public is not.

Fortunately there is quite a lot of evidence that people do not take too much notice of what they read and what they hear. On the other hand, they are very much influenced by what they see on television. There is often a tremendous conflict on television between somebody saying something and somebody having an image, and this conflict can really distort the message. There is a lot of very interesting work being done on this.

Sir Douglas Black: Relevant to Dr Lock's last point, I was at a meeting with representatives of the media about 18 months ago and it was pointed out that whereas 10 or 15 years ago people had their opinions largely formed, if one believes such a thing to be possible, by the newspapers. Now this is done very much more by television news and programmes. What always makes me relatively unconcerned by the media is the very instantaneous way in which they work. I do not worry too much about something that happens only once because something else will happen the next day and drive it out of people's heads. That is why I am not scared to meet them.

Dr A. B. Wilson (Llandeilo, Dyfed): Picking up the comment about people being impressed by the visual – I do not know how many people saw the recent programme on the CRM release, but I found the group of doctors that were a part of the interview system really came over as naughty boys acquiescing to the expert views coming from the CRM. This is a role of the profession – that obviously they would influence the viewer's interpretation of events.

Dr Lock: It is quite a technique. Anybody can be made to look like a nasty fascist. We have known that since Eisenstein's films following the Russian revolution. The way they are shot with a fishtail lens, so that people have great bloated jaws and fat cigars – people can be made to look

very silly merely by camera angle. It is something that perturbs me
considerably from the point of view of TV, because people can be
made to seem villains or goodies merely by the way they are shot.
This is something we need to know about as well, and to take
cognizance of it.

Prof. Dollery: I suppose that the answer is that we shall all have to have training in
appearing on the television as part of our primary education.

Dr Lock: Perhaps the other factor is keeping the medical profession informed of
activities such as those of the CSM and CRM. We have been told
that most doctors do not know of the existence of these organizations. I suppose if that group (referred to by Dr Wilson) was a
random selection of GPs, and one imagined oneself as one of them
just plumped into that situation and was told that this was the view
of an expert committee of the government, one would be a very
unusual character to say, 'What a load of boloney', under such
circumstances. They were almost set up for passive acquiescence by
the group.

Dr W. Inman (Committee on Safety of Medicines): Dr Lock attacks, in the nicest
possible way, the response from the Department of Health over the
Debendox affair. I am on the fringe of a change of career and can
risk commenting on my 16 years of experience as a senior professional officer working for the Department. It is a justified
criticism that the senior officers are not generally allowed to be in
contact with the press. We have a little rule, the Official Secrets Act,
but not many of us worry too much about that in our private
contacts, or even some of our public ones. But, traditionally, the
officer is separated by a chain of junior officials, starting usually
quite low down and working up to Under-Secretary, before any
answer is given, and this takes time. Also, there is traditionally a
defensive posture which tends to protect the minister but not
answer the question.

A great deal more could be done by experienced professional
people towards what Dr Lock is suggesting, and this is something
that the Department will hopefully consider as time goes by.

Dr Lock: One recognizes the difficulties, particularly the legal ones. Obviously it is a
sort of consensus statement. But I do believe it should happen
more, and I do think, as Professor Dollery said earlier this morning,
that if stuff is concealed in a lot of garbage, then investigative
journalists suspect that there is something underneath it, and they
will burrow away, and there may or may not be something in the
woodwork. We just do not know.

Prof. Dollery: I do not know whether anybody from industry would care to comment
on their relationship with the media, but it has seemed to me that
when pharmaceutical companies interface with the media, sometimes they do not do it very cleverly, particularly if they are under

criticism. I know it is extremely difficult, if one is being harassed by a journalist or a television reporter, but some of the people who have appeared as industry spokesmen have looked as though the expression on their faces has convicted them almost before they said a word. I do not know whether it is the same in industry as it is in government, in other words that there is a chain of public relations people whose job it is to keep the press as far away as possible from the senior scientists or executives who might be able to give a sensible answer.

Would anybody from industry respond to that?

Dr T. Vossenaar (Organon International): We have tried to get contact with the press for many years. We have a little office with a lawyer, a press man and a chemist who was not so good at chemistry any more, and we failed at the beginning because we simply had too much good faith and we thought that our message would get across. Then we trained our people and we started to discover the soft spots of the press, and the tactics and the policies we had to deal with. We picked out a number of people in the company and trained them to appear on television – they went on a television course. That materially influenced our relationships. There is no doubt about it. Still, we had problems because the press is, in essence, suspicious of us, even when we have a good message. We try to be as honest as possible and as honest as policy allows us to be honest, but sometimes it is very difficult to bring over the message, because the press always feel that our primary motivation is making money.

I subscribe to the opinion that anyone who really wants to build up a good relationship with the press and with the media must have handpicked people who are given a good training, so as to know how to deal with them. Otherwise they will be torn to shreds. They will be dealing with quite intelligent people.

Sir Douglas Black: I agree very much that when one is talking about general issues then one has to use the professional help of public relations people, administrators, and so on. It is very different at the level of the doctor and the individual patient. I have seen a lot of difficulty with patients' complaints and I have even come across instances where the consultant was advised by the administrator not to talk to the patient about it. This seems to me to be exactly the wrong way round. One should have a good try first of all at a discussion with the patient before one brings in the apparatus of public relations people, administrators, and so on.

Dr J. Davoll (Conservation Society): I suspect the press is not really committed one way or the other, except to providing novelty. A wonder drug is a novelty. I do not suppose that the drug industry really rushes in to criticize exaggerated expectations that might be raised by publicity for such a drug, any more than environmental groups rush in when they see something published that they feel will help their cause and which they know to be exaggerated. I am afraid that is what happens with these statements. Then of course we all complain when they turn round the other way. But the media are rather a neutral force, interested in transient phenomena rather than in the long-term processes, which are much more interesting. It is very important to have trained people to talk to them who are well aware of this because they can be quite tricky to deal with. They will quote one out of context on things if they think it provides a striking headline.

Dr Lock said something that rather worried me. He spoke of combating emotional statements with emotion. I am well aware of how far this is done by environmental groups, including those with whom I agree and those with whom I disagree, and of course, I feel rather differently about the two groups. Nevertheless, it does seem to me better to recognize that people have emotions that will motivate them to undertake various campaigns. I do not think it excuses them in then discarding reason as they conduct the campaign. That is really of what Hume meant when he said that reason is and should be the slave of the passions. He did not mean that reason was to be abandoned altogether, but that it was to be used in a particular way, with regard to the rules of reason, but recognizing that what one is trying to achieve is motivated by things that are beyond reason.

Dr Lock: I see the point, and we believe that our lives can be ruled by reason. But consider the situation round the Cabinet table when Ennals talks about seat belts, the Blennerhassett Report, smoking, etc., which all issues on which I personally feel angry. We know that a week is a long time in politics, and similar glib nonsense, but I suspect that if Ennals had thumped the table and said that people are dying, that within the last 30 years three times as many people have been killed by the cigarette in the UK than we killed in the whole of the 1914–18 war. Facts like this. That is what I mean by emotion. Emotion with reason, but still emotion. There has been far too much coolness on our side. When I think of 12 children last year dying of pertussis it also makes me angry. I think somebody is responsible for that.

Prof. Dollery: I have been personally worried by one or two new drugs apparently being announced at press conferences before they have been fully reported in the accessible medical literature. I suppose it is a temp-temptation for a pharmaceutical company to do that, if they are proud of a new product, but some of the statements that appear as a result of the briefings at those press conferences are almost as inaccurate in one direction as some of the criticisms that arise out of drug toxicity in the other.

It is a point to bear in mind.

Mr J. Spink (Wellcome Foundation): I would agree entirely. This sort of thing must not happen.

There is a strict rule in the ABPI Code of Practice that this should not happen, but sometimes it does without the manufacturer knowing about it.

Prof. Dollery: I read the newspapers always with suspicion. I wonder who has put up a journalist to that story. If it is a major news item one should not read it with that suspicion, but the less important items are usually there because somebody has encouraged the reports. When they appear in several newspapers simultaneously, along the same lines, one assumes that somebody in the company concerned must have been the source and that it was a policy decision.

Sir Douglas Black: Could it not equally have been whoever was doing the clinical trial?

Prof. Dollery: In that case it would usually be ascribed to him.

Dr D. Jack (Glaxo Holdings Ltd): Since no one else has spoken for industry I should say something or be guilty by silence.

When a new drug is first introduced, that there should be a press release would seem to be entirely natural. What is important is what is in it and the essential thing is that what is said about the drug should be right. If frankly misleading claims are made, then that is another story altogether. I have not commonly seen misleading statements made about drugs introduced recently. I am not aware of it to any great extent.

Prof. Dollery: I had one or two incidents in mind. I would not say that they were deliberately misleading, but what was published was quite unbalanced, which can amount to the same thing. I am not saying that there was an untruth said, but there was a very partial truth said. Whether that was in the original press release, or whether it was how the journalist chose to handle it, is often hard to say.

Dr Lock: I am basically very hopeful. Journalists exist to make a living. They exist to write stories. If we can put into their minds the stultifying influence of the bureaucracy, the way that we are wasting animals, the way we are wasting civilized expert lives in this terrible process and to add that we are not looking towards outcomes at all, then I think we could probably change things. I am thinking of the situation with ethical committees about 15 or 20 years ago. There was a lot of public disquiet aroused by Papworth's Book, *Human Guinea-pigs* and quite a lot of that was justified. On the other hand, quite a lot of it was not, but we sorted ourselves out. We now have ethical committees in all the hospitals. We never hear a shred of an ethical story these days. It is a great success for the College of Physicians and for the hospital ethical committees and the World Medical Association.

I have a feeling that if we got the process right, with somebody like Dr Inman masterminding it, we might swing the whole story about the drug industry round the other way. I am quite optimistic.

Sir Douglas Black: I think I might be wise, because one never knows what is to happen to one, to qualify some of the things that I said, or rather implied, about lawyers. Obviously if something goes wrong with a patient in the course of treatment, and if they cannot extract a satisfactory explanation from the chap who is responsible for the care of their illness, then they have an inalienable right to get legal advice. Equally the lawyer has a right to charge a customer a fee for that. What I was really criticizing was the commission principle whereby they can get a share of the damages. Just as Dr Lock recognizes that journalists must live, so I recognize that lawyers must live.

15
The influence of the medical profession

SIR DOUGLAS BLACK

This may be exercised in two ways, which are best considered separately. The first to be considered will be the corporate influence of the medical profession, and then the responsibility of the individual doctor responsible for the care of a patient.

CORPORATE INFLUENCE OF THE PROFESSION

There are three areas in which this can be exercised – in advice to Government, in the education of doctors, and in the education of the general public. But before describing these, there is a rather difficult question to be faced – who represents the medical profession, in all its rich diversity? There is no single body to which all doctors adhere and this should not be regarded as a disaster, indeed it is probably inevitable, given the diversity of medical tasks and the individualism of many doctors. The nearest approach to a representative body is the British Medical Association, to which the majority of practising doctors belong. The BMA deserves support, both in its desire for an increase in membership, and in its firm rejection of a 'closed shop' in medicine. The BMA is the only body empowered to negotiate with the government on terms and conditions of service and although some take objection to this it seems only sensible to have a single, undivided voice in this contentious area. But it is equally important to have alongside the BMA other bodies of stature which can consider, so far as possible in isolation from pecuniary considerations, the educational aspects of medicine and its standards of practice. The independence of the universities and the Royal Colleges is something to be cherished, even if it may sometimes give an impression of divided counsels. So far as consultants are concerned, the Joint Consultants' Committee is a useful forum in which the Colleges and the Central Committee of Hospital Medical Specialists (CCHMS) of the BMA play an equal part in considering a range of problems in our hospitals, and in making representations to the Health Departments. Among general practitioners, there are useful contacts between the Royal College of General Practitioners and the General Medical Services Committee (GMSC) of the BMA.

The debates in these bodies, while sometimes falling short of complete unanimity, usually lead to a degree of harmony and fortunately the theme of risk–benefit analysis in drug research is one on which there is virtually complete agreement within the profession. The issues are recognized as serious, and strong, united statements have been made. Moreover, the problems which we have been discussing in this meeting are well and sympathetically understood within the Health Departments. This report draws heavily upon the consideration within the Royal College of Physicians of the advice which it has tendered to the government on the application of 'strict liability' to the adverse effects of drugs, as recommended in the Pearson Report, and in draft EEC legislation. On the advice of clinical pharmacologists among our fellows, and with particular help from Drs J. W. Black, D. R. Laurence and D. W. Vere, the college prepared a paper on the dangers of applying strict product liability to drugs, which has been published in the Law Society's Gazette, submitted to the Medicines Commission, approved by the Joint Consultants' Committee and circulated to UK members of the European Parliament.

It is rare indeed for a pharmaceutical product to be intrinsically faulty, though human error could conceivably lead to faulty labelling or deterioration during storage. The great majority of adverse reactions arise when the product itself is sound, but when there is an unforseen interaction between the individual patient, the illness in its changing course, and the drug in its various formulations and dosage schedules.

Patients resemble Cleopatra in this, even if in nothing else, that they are infinite in their variety. Variation begins at the level of compliance – how much of what is prescribed is actually ingested? It extends through the processes of absorption, distribution and metabolism, all of which affect the amount of the drug which actually reaches the target organ. This variability is reflected in the several-fold variation in steady-state plasma levels in different patients, given the same drug in the same dosage[1]. Age, bodyweight, activity of acetylation and extent of induction of hepatic microsomal enzymes can all influence the response, more so for some drugs than for others. One might hope (or fear) that after the micro-electronic revolution all these variables could be fed into a computer, with the end-product an 'individualized dosage schedule'. In the meantime, decisions have to be taken, sometimes rapidly and the first indication of abnormal responsiveness by a patient may be an adverse reaction. In chronic illness, there is more opportunity for cautious 'trial and error' but the longer duration of treatment brings with it the possibility of slowly developing adverse reactions.

The nature of the patient's illness may be highly relevant to the incidence of side-effects. Gastro-intestinal disease may impair absorption, so that the dosage is increased to produce a therapeutic effect; if absorption then improves, adverse effects may appear. At the other end of the metabolic chain, impaired function of the liver or the kidneys leads to accumulation of drugs in the body, so that side-effects appear at conventional or even low dosages. When the degree of renal function impairment is known, dosage can be adjusted on the basis of nomograms for particular drugs but there are many situations in which this is not practicable, or at least not practised.

Drugs are given in different forms, by various routes, and often in combination. Response to the same chemical may be influenced by the physical form in which it is given or by the way in which it is compounded with 'filling' to give a bulk which can be swallowed. The different routes of administration may lead to complications. Oral medication may cause nausea; but parenteral medication can be associated with thrombophlebitis or with capricious absorption from an intra-muscular or subcutaneous depot. One drug may interact with another at the various levels of absorption, metabolism, end-organ effect, and elimination, challenging human memory up to and beyond its limits, so that we have in this area both massive works of reference and devices such as the Goldberg disc.

Add to this the possible interactions of drugs with articles of food and drink, the possibility that several doctors may be prescribing for the same patient, possibly with imperfect communication between them and the permitted substitution of one formulation for another and it is not surprising that adverse reactions are common. What is surprising is that intelligent men should apparently regard this labyrinth as capable of legal resolution, so that 'strict liability' can be responsibly assigned. Without necessarily accepting the underlying proposition that if an illness gets worse, compensation must be paid, our college suggests that a 'no-fault' or 'common fund' system of compensation for clear-cut serious adverse effects of drugs would be fairer, and very much more practicable than compensation which involved inconclusive legal arguments on the allocation of 'strict liability'. There will, of course, be rare instances where a patently excessive dose has been given, or a well-recognized interaction has been ignored and in such cases, the prescriber, or possibly the dispenser, is clearly at fault. But in the great majority of cases, it is likely to be impossible to ascribe an adverse effect with precision to abnormal susceptibility in the patient, genuine complication of the illness, and direct effect of the drug, or to an interaction between any two or all three. For example, if a patient on a mono-amine oxidase inhibitor, having been warned against taking cheese, red wine, etc., has a reaction to pickled herring, who is to blame – the manufacturer of the drug, the doctor who prescribed it, or the delicatessen owner who supplied the tyramine?

In the course of undergraduate education, students should be made aware of the complexity, and possible risks, of giving a drug or drugs to patients. All medical schools should have a Department of Clinical Pharmacology, which should carry the main responsibility for inculcating the principles of drug action and practical therapeutics but it is just as important that clinical teachers in general should draw attention to the considerations governing prescribing in their particular specialties. In other words, the approach which is developed and specifically taught in a department of clinical pharmacology should also be pervasive in medical teaching generally. Similar considerations apply in postgraduate training and in medical practice. It seems to me unrealistic to expect to have a clinical pharmacologist as such in district hospitals with four physicians or even fewer but for one of them to have a special interest in clinical pharmacology is highly desirable. Similarly, courses for general practitioners should lay particular emphasis on therapeutic principles.

The education of the public is also of importance. The tradition of 'a bottle of medicine' (now more often some tablets) for everything dies hard. Also, it takes much longer to convince a patient that he needs no medication, than to prescribe some innocent-seeming nostrum. The public should be made aware by all suitable means that on the one hand there is now a considerable range of potent drugs for many illnesses but on the other hand, the very potency of modern remedies brings with it an inescapable element of risk. People are accustomed to taking risks in many contexts: in the home, in the factory, in travel by road, rail, sea and air. It should not be impossible to gain acceptance of the notion that the treatment of an illness is not an oasis of absolute safety in a world full of hazard. For this reason, articles in newspapers and journals, programmes on radio and television on medical treatment are to be welcomed, provided that they acknowledge plainly that the therapeutic situation is a risk–benefit situation, not an area of unalloyed benefit.

RESPONSIBILITY OF THE INDIVIDUAL DOCTOR

The only ways in which a doctor could avoid all adverse effects of the drugs which he prescribed would be by embracing homeopathy, or by reverting to the era of therapeutic nihilism, which briefly intervened between the catastrophic measures of earlier centuries and the drug explosion of today. He would not, however, meet the reasonable expectations of his patients, and he would be limited to seeing the not inconsiderable number of cures which are achieved by nature alone, moreover, he would be depriving himself of many useful therapeutic interventions in potentially fatal diseases. By accepting, as of course in practice he would, the benefits of modern therapy, he would also be accepting the risks. What can he do to contain these within acceptable limits?

Some long-established principles still hold good. He must know as fully as possible both the nature of the illness with which he is dealing and the characteristics of the patient for whom he is going to prescribe. He should have a considerable acquaintance with what he is about to use, with its properties, desirable actions, and undesirable actions (including both those which are necessary accompaniments of the desired action, and those which are uncommon, possibly based on individual susceptibility). He should not be ashamed of refreshing his memory from a textbook or card-index in front of the patient. He should be wary of new drugs, whose benefits and risks may not be fully established by experience. A limited repertoire of well known drugs is preferable to attempts at variety and catholicity in prescribing. If the patient has already been seen and treated by another doctor, he should take pains to discover what the patient is taking, not only for current illness, but also for any other condition on a long-term basis (the referral letter should of course contain this information, but it may not, and we all know the fall-back position of trying to identify a cascade of tablets from an atlas).

In the course of the history, patients should be asked about previous reactions to drugs, and any history of allergy to other agents, with of course particular attention to any drug which the doctor has it in mind to prescribe. The regime should be as simple as possible, both to lessen the chance of interactions, and to increase the chances of compliance. A careful history and examination lays the foundations of trust and these should then be built upon by an explanation of what is thought to be wrong and what treatment is suggested, with the reasons for recommending it. The regime should then be outlined in detail, including any modifications of diet or activity which it entails. If it is at all complicated, the patient should be given it in writing. If there is an unavoidable side-effect, for example those linked with the therapeutic action, these should be explained. More judgement is required when it comes to uncommon side-effects. If we stress the risks overmuch, the patient may decline to accept them, whilst on the other hand, we are disturbed when a rare side-effect occurs. On the whole, it is better to err on the side of under-statement, for patients will generally accept the explanation that a side-effect was rare and unexpected. Of course, if 'strict liability' comes in, it will give medical practice a violent push in the other direction, not the least deplorable of its likely effects. Newer drugs are often accompanied by 'data sheets', which may list possible side-effects in some detail; these are helpful to the doctor, but need not be communicated in their alarming entirety to the patient, though again this might be forced upon us by ill-considered legislation.

The problems of prescribing for chronic illness, especially in the elderly, are compounded by the tendency for therapy to grow by accretion, as one doctor is seen after another. Therapeutic benefit is then likely to come from vigorous pruning of the medication. It is usually better not to pursue the draconian course of stopping everything at once, even if it occasionally works magic. It seems to be better to pick off disposable items in ones or twos, observing the effects.

Returning for a moment to the question which forms the alternative title of this meeting – 'How safe does a drug have to be?' The answer runs on these lines – 'Certainly not absolutely safe, which would imply that it was totally ineffective. But as safe as reasonable precautions by all concerned can make it, consistent with appropriate therapeutic benefit. Clearly, the safety criteria for "over-the-counter" remedies for headache and indigestion must be more rigorous than those for drugs used in the treatment of endocarditis or cancer.'

Reference

1. Prescott, L. F. (1979). Variability in response to drugs – pharmacokinetic factors. In Davies, D. M. and Rawlins, M. D. (eds.) *Topics in Therapeutics*, 5 (London: Royal College of Physicians; Pitman Medical)

Summary and Conclusions

C. T. DOLLERY

The programme says 'Summary and Conclusions' and making either is very difficult in a meeting that has covered such a diverse range of subjects as this one has.

I shall begin by saying that I thought the lectures that we heard were of exceptionally high quality, both in their delivery and in their content. The murmurs of approval that we heard around the audience showed that most people agreed with the opinions that were being expressed.

I then fell to wondering if, had the reporter from the *Observer* who wrote about Debendox been in the audience, would he have been contrite and altered his opinions. Even more importantly, if there had been a cross-section of readers of the *Observer* who had read the original reports, would they have changed their minds? And I concluded that they would probably not have been convinced. Why not? Mainly for the reason that so many speakers have mentioned and that is, that the presentations, although well argued, have been long on opinion and short on data; and opinion is essentially ephemeral, and when weighed in the balance it is no better than somebody else's opinion. People can always be found who will profess almost any opinion, and one can only in the end judge which of those opinions are correct and which are not by weighing them against data.

I ought to say a word at this point about risk–benefit and cost–benefit. The original title of the meeting had cost–benefit in it, but it was changed in the revised programme to risk–benefit. They are not exactly the same thing, but they are related. Sir Edward Pochin told us that there is a better history of looking at cost–benefit in relation to engineering and the hazards of nuclear radiation than there is in medicine. Of course it is easier to try to calculate the cost–benefit of improving a road junction (which the Ministry of Transport does) or the cost–benefit of putting in a bridge with a particular safety factor. That is commonly done. Perhaps the accident to the 'Flotel' in the North Sea late in March illustrates that such calculations can be fallible, but they are possible. One puts into the calculation some assessment of the probable extreme risk over a period of time, and then one adds a safety factor to it, which on many engineering structures is 2 or 3 to be on the safe side. One of the most interesting situations where the factor is smaller is on the wings of aircraft which are given a safety factor of only 1.5 times. The interesting reason for this is that aircraft would not be able to take-off because of the weight if they were made much stronger. There may be an analogy there with the safety of drugs. We might easily get into a situation where we bought additional safety for drugs at such a high cost that their development would cease and that has been much of the thrust of this meeting.

But if we are talking about cost and risk–benefit in medicine, one of the great difficulties is that we are comparing unlike quantities. We are comparing increased survival, or relief of symptoms, in one patient with the causation of different disease and symptoms by the drug in other patients. The information about both aspects is often very uncertain, but even if it were certain and it could be made much more certain, there would still be the problem of how to compare the one with the other. All of us can recognize, particularly in the context of treating solid tumours, that there can come a point when the misery inflicted by treatment is so great that one could believe, and some patients will say, that they would rather die than continue with it. So there must be some point of time when the two things can be weighed, but it is not easy, and those like Alan Williams, who both Douglas Black and I know well, will say that the only way of comparing unlike quantities of this sort is using the only common currency we have – money. Those who study cost–benefit analysis try to weigh these unlike quantities in money terms, for example, by asking someone who has a hernia how much he would pay today to be free of discomfort. By asking a lot of people one would get some extreme and silly opinions, but in the end some sort of consensus would emerge, and that could be weighed against the cost of surgery and the effectiveness of surgery in curing a hernia.

If such calculations are done, they lead to interesting results. Some of the simplest procedures in medicine, such as giving reasonable dental care so that people do not lose their teeth or repairing a hernia, or varicose veins, look much better in terms of cost–effectiveness or cost–benefit than some of the more sophisticated procedures in medicine where the costs are high and the benefits not so clearly made out.

I am not here to advocate that approach. It is clearly fraught with difficulty. But it is interesting that although we have been discussing risk–benefit throughout the meeting, that nobody really has set out anywhere to try to weigh the one against the other. In the end one has to do so and one is up against the problem of comparing things that are not measured with the same scale. it would be interesting to see some calculations doing this in relation to drug efficacy and safety, and I believe some people are even beginning to try to do it in the treatment of tumours where the balance is at its finest.

I turn once more to the lack of a numerical basis for so much of what we have discussed. I shall make two assertions neither of which will be much liked. The first is that the benefits of drug therapy in most cases are less than we think they are. The second is that the risks are usually greater than we know. I should like to try to justify those because they are challenging.

The benefits which we know with reasonable certainty are derived from randomized controlled clinical trials. I shall come to the question of the dearth of those in a moment. But we also know, from such studies as have been done, that the benefits that are achieved in the ordinary practice of medicine from the use of therapeutic procedures are usually less than are achieved from using the same procedures in randomized controlled trials because they are applied with less skill to less appropriately chosen patients, and often with less persistence. Thus, one can say that the benefits are less than we believe. On the other hand, it is clear that there are still undocumented risks of treatment, whether by drugs, surgery or investigative procedures, so that the risks are greater than we know. I believe one of the problems that we suffer is that we have overclaimed the benefits of treatment in the past.

I should like now to make it clear where I stand. The balance sheet of drug treatment is a strongly positive one, but it is not as strongly positive as some of the most enthusiastic advocates have said, and one of our problems with the public and the media is that they rightly suspect that we have made excessive claims. How is this situation to be remedied? There is only one remedy that I can see and that is to improve our knowledge and our information base about the risk and benefit of treatment. I shall discuss that under three headings.

The first is concerned with animal toxicity tests. I share Dr Dayan's scepticism about the value of much of the animal toxicology we do now in predicting toxicity in man. That is not to say there are not excellent models in animals of many kinds of human toxicity, but these models are much weaker in making useful predictions than in reproducing known types of toxicity. For example, I do not have entire confidence that the existing teratogenicity tests that are done in animals, which are very effective at detecting effects due to thalidomide, would necessarily detect teratogenicity of a new drug that was to be given to pregnant women.

But it is no good just criticizing toxicity tests and in a sense criticizing regulatory bodies. Regulatory bodies are essentially passive organizations. Having sat on one for 7 or 8 long years, I think I can say that with some confidence. They respond to the general scientific situation around them and the opinions that are given to them. If there are problems, as I think there are, over such basic matters as the precision, and accuracy, reproducibility of toxicity tests, then the only people who can generate data to validate that view are the people who work in the field, in the pharmaceutical industry. Those of us who are interested in toxicology, who work in academic units, do not have the large animal holding and drug administering facility that is necessary to do such studies. The industry has excellent ones.

Years ago, when I was a member of the committee of the European Society for the Study of Drug Toxicity, now the European Society of Toxicology, a study was sponsored which has already been mentioned. A compound was circulated around ten or eleven of the major companies in Europe to be subjected to teratogenicity tests. The results were interesting because there was one company that did not find it to be teratogenic, and two where the results were doubtful, although this particular substance was a well known teratogen. It seems to me that the industry, rather than blaming the regulatory authorities for all of their problems, could serve their own cause by sponsoring such studies within the industry, so that instead of confronting the regulatory body with an opinion which is clearly partial because they are on one side of the argument they could confront them with scientific evidence which is very much more difficult to ignore. Why has nothing of this kind been done? I do not know. I have talked to people in industry about it and I have been given a variety of opinions related to the pressure of work, the priorities, the legal situation about collaboration with other companies and so on. I can see that all of these are problems, but I doubt that they are so substantial that they would prevent such collaboration taking place, and I would commend a new initiative.

But having said that about animal tests, I have to go on from Dr Dayan's viewpoint and say that I put my chief faith in clinical studies. That is one reason why I have strongly supported the kind of criticisms that Professor Breckenridge was making of the delay in the CSM procedures for clinical trials, which to me seems quite intolerable and unnecessary. Unlike Mr Ennals who put forward opinions here that are somewhat different to those upon which he acted whilst in office, I can say that when I was a member of the CSM I was a strong advocate of that opinion, and, in another context, some years ago I was able to persuade the CSM that it would be a good idea to have a Senior Medical Officer as a research officer to the committee, mining away in the files of data. But at that time an objection was brought up that all of the data was given under assurances of commercial confidentiality, and that it could not be used to identify individual structures unless the companies responsible would release it. When we sit together as scientists we may feel that all reasonable men would agree to release such data, but the practical matter is that when one talks to managers in industry, and particularly to the lawyers, there are always some who will not agree to release the work and so it is very difficult to do a study based on the regulatory authority.

But there is nothing whatever to stop the pharmaceutical industry, or groups of companies, doing it. I would commend to Dr Brimblecombe, that if he cannot get this study done through the CSM, and I believe it will be difficult, then the other kind of initiative mentioned, perhaps through the ABPI, or through consortia of companies doing major amounts of research, is much more likely to be effective than trying to persuade everybody to agree that the information that used to be in Finsbury Square and has now moved to Market Towers can be made generally available.

However, that is an aside, and I come back to the question of clinical studies. It seems to me that it is only from good clinical trials that we can answer questions about both risk and benefit. Nowadays clinical trials are often done which contain substantial numbers of patients. Admittedly such trials are sometimes not done in the pre-marketing era but afterwards and a good example would be the very large trials that are being done on beta blockers, sulphinpyrazone, aspirin, and dipyridamole, and other agents of this sort in the primary or secondary prevention of myocardial infarction. These trials often contain several thousand individuals and are an excellent source of data about efficacy which usually is published with the result of the trial, but should be an equally good source of accurate information about side-effects and toxicity. Unfortunately the side-effects, toxicity and reasons for drug withdrawal are usually not nearly so well-documented in the trial reports as is the primary conclusion about efficacy. I would commend again to those who are working on the clinical trials side of the pharmaceutical industry that there is much to be gained from improving still further the way the trials are done so that more information about side-effects, withdrawals, and as Dr Inman said, events, are documented in those trials. Let me give a simple example. I have been associated with the MRC hypertension trial, which is a large trial and will eventually have about 18 000 people in it. It currently has about 11 000. Either bendrofluazide or propranolol, and identical placebos, are being compared. The trial has not yet reached a conclusion about efficacy, but along the way it has collected the best information I am aware of in relation to those two drugs about side-effects, their severity in the sense of how many patients have to be withdrawn because of them, and there is very accurate information, because there is a placebo group and therefore the noise level can be subtracted, and one knows exactly how many patients are on the drug so that a very good estimate can be given of incidence. We have learnt that if propranolol is given to people with no history of asthma, about 1 to 2% will have to withdraw because they develop wheezing. We have discovered a new side-effect of bendrofluazide. There were an appreciable percentage of withdrawals in men around 1 or 2% owing to impotence, and using questionnaires to back that up it became quite clear that bendrofluazide can cause that impotence. That kind of trial is not unique. There are many large-scale clinical trials going on. If we collect good quality data from such trials, then at least for the drugs that have been the subject of them, we should have excellent risk–benefit data, valid up to events that are occurring with an incidence of around 1 in 1000. I agree with Dr Inman that such a system will not detect events which are less common than that, but most of the kinds of toxicity that interest us can be looked upon as having an iceberg effect. In other words, for every patient that is detected as being ill due to the drug, there will be a number of others who are suffering some inconvenience and symptoms but not so severe. So the more sensitive the methods, the more likely that things will be picked up with smaller numbers.

Where does this all leave us? If I am to argue that the chief thrust of safety data will have to come from man, there are some uncomfortable conclusions one draws as well as the comfortable ones. The people who have made the comfortable one would be those, like Dr Brimblecombe and Dr Dayan, who said that we must get to man early, with more compounds and less fuss and they are right. That will mean some saving of time and expenditure at that stage of drug investigation. But if we look at the costs of drug studies, it is clear that the clinical studies are often very much more expensive than the basic investigations of toxicology, particularly if the full cost of them has to be carried, as a commercial company often has to do when it is paying for trials. It may be somewhat easier for a body like the MRC which is often paying only marginal costs and using the existing machinery of the NHS. It would not be right to delude anyone into thinking that the kind of approach I am advocating will necessarily cost the state less money. It might well cost more. What it ought to do is to produce much better quality information at the end of the day because the studies will be done in the correct species, man, and in the correct disease, a human disease. That is the way we have to go, and I can perhaps claim a miniscule amount of action in support of my opinions in that when the new secretary of the MRC was appointed, I made an appointment to go and see him and say that one of the things I felt he ought to do was to try and be more active in sponsoring large-scale long-term clinical trials so that we are better able to answer the questions about efficacy and safety of many of the medicines that we now use or will use in the future.

Supposing we can slowly achieve that, and it will be relatively slow. What should we do with the information? I believe passionately that we must adopt the approach advocated by Dr Lock. I do not think that we shall change the present adversary position with the consumer groups, and with the press, unless we are prepared to be open with them and to be responsive to their criticism. It would be wrong to think that all of the criticism of medicine, or of the pharmaceutical industry, is necessarily ill-directed or wrong. It may well be that more information about drugs will show that some of the drugs we are now using have little benefit and some risk, and therefore should be removed from the market. Or perhaps some that have obvious benefits have larger risks than we knew which raise a question about their use in mild disease even if they should be continued in severe disease. Such questions may have a major economic impact upon the pharmaceutical industry because if a drug is selling to 100 000 patients at a particular price and that is honed down to 20 000 people who really need it, it might cease to be a profitable product for the company concerned and would either have to go out of use or to be sold at a much higher price.

Those are questions that will have to be resolved, first we must get better data. We must be prepared to conduct a public argument about risk and benefit, and then we must take the consequences, because eventually everything we do is paid for by the general public of which we are part.

Index